The
Parthenon
Paradox

The Parthenon Paradox

Rivers of Redemption

PETER BARBER

The Parthenon Paradox
Copyright © 2025 by Peter Barber
All rights reserved.

No part of this publication may be reproduced, stored in a retrieval system, or transmitted in any form or by any means—electronic, mechanical, photocopying, recording, or otherwise—without the prior written permission of the copyright holder, except for brief quotations in reviews or as permitted by law.

ISBN:
978-1-916574-99-1 (paperback)
978-1-916574-98-4 (hardback)

Cover artwork by Charly Alex Fuller
Book design by wordzworth.com

Dedication

To the extraordinary people of Pefki, your kindness during one of the most challenging chapters of our lives was nothing short of overwhelming.

To Mary and Theodora, who worked tirelessly to help us restore our home.

To Adonia, who opened her taverna every day, ensuring we were fed with warmth and care.

To Marily, who graciously offered us her finest room in her beautiful hotel when we had nowhere else to turn.

To Omorfulas. You are always there for us.

And to the many others, whose names may not be written here but whose acts of compassion will forever remain etched in our hearts. You showed us the true meaning of Greek kindness.

This book is dedicated to all of you, with gratitude that words cannot fully express. You are living examples of "philoxenia", the ancient roots of Greek hospitality. Thank you for your generosity, your humanity, and your unwavering support. You will never be forgotten.

With love and appreciation,

Peter and Alex

Contents

Dedication		v
Chapter 1	The Girl of My Dreams	1
Chapter 2	Soulmates	18
Chapter 3	Meet the Barbers	40
Chapter 4	Gossip and Intrigue in a Greek Village	56
Chapter 5	The Tale of the Sneaky River	74
Chapter 6	The Calm Before the Chaos	101
Chapter 7	Celebrating a Life of Greatness	114
Chapter 8	The Day the Gods Came to Visit	131
Chapter 9	The Gods Hadn't Finished with Us Yet	148
Chapter 10	A New Beginning	160
Chapter 11	Life in the Pokey	175
Chapter 12	Catch Us If You Can	198
Chapter 13	Oh No! Another Last Straw	211
Chapter 14	The Wicked Witch of the Village	226
Chapter 15	Truth Beneath the Surface	239
Chapter 16	The Turning Tide	265
Chapter 17	The Olive Branch Strategy	277
Chapter 18	Peace Among the Ruins	293
Author's Note		305
Credits and Gratitude		307

CHAPTER 1
The Girl of My Dreams

Humans once had four arms, four legs and two faces. Zeus split us in half as a punishment for our pride, and we were destined to walk the Earth searching for our other half.

– **Plato**

The storm started like any other. Dark clouds gathered on the horizon and distant thunder rumbled over the mountains. But as the sky darkened and the winds grew stronger, it became clear that this storm was different. Rain poured down, turning the cobblestone streets into rivers within minutes. The villagers of Pefki, used to heavy downpours, went about their well-practised tasks, securing shutters and bringing in laundry, unaware of the life-changing disaster that was about to strike.

Unknown to us, this storm was brewing with a ferocity the village had never witnessed before. The raindrops pounded against the rooftops like a relentless drumbeat. The winds howled through the trees, stripping the branches of their leaves. Debris cluttered the narrow alleyways, carrying a sense of foreboding. The villagers hurriedly completed their preparations, oblivious to the havoc that awaited.

As time went by, the rain continued without ceasing. The previously dry ditch behind our garden transformed into a furious torrent. Water overflowed its banks, engulfing our garden and inching perilously close to our house. The long-standing olive groves, peacefully growing on the nearby hill for centuries, surrendered to the relentless downpour; the soil eroded beneath their roots, leaving them without a foundation.

By midday, the situation worsened. The village square, typically a bustling hub of activity, was suffering. Water surged through, sweeping away tables and chairs from the kafenio. Anastasia's bakery, a cornerstone of the village, had water lapping at its doorstep. The goats, usually so mischievous and spirited, huddled together on higher ground, their bleats lost in the howling wind.

Our home was now in the path of the raging water. The garden we had lovingly created for years was submerged. Plants, flowers and trees were uprooted and swept away. But this was just the beginning. The full force of the water from the mountains had yet to reach our paradise. When it finally came, it was like a biblical event. A wall of water hit us like a tidal wave. It smashed into our house with unstoppable force. Our wrought-iron gates, air conditioning units and garden furniture were taken away as if they were matchsticks.

The water surged through the doors and windows with a deafening roar, obliterating everything in its path. Furniture and cherished possessions were tossed about like debris in a tempest. The relentless current ripped the plaster from the walls, leaving behind exposed brick and shattered remnants of our life. Kitchen units and appliances were submerged, disappearing under the churning, muddy water.

The house groaned under the strain, windows shattering as the floodwaters poured in, filling every room with chaos. The memories built within these walls were being dismantled in a matter of minutes. The roaring water seemed to laugh at our helplessness, each surge a cruel reminder of nature's unforgiving power.

We were in big trouble. We were going to lose our home. All we had worked for over the years was going to be washed away, and we were powerless to intervene. The dream we had built together, piece by piece, was crumbling.

We were going to lose everything.

We loved living in the picturesque fishing village of Pefki, on the beautiful island of Evia. It embodied the quintessential Greek dreamscape, with its enchanting sights of cobalt blue waters and charming whitewashed buildings.

The gentle lull of the waves and the distant cries of seagulls created a soothing melody in the air. The aroma of freshly caught seafood wafted through the streets, igniting our senses and enticing our taste buds. Every moment spent there felt like a blissful escape into a paradise we never wanted to leave. We didn't have to; we had built our home here.

As you look out from any point in the village, the historic straits of Artemision inspire a kind of reverent awe, as if the sea itself remembers the clash of ancient oars. Here, amidst these sapphire waters, the Greek fleet once stood defiantly against the Persian Empire in a battle of both wits and will. A prelude to the heroics of Thermopylae. The scent of pine mingles with the brine of the Aegean, and the tang of ozone sharpens the memory of ancient war cries carried on the wind. The waves, now gentle, once mirrored the disciplined lines of Athenian triremes, flanked by the fearsome warriors of Sparta. In the distance, the emerald islands of Skiathos and Skopelos offer a glimpse of other tranquil havens, untouched by the echoes of history yet forever linked by these myth-laden waters.

But Evia is unlike the polished, tourist-centric islands you might imagine. Here, the rhythm of life beats to a different drum, one that still dances to the old Greek songs. While it's welcoming to visitors, the journey to get here requires a little more effort, and that small barrier has kept it refreshingly authentic. Evia has never bowed to the whims of mass tourism; its heart lies in agriculture and the steady pull of the sea. Instead of lines of rental cars and tourist buses, you'll find pickup trucks and tractors parked outside the village tavernas, where the locals gather over a shared meal and the stories flow as easily as the ouzo. We found solace in this simplicity, a life stripped down to its essentials.

Our home in Pefki became a retreat, a sanctuary from the noise and haste of the city. Tucked between the pine-clad mountains and the quiet outskirts of the village, our whitewashed refuge held a rare tranquillity, as if it were a part of the landscape itself. We would stroll to the harbour each day, where the fishermen returned with their catch, hands calloused by the salt and sun, embodying a tradition that felt as eternal as the tides. The scene was a reminder of a simpler time, one that Pefki seemed determined to keep alive.

Alex and I were sitting on the sunlit patio of our house. We were surrounded by vibrant bougainvillea. The aroma of freshly brewed coffee mingled with the scent of sea salt on the gentle breeze. The symphony of tzatzikis and cicadas filled the air, blending with the sound of crashing waves in the distance. In that moment, I felt a deep sense of belonging. The warmth of the sun on my skin reminded me that I was now part of this ancient culture. I was no longer an outsider; I was a local. I had married a Greek, and with it came Greece.

As a child, I was obsessed with the stories and legends of the brave Spartans. The tales of Hercules, the stories of Greeks and Trojans, fascinated me. Unlike my childhood friends, my heroes didn't kick a football around a muddy field on a rainy Saturday afternoon. They fought for justice under perfect blue skies, overlooking the sparkling Aegean Sea. Now, not only was I here, but I owned my own house here. Building our dream home was a struggle, but with Alex by my side, and against all odds, we had achieved it.

Originally, buying land here was an accident. It wasn't really our fault. Our dogs, Jack and Bella, were to blame. We wanted to go on a holiday away from our home in Glyfada. It was August and the heat was unbearable, reaching temperatures of forty degrees. The islands always have a cool sea breeze, unlike the mainland. However, the challenge was finding a pet-friendly hotel in Greece, which was quite rare. After searching through various websites, we finally found one in Pefki, North Evia. Alex and I were familiar with the village because we had visited briefly when we were searching for marble tiles for our building in Glyfada. We remembered it as a beautiful place, so we decided to spend our holiday there.

As we drove off the ferry and left the mainland behind, the shift was immediate and unmistakable. The heat of Athens melted away, replaced by a cool, refreshing breeze, as if the island itself were breathing differently. I remember Alex leaning out the window, pointing out the goats that roamed freely across lush, grassy fields. They ambled between pine trees, their horns catching the light as they grazed lazily. Some of the trees had small plastic bags tied around their trunks, and Alex explained that the locals collected resin here for making retsina, the distinctive local wine. It was a detail I hadn't noticed before – a small but telling sign of life carrying on unchanged by time.

As we approached Pefki, the road curved beneath a grand archway of ancient Pefka trees. It was like entering a hidden world, the dense canopy above us filtering the sunlight into soft, dappled patterns. We rounded a gentle bend, and there it was: the shimmering blue Aegean Sea, opening up before us. The village harbour lay nestled against the shore, vibrant fishing boats bobbing in the water, their colours as vivid as the wildflowers dotting the roadside. It was a scene straight out of a postcard, but it felt real in a way those pictures never do, as if you could almost reach out and touch the salt-tinged air.

We slowed as we passed the stone harbour wall. Across the water, the towering mountains of the mainland seemed to dissolve into the horizon, their green slopes fading into the grey, rocky peaks too high for any trees to take root. Alex pointed out Skiathos to our right, its hazy outline shimmering in the distance, while Skopelos lay just beyond, a faint shadow on the edge of the perfect blue sky. The familiarity of the view was comforting, yet it felt new to us all over again.

As we continued down the road, the bustle of the village began to surround us. Waiters darted back and forth across the street, balancing trays laden with seafood and glass carafes of wine destined for sun-kissed diners lounging at tables perched above the sandy beach. The sea here was a shade of blue I'd forgotten existed, clear enough to see the pebbles below, and inviting in a way that made you want to abandon everything and dive in immediately. We drove slowly, taking it all in, the tall palm trees swaying gently above us, framing the view like a painting.

We felt like we'd arrived in a different world entirely, one where the usual rush of life had no place. It was a return to simplicity, to a place where time stretched out like the waves lapping against the shore.

Leaving the village behind, we drove along a road that ran parallel to the shingle beach. Although it was midsummer and the height of the tourist season, the beach was almost deserted. We'd landed in paradise.

After our initial enthusiasm, buying our land was difficult. With no savings and a time limit to come up with the money, we faced significant difficulties. But Alex had her heart set on owning a small piece of this island. We used our holiday money to put down a small deposit, which curtailed our visit and left us wondering if it was the right choice. I returned to England to try and raise the rest of the funds, while Alex worked tirelessly in her beauty therapy business in Glyfada. Meanwhile, I continued my work as a building surveyor in England. Despite these efforts, we were unsure if we would succeed within the time limit.

But we did it. We owned land on a Greek island. Although we eventually managed to scrape together enough money to purchase the plot by cashing in my pension, we were left with the daunting question: what were we going to do with it now? We hadn't fully thought through how we would ever afford to build anything on the land. The uncertainty weighed heavily on us, overshadowing the excitement of owning a large plot of land. We hoped that with hard work and determination, perhaps one day we might build something, but the path forward was far from clear.

It all started two days into our holiday. We were sitting at a taverna by the sea, sipping ouzo and enjoying the slow pace of life, when Alex suddenly dashed off to a shop across the street. I thought nothing of it until she returned with a look of excitement I'd seen only a few times before.

"You have to come and see this," she said, practically pulling me out of my chair.

We found ourselves standing on a sunlit patch of land, wildflowers swaying in the breeze, with a view of the Aegean that took our breath away. "This is it," Alex whispered. Her heart was set on it before I'd even caught my breath. It was one of those impulsive holiday decisions people make, the kind you laugh about later when you're back home – except we weren't laughing.

As the ferry pulled away from the island, we were filled with a mixture of excitement and dread. We had no savings to fall back on and a tight deadline to come up with the rest of the money. I started to wonder if we'd made a huge mistake. The fantasy of owning a slice of Greek paradise was quickly overtaken by reality. What had we got ourselves into?

Beneath my feet, the warm Greek earth feels almost unreal, even now. Twenty years later, I still pinch myself, wondering how I ended up here, trading the drab predictability of England for this life filled with sun, salt and spontaneity. My old life feels like a distant memory – full of routine, like being stuck in a queue that never seemed to move. It was all about making ends meet and following a script: the daily grind, the polite nods at the office, the weekends that felt like a brief gasp of air before diving back under.

I had friends, of course. We'd gather at the local pub, chatting about football scores or complaining about the weather, sticking to the kind of safe topics that keep everyone comfortable. It was small talk that filled the silence but rarely touched on anything real – the kind of talk that fills the time but doesn't really fill the soul.

Life was comfortable and predictable. Until I stepped off the plane at Athens airport that first time and realised there was a different kind of life waiting for me.

It's not that I didn't care about my friends, or they didn't care about me. It's just that our lives were wrapped up in the everyday routine, and there wasn't much space or time to explore anything more meaningful. We were all just trying to keep our heads above water, managing jobs, family obligations and the day-to-day grind. We didn't often pause to ask how we were really doing or what we truly wanted out of life.

Looking back, those friendships feel more like connections of convenience rather than the deep bonds I've found in Greece. Here, friendships are about sharing not just good times but also struggles, joys and dreams. It's about opening up, being your true self, and supporting each other through the ups and downs. That's the kind of connection that's transformed my life in ways I never imagined back in England.

Life in Greece is something else entirely. It's like someone turned the volume up. The culture here is all about enjoying the moment and really living. Every day is full of laughter with friends, family gatherings that go on forever, and just soaking up the simple pleasure of a long meal by the sea. It's added a depth and joy to life that I never knew was missing.

I used to feel like just another cog in the machine, but here, I feel alive. The Greek way of life has splashed colour all over my days, replacing the grey routine of the past with vibrant moments of joy and contentment. I've found a real sense of belonging and purpose in Greece that makes every day an adventure. Life isn't just about getting by any more – it's about truly experiencing and savouring every single moment.

Alex and I still spend time in England, but things are different now. With my new-found culture and imbibed Greekness, I have changed, and my friends have opened up to me like never before. In the old days, our interactions provided a sense of familiarity and comfort, but they lacked the intellectual stimulation and depth that I didn't realise I secretly craved. It seemed that for most English people, including myself, this surface-level socialising was the norm, and delving into philosophical discussions was considered unnecessary or even pretentious. As part of my British life, I had to be content within the confines of my familiar insular existence.

But my Greek family changed all of that. In a Greek family, they actively promote philosophical discussions. It's a necessary part of everyday life. Alex will have a conversation with a complete stranger and ask the most direct questions. How much do you earn? Are you in love with your partner? Are you happy with your life? In Greece, this is normal, but in England, we tend to restrict ourselves to safe subjects like the weather, snippets of news, and potholes in the street. We don't like to open up too much; we find it impolite to stray into personal details. Now, my old friends have become new friends. We no longer feel embarrassed to talk about sensitive subjects; we discuss philosophy. Like me, it was clear they also felt restricted and uncomfortable, but now they feel free to chat quite happily about any subject. This has caused relationships to bloom. They take away with them the freedom to express themselves to others, so in our small part of England, a little bit of Greek culture is now developing.

Alex, my Greek wife, gave me the most extraordinary gift. She gave me Greece and, above all, a licence to open my mind. Little did I know this gift would profoundly alter every facet of my existence. Suddenly, my life turned into long sunny days of laughter, philosophy and love. I used to worry about the rain ruining my day; now I'm more concerned about running out of tzatziki.

Alex has a captivating presence that can light up a room – or, depending on her mood, send you scurrying for cover. Her eyes are always full of curiosity and challenge, like she's about to drop a philosophical bomb that will either enlighten you or make you feel like you've been living under a rock. She loves debating and sharing interesting ideas, and her thought-provoking questions help me understand complex concepts. It's like living with a charming cross between a university professor and a Socratic philosopher.

Even our arguments are educational. She'll patiently guide me through my flawed reasoning with the skill of a seasoned teacher explaining algebra to a particularly dim student. "Have you considered this perspective?" she'll ask, eyes twinkling with a mixture of amusement and pity. It's as if she's said, "Bless your heart, but that's not quite it, is it?"

Despite her intellectual prowess, Alex is never demanding. She doesn't need to share her opinions; she just asks questions that require careful thought.

Alex's kindness and generosity are legendary. One summer evening, we were at a taverna, and Alex caught the eye of a young waitress with her stunning dress. Alex noticed the admiration and struck up a conversation. The next day, she returned with the dress washed, ironed and ready to pass on as a gift.

More recently, one of her friends admired her designer sunglasses. I had bought these for Alex as a present at an upmarket airport store. "Try them on," Alex suggested, and before her friend could even blink, Alex had declared that they suited her perfectly and gifted them on the spot. It's like living with a fairy godmother, except she turns your admiration into reality instead of pumpkins into carriages.

But beware: Alex is also fiercely loyal and protective. Our friends and blended families quickly learn that her instinct is that of a lioness protecting her cubs. Her generosity is matched only by her ferocity when crossed. If you wrong her, you'll see those fiery eyes flash, a signal that you've stepped on a landmine. She doesn't just react; she strategises, ensuring that justice is served with the precision of a military operation. Cross her, and you'll find yourself at the mercy of her relentless pursuit of retribution, delivered with a smile that would make a Bond villain proud.

Alex's passion and intensity are magnetic, drawing people in and captivating them. Her unwavering support and love for her family and friends are evident in the countless ways she goes above and beyond. She is not just my wife, but also my mentor, challenger and greatest advocate. Life is richer, more meaningful and infinitely more stimulating with Alex by my side.

I first saw Alex in Northwood, a leafy suburb of London. I was sixteen, and she was fifteen. Her parents, Debbie and Zissis, had just moved the family there for Zissis's new job overseeing a cruise company's London sales office. They settled into a house on Elm Street, right in the heart of Northwood. Meanwhile, I had just started working at a butcher's shop after leaving school, unsure of what I wanted to do with my life. University wasn't an option because of my grades, and I wasn't ready for college either. One day, I spotted a job ad for a trainee butcher, applied, and got the job. It was a short train ride from my home in Watford, which made it convenient. But after a few months, I realised there wasn't much room for growth. So, I decided to enrol in college to study building surveying, which eventually became my career.

Every morning, I watched Alex and her friends walk past the butcher's shop on their way to Potter Street comprehensive school. She always gave me a friendly wave. To me, she was the most captivating creature I had ever seen. Her olive skin and long brown hair flowing over her shoulders made her stand out. She exuded elegance and had a unique charm that drew me in. I'd had crushes before, but this was different.

There was something inexplicably familiar about her, as if I had known her in a previous life. Deep down, I felt she was my soulmate. It seemed like we had been destined to be together forever.

Every day, my heart raced with anticipation. I yearned for even the slightest exchange with the girl who had stolen my heart. Her radiant smile was like a ray of sunshine, brightening up my existence. I would often find myself lost in daydreams, imagining what it would be like to hold her hand, share moments of laughter, and explore the depths of our souls together. Each morning, I positioned myself near the shop window. As I cleaned or arranged trays, I hoped to catch a glimpse of the girl of my dreams.

One morning, as she walked by with her friends, Alex's wave was accompanied by a bright smile that seemed just for me. My heart leaped. I fumbled with a tray of sausages, nearly dropping them. My boss gave me a curious look, but I didn't care. That smile kept me buoyant for the rest of the day.

A few days later, a girl in school uniform stepped into the shop. It was Emma, one of Alex's friends. She handed me a small, elegant envelope. My hands trembled slightly as I took it, glancing at the neat handwriting that spelled out my name.

"Alex asked me to give you this," she said with a knowing smile.

I managed to stammer a thank you, and Emma waved before leaving the shop. I stared at the envelope, hardly believing what had just happened. It was an invitation to Alex's birthday party the following Saturday.

I spent the rest of the week in a haze of excitement and nervousness. What kind of present should I get her? What would I say when we finally met face to face? Should I try to be cool and laid-back, or just be my usual, clumsy self? The weekend loomed ahead, holding the promise of answers and the potential to change everything.

Finally, Saturday arrived. I carefully followed the directions on the invitation and arrived at the house. Wanting to avoid being the first one there, I hid around the corner until I saw others arriving, and then I hurried over to join them. When Alex opened the door, my heart skipped a beat. She looked absolutely stunning, dressed in a short glittery skirt, a belt made of wooden beads, a tight gold Lycra top, and a gold scarf to complete the ensemble. She kissed her guests on the cheek as they entered the hallway. I felt myself blushing as I waited for my turn.

She put her hands on my shoulders, said, "Geia sas, to ónomá mou eínai Alexándra," then kissed my bright red cheek.

Her mother arrived behind her, shook my hand and welcomed me. She put her arm around her daughter and said, "Welcome! We are Greek. Alexandra does not understand much English yet, but she is learning. She said her name is Alexandra. What's yours?"

I shook Alex's hand and introduced myself. With that, she smiled and turned away to join her other guests.

I didn't speak to Alex again that evening, and I left the party alone. It hadn't gone the way I'd hoped, but at least we'd spoken, and she might remember me the next time she walked past the butcher's.

The following Monday, I waited by the shop window for her to pass. She didn't come. Nor did she appear the next day, or the one after that. After a torturous week, I found out that she and her family had suddenly left England and gone home to Greece. I had no address for her and no way of getting in touch. I was devastated. But somehow, that short meeting promoted a bond that would stay with us forever.

We both went our separate ways, carving out different paths in life. In my early twenties, I married and settled into a typical suburban life. My days were filled with routine until my late thirties, when everything changed. My wife succumbed to a long illness, leaving me a widower. The loss was profound, and I found myself adrift, seeking solace in my career as I tried to rebuild my life.

Yet over two decades, the memories of Alex remained vivid, as though etched with permanent ink. I could still picture her, an image of unparalleled beauty. Our meeting had been fleeting, limited to a single conversation, but it left an indelible mark. When she introduced herself in Greek, her words flowed with a melodic rhythm, her mother translating with a kind smile. That brief moment, infused with her grace and charm, always carried a touch of nostalgia for me.

CHAPTER 2

Soulmates

Love is born into every human being; it calls back the halves of our original nature together; it tries to make one out of two and heal the wound of human nature. Each of us, then, is a "matching half" of a human whole ... and each of us is always seeking the half that matches him.

– Aristophanes

Just before my fortieth birthday, on a bitterly cold winter day in my hometown of Watford, I saw a young man struggling to push his stranded car. I stopped my car and offered to give him a hand. The wind was piercing, howling through the air, biting at our cheeks as we exerted our strength. The car refused to budge, but with determination, together we managed to get it moving, and with a bump, we successfully jump-started it. Grateful for my help, he invited me to his nearby home for a warm cup of coffee, a small gesture of thanks.

We had no idea that this seemingly small moment would lead to something life-changing.

As we chatted over coffee, the conversation took an unexpected turn. There was something about this chap that made me feel comfortable, like a long-lost friend, even a brother. He introduced himself as Christos, here to take a training course at the university where he first qualified as an electrical engineer, catching up on new developments in his field. He mentioned he was Greek. I casually recalled meeting the most beautiful Greek girl years ago.

"Where was this?" he asked. "In Greece?"

"No, it was here in England. Over twenty years ago I worked in a butcher's shop. This beautiful girl would walk past the window every morning. We never really spoke, but I was in love. A teenager's infatuation, I suppose."

"Ah yes, we have all loved and lost." As Christos reminisced, his eyes wandered off into the distance, lost in the memories of his youth. After a moment, a wistful smile tugged at the corners of his lips. "Her name was Sophia," he said, his voice laced with a hint of nostalgia. "She was the girl who lived in the next street when I was growing up. We were inseparable back then, exploring the neighbourhood, getting into mischief together. But life has a way of taking people on different paths, and eventually, we drifted apart."

There was a touch of sadness in his eyes, a reflection of the deep bond they once shared. It was clear that Sophia held a special place in Christos's heart, even after all these years. As the memories flooded back, he couldn't help but wonder where she might be now, how her life had unfolded.

"So, tell me about your lost love," he said.

"Her name was Alex. I was working not far from here in Northwood. But since I first saw her, I never managed to get her out of my mind."

"That is a coincidence," he told me. "We lived in Northwood for a short time many years ago." A smile played across his lips. There couldn't have been many Greek families living in the small village of Northwood at that time. "That's my sister's name. Do you think it may be the same girl?"

"Of course not," I said. "She went back to live in Greece, and we haven't spoken since. She's probably married with a couple of kids now. I had my chance and let it go. Life moves on, we have to move with it."

I finished my coffee and got up to leave, when a woman entered the room. Christos introduced me. "Mana, this is Peter. He helped me start the car." The woman held out her hand, but as I took it and looked at her, I was overcome with a sense of familiarity. It was her – the woman who had greeted me at that unforgettable party a lifetime ago. She was Alex's mother.

I sat back at the table. "Is your name Debbie?"

"Yes, how do you know?"

"I met you many years ago in Northwood. I came to a party at your house."

Her eyes narrowed as she tried to remember. She looked into my eyes. Suddenly, a look of recognition spread across her face. "You were the butcher's boy! I remember you."

I had a million questions that had been simmering within me for over two decades, swirling like a tempest. Where would I begin, amidst this whirlwind of curiosity? But as I mustered the courage to speak, the question that escaped my lips felt tame, lacking the intensity that churned within me.

"How is Alex?" I asked, trying to cloak my true emotions behind a veil of nonchalance.

"Ask her yourself," Debbie said. "She's upstairs, I will get her. Wait there."

And then, the realisation hit me like a thunderbolt. Alex, the girl who had haunted my dreams for years, was here, just in the next room.

I was terrified, unable to believe what was happening. How could this be? My instinct screamed to flee, but an unseen force kept me rooted to my chair, paralysed by a mixture of fear and anticipation.

Then, a perfect English accent pierced through my tumultuous thoughts, pulling me back to reality. There she stood before me, radiating an ethereal glow.

"Hello, Peter," she said warmly, her voice music to my ears, sending shivers down my spine. It was Alex, standing there, even more breathtaking than I remembered.

I instinctively reached out my hand for a customary handshake, but she disregarded it entirely. Instead, she wrapped her arms around my neck. Softness met my cheek as she planted a gentle kiss, leaving me breathless.

At that moment, I realised she had transformed into an

even more resplendent version of herself. Her long chestnut hair cascaded over her shoulders, each strand seemingly infused with sunlight. Her eyes, a mesmerising shade of brown, shimmered with a captivating blend of curiosity and wisdom, revealing maturity beyond her years. She was a vision of loveliness. I was in love all over again.

We hadn't met in over twenty years. Our reunion felt like stepping into one of the many dreams she had haunted, only this time, I never wanted to wake up. As we talked about our past lives and shared experiences growing up, I felt like I was floating, suspended in time. Her words felt genuine and true, peeling back the layers of time and revealing who we had become.

She spoke about her life since we last met, her voice filled with both wistfulness and resilience. She had married at twenty-one, but the marriage lasted only a year. The way she told it, with a mix of sorrow and acceptance, made my heart ache for her struggles. I shared my own stories too, talking about my years of suburban routine, the love I had known, and the profound loss that had changed my life. Our words wove a tapestry of our individual journeys, each thread showing the paths we had walked alone.

It was a slow and deliberate unravelling, each revelation bringing us closer to understanding the person sitting across from us. We laughed at the absurdities of our youth, sighed over missed opportunities, and marvelled at the strange twists of fate that had brought us to this moment. With every shared memory, every confession and every heartfelt exchange, it felt as though the universe was aligning our paths once more.

In that instant, as our eyes locked and a silent understanding passed between us, I knew that destiny would not deny me any longer. The girl of my dreams, now a woman of depth and grace, was here with me. And this time, I was determined not to let her slip away.

The next day, we met at a cosy Italian restaurant nestled in the heart of the town. As we settled into our seats, the aroma of freshly baked bread and simmering sauces wafted around us, creating a warm, intimate ambiance. Alex was living and working in Greece, running her own beauty therapy business. She had returned to England for a couple of weeks to visit her mother, who was staying with Alex's brother. But our time was limited; she was set to return to Greece in just two days.

Throughout the meal, we exchanged stories and laughter, finding a natural rhythm in our conversation. I quietly knew by the end of the evening that this was the person I wanted to spend the rest of my life with. Every glance, every shared smile, reinforced that feeling. I hoped Alex felt the same; the ease and comfort we found in each other's company were undeniable. But she didn't know when she'd be able to return to the UK, since this visit had drained her savings and she needed to get back to work.

I had to check myself to make sure this wasn't just a rekindling of a teenage infatuation. Alex had been in my thoughts since our first encounter over two decades ago. Back then, our interactions were limited to fleeting waves as she passed by the butcher's shop on her way to school. This time, however, we needed to be certain.

True to her direct nature, Alex suggested I come to Greece and stay with her for a while so we could truly get to know each other. It was a bold proposition, but it was typical of her upfront approach to life. She must have seen some potential in me worth taking the risk for. Her eyes, filled with hope and determination, conveyed that she was serious. Without hesitation, I agreed.

As we walked out of the restaurant, the cool evening breeze swirling around us, I felt a sense of excitement and anticipation. Our paths had diverged for so many years, only to converge again at this very moment. The prospect of visiting Greece, of experiencing Alex's world, filled me with a sense of adventure and hope. I knew that this journey was not just about seeing a new place, but about exploring the possibility of a future together.

I arrived at Athens airport feeling nervous as I passed through passport control and waited by the baggage carousel. The hum of the conveyor belt and the clatter of suitcases served as a backdrop to my swirling thoughts. I had to pinch myself. Was I actually here? Was Alex outside in the waiting area as arranged? It had all happened so fast. My past life became a blur, a distant memory overshadowed by the whirlwind of recent events.

As I passed customs, my heart pounded with anticipation. I anxiously looked around, hoping to see her. The crowd seemed to move in slow motion, every face a potential letdown. I hoped she hadn't had second thoughts. Doubts started creeping in, each second feeling like an eternity.

And then, amidst the sea of unfamiliar faces, I spotted her. Alex stood there, a radiant beacon of warmth and beauty. Her smile was like a sunrise, banishing the shadows of my worries. She waved enthusiastically, her eyes sparkling with excitement.

I quickened my pace, my suitcase dragging behind me, my heart lifting with every step. As I reached her, she enveloped me in a hug that felt like coming home. The scent of her hair, the touch of her hands on my back, all reassured me that this was real, we were here together, and that the future we were about to explore was just beginning.

"Welcome to Greece," she said, her voice a melodious blend of happiness and promise.

"I'm so glad you're here," I replied, my nerves melting away in the warmth of her presence.

We walked out of the airport into the Greek sunshine, the world around us buzzing with life. With Alex by my side, I felt ready to embrace whatever came next. This was our moment, and I knew without a doubt that I was exactly where I was meant to be.

After a short taxi ride, we arrived at her home in Glyfada. The first thing I noticed as we left the taxi was the overwhelming perfume of the jasmine hedge that spread across the front of the house. The scent was intoxicating, wrapping around me like a warm embrace and instantly making me feel at home. We entered through the wrought-iron gate and stepped into a sun-drenched courtyard, shaded by a canopy of vibrant bougainvillea that seemed to bleed a deep, passionate red against the blue sky.

The country itself was stunning, but Alex was even more breathtaking. Her presence was like the jasmine, captivating and unforgettable. Each evening, as the sun dipped below the horizon, we found ourselves drawn into deep conversations that stretched into the late hours of the night. We talked about everything – our dreams, our fears, our pasts, and our futures. There was an ease in our communication, a natural flow that felt as though we had been having these conversations for years rather than days.

By the time I had to leave for England, it was clear that our futures were intertwined. It wasn't just the easy rapport or the shared laughter; it was the sense of finding someone who understands you at a level deeper than words. As I stood at the airport, ready to board my flight back to England, I realised that this was not just a fleeting romance. It was the beginning of something profound and lasting. We had discovered each other anew, and there was no turning back.

We began to make plans for our lives together. I suggested that I could work in England during the week while she continued her work as a beauty therapist in Athens, and I could fly to Greece on weekends. Fortunately, cheap air travel made this possible, allowing me to commute between our two worlds. It would be tiring but worthwhile, giving me time to adjust to Greek culture while being with Alex.

Although Alex loved the idea, she had reservations.

"How can you fly every weekend?" she asked. "I would

love you to be with me, but you will get exhausted." I could see she was conflicted. "It would be wonderful to spend every weekend together, but such a long journey every week would certainly take its toll."

"Look, let's try it for a month and see how it goes," I replied.

I became EasyJet's top client. I would fly out of England to Athens on the Thursday night flight at 10 p.m. Alex would meet me at the airport at 3 a.m. on Friday mornings, and we would spend the weekend together. On Monday, I would catch the 7 a.m. flight back to Luton, arriving at 9 a.m. because of the time difference. I would then work eighteen hours a day until my return on Thursday night back into Alex's arms.

This routine turned into my regular commute for two years. I developed such familiarity with the flight crews that I knew each of them by name. They would even save a seat for me, well aware of the exact moment I would board the plane.

During my initial visits, Alex and I had the house to ourselves. Her mother, Debbie, was still in England, her brother, Christos, was finishing his university course, and her father, Zissis, was away with his work as a cruise director. This solitude gave us the perfect opportunity to get to know each other intimately, without the distraction of a busy household. We spent our days exploring the local area, and our evenings were filled with long conversations under the stars. But this peaceful interlude was short-lived, and soon enough, the house was buzzing with life as the family returned home. Debbie arrived like a hurricane. As soon as her friends and relatives realised she was back, the house became a centre of activity. The peace and quiet of when it was just Alex and I living there was suddenly gone. The sounds of conversation and laughter echoed through the house as a constant stream of family members and friends visited. They passionately debated politics, shared heartfelt stories, and exchanged philosophies. The kitchen quickly became my favourite place, a bustling hub where the tantalising scent of garlic, olive oil and freshly baked bread wafted through the rooms.

The music, too, was an integral part of the home. The sounds of bouzouki and traditional Greek folk songs filled the air during family gatherings and celebrations, adding to the festive atmosphere.

Living with a Greek family was an explosion of vibrant sights, rich scents, lively conversations and unforgettable tastes. Each day brought new experiences and deeper connections, leaving an indelible mark on my senses. I felt an intense sense of belonging, as if I had been embraced by a new family and culture that welcomed me with open arms.

In a Greek family, there's an extraordinary tradition of openness and honesty unlike anything I'd known before. From a young age, children are encouraged to express their emotions freely, and this candid communication continues into adulthood. Family gatherings often feel like open forums where no topic is off-limits – whether it's hopes, fears, or deeply personal issues. It's not seen as oversharing; it's simply how they connect and build trust.

This level of honesty forges strong bonds. Celebrations are filled with heartfelt cheers and spontaneous dancing, as joy is shared with genuine enthusiasm. Conversely, in tough times, no one is left to face struggles alone. Whether it's financial troubles or health scares, the entire family rallies together with unwavering support. As the saying goes, "Eímaste oikogéneia, kai aftó simaínei óti den eísai poté mónos" (We are family, and that means you are never alone). It's a mantra that embodies the spirit of unity in even the darkest moments.

The sense of community often extends beyond blood relatives. Close friends, neighbours and even colleagues are embraced as part of the wider family network, welcomed into the fold with the same warmth and sincerity. A family dinner might easily include a mix of relatives and lifelong friends, all gathered around the table, sharing food, laughter, and life's ups and downs.

In a Greek family, life is lived out loud and in the open. This culture of transparency and shared experience creates bonds that are deep and unbreakable. Whether in moments of joy or hardship, the family stands together, a testament to the strength that comes from truly knowing and supporting one another.

It took me a while to grasp this cultural difference and get used to it. According to Alex, I was still "far too English", carrying the emotional baggage of my English upbringing where feelings were hidden away like dirty laundry. Growing up in England in the early nineteen sixties, we were trained to keep our emotions under wraps, to maintain the so-called "stiff upper lip" and to live by the motto "big boys don't cry".

So, Alex decided to take on a new project: converting me

into a more emotionally expressive human being. "I'm going to open you up," she declared, rolling up her sleeves like a mad scientist, ready to dissect my British reserve.

The first step in her plan was a visit to the local lap dancing club. Alex paid a naked woman to sit on my lap and wriggle. "It's okay to feel things," she told me afterwards. "This is living. You need to brush away your embarrassment and embrace life. You are not going to have an affair with this girl. It's just a temporary emotion. It shows you're human."

I stood there, bewildered. "Alex, I really don't need this," I said, feeling my face flush. I wasn't sure if it was embarrassment or anger that I felt. But Alex had got her way. It was certainly an emotion.

She kissed my red cheek. "That's progress, my love. At least you're not bottling it up!"

Next, she planned a weekend in Mykonos during the XLSIOR International Summer Gay Festival. "We're going to dance in the town square," she announced with a gleam in her eye.

When we arrived, the vibrant energy of the festival hit me like a tidal wave. Alex dragged me into the crowd, and soon we were surrounded by people dancing with abandon. "Just let go!" she shouted over the music, her arms flailing wildly to the beat.

"Alex, I feel like a floundering chicken!" I yelled back, trying to imitate her moves but feeling utterly ridiculous.

"You look fantastic! Keep going!" she encouraged.

After that, we visited a transgender nightclub. As we walked in, Alex grinned at me. "Ready for another round of emotional liberation?"

"I think I'm as ready as I'll ever be," I said, trying to muster some enthusiasm.

We sat down, and soon a performer came on stage, dazzling the audience with an incredible show. I found myself clapping along, feeling more comfortable as the night went on.

"See? You're loosening up," Alex observed.

"I have to admit, I love this," I said, genuinely enjoying the experience.

The final stop in Alex's emotional boot camp was an afternoon at Super Paradise Beach – a place where clothing was optional, and vulnerability was embraced. As the small transport boat approached the shore, my nerves started to take hold.

"Alex, are you sure about this?" I asked, my voice tinged with anxiety.

"Absolutely," she said with a confident smile. "It's about embracing vulnerability and feeling free. Trust me on this."

I hesitated, looking around at the carefree people on the beach. "Do we really need to get undressed to understand that freedom?" I asked, trying to find a way to ease my nerves.

Alex laughed softly. "Not necessarily. Sometimes it's about appreciating the freedom of others and understanding what that openness means to them."

Taking a deep breath as we stepped onto the beach, I felt a strange mix of liberation and terror wash over me as I slowly began to appreciate the experience. While I still felt exposed, I realised that the real lesson was in observing the freedom of others and understanding that vulnerability can be powerful, even if it's not in my comfort zone.

"I feel like I've lost something important," I joked, trying to lighten the mood and cover my nervousness.

"Yes, your inhibitions!" Alex gave me a playful nudge. By the end of the afternoon, I realised Alex's project was working. I was opening up.

"Alex, I think I'm starting to get the hang of this," I said as we walked back to our spot on the beach.

She smiled, clearly pleased. "I knew you would. You just needed a little push."

"A little push?" I laughed. "I feel like I've been thrown off a high building."

"Well, sometimes you need a good shove to get things moving."

Looking back, I had to admit she was right. These experiences had opened me up in ways I never thought possible. And with Alex by my side, I knew I'd keep growing, one adventure at a time.

Our trial month of commuting had quickly turned into two years, and before we knew it, we were standing together at the altar, committing to a life that would merge not just our hearts but our cultures. The wedding itself was a beautiful blur of Greek music and English traditions – a celebration of the life we were building together. It wasn't just a promise between the two of us; it was a merging of two families, two ways of life.

But it wasn't all one-way traffic in merging our cultures. I, too, had something to bring. English culture, with its own unique traits, had a lot to offer our Anglo-Greek marriage. While Alex's plans to "open me up" were well underway, marriage brought a new layer of integration. Now, surrounded by the warmth and openness of her Greek family, I found myself embracing a different kind of life – one where shared meals and deep conversations became the norm, and where I was learning to shed my English reserve, bit by bit.

Greeks appreciate many aspects of English culture, and our honesty is one of them. This is highly valued, because in Greek society, trust and integrity are essential in building and maintaining strong relationships. Throughout my life I have always strived to live with honour, keeping my promises and being true to my word. These qualities were respected by the Greeks, not only when it came to being a visitor or a friend but also as a member of the family.

Living with a Greek family taught me that it's essential to openly feel and express emotions rather than internalise them. However, English culture brought its own kind of emotional strength to the marriage. While Greeks are known for their passionate expression, the English sense of restraint can add balance and calm to a relationship. This doesn't mean suppressing emotions but rather approaching situations with a level-headedness that can be very grounding.

English humour, with its dry wit and subtlety, was another gift to our marriage. It's a way to find lightness in challenging situations, bringing laughter and perspective when things get tense. This sense of humour resonated with Alex, adding an extra layer of joy and connection to our relationship.

Also, the English appreciation for personal space and independence complemented the close-knit nature of Greek families. It offered a gentle reminder of the importance of individual time and self-reflection, which enriched our shared experiences.

In our marriage, these English values blended beautifully with the vibrant, expressive Greek culture, creating a partnership that honoured the best of both worlds.

Alex had grown up in Glyfada when it was still a village, playing on dusty roads and forming lifelong bonds with the community. Over time it had changed, losing its small village charm to become an upscale suburb of Athens favoured by the wealthy. Despite many of our friends and neighbours taking advantage of soaring real estate prices and moving to the islands to reconnect with a more authentic Greek way of life, we remained steadfast in our decision to stay put. Alex was born here. This was her village, and whatever it would become in the future, it was her home.

Alex's roots run deep in Glyfada; the memories tied to that street were too many to let go. For me, it was where I first experienced Greek culture, welcomed with open arms by Alex's family. Debbie was the heart of it all, tirelessly cooking for a constant stream of visitors who gathered under the blooming bougainvillea to share stories and laughter. Her delicious Greek dishes filled the air with a fragrant aroma as she bustled about the kitchen wearing nothing but her knickers and bra. From her window, Debbie, whose real name is Despina but everyone called her Debbie, would often engage in lively conversations with neighbours down the street. Her voice was so powerful that not even the roar of aeroplanes departing from the nearby airport could drown her out.

Our old house was simple. It was a crumbling wreck, but it was full of love. The lower section of the house, where Debbie and Zissis lived, was particularly dank and dilapidated. It was a semi-basement, reached via an entrance to the side of the building, down three marble steps. The entrance was marked by a cast-iron lattice door panelled with multicoloured stained glass. The intricate patterns of the stained glass cast a beautiful mosaic of colours onto the bare stone floor, which was randomly scattered with rugs which added a bit of warmth to the otherwise cool environment.

In spite of its flaws, the semi-basement had a certain charm. It was always dark and shaded down there, mostly as a defence against the scorching Greek summers, allowing the home to stay cool. The temperature remained surprisingly pleasant even during the peak of summer, making it a popular refuge for the family and visitors alike. Although there were windows in every room, these always had the shutters closed to stop the relentless sun from penetrating and turning the space into an oven.

The house always had a musty smell, a constant reminder of the dampness that caused large chunks of plaster to fall off the stone walls. To cover the bald patches, polythene was stuck on with masking tape, creating an almost patchwork effect. Framed old photographs, oil paintings, and a poster of the harbour in Castella, Debbie's home town, were hung over the polythene, adding a touch of nostalgia and personal history to the otherwise stark walls.

In one corner of the living room, there was a small table adorned with a hand-painted wooden icon of the infant Jesus cradled in Mary's arms, both with shimmering gold halos. Little oil burners created a soothing ambiance, their flames dancing in eternal reverence. The room was filled with the fragrance of everlasting incense, reflecting the spirituality within these walls. Beside the icon, there were neatly arranged rosary beads, another sacred icon and a cluster of postcards featuring lesser saints. This sacred space was a common sight in Greek houses, with an always-lit oil burner and one or two icons of favourite saints. In our case, because of the family's seafaring history, it was dedicated to Saint Nicholas, the patron saint of sailors.

Despite its physical state, the house was a place of warmth, filled with the sounds of animated conversations, laughter, and the occasional outburst of song. It was a sanctuary where the family gathered to share their joys and sorrows, making it a home in the truest sense of the word.

This is where I cut my teeth on true Greek culture. But things in this idyllic Greek village were changing. We held back the steamroller of progress as long as we could, but two years before the 2004 Olympics came home to Greece, we finally relented. Our house was the last one standing on our street.

All of our neighbours had demolished their family homes and replaced them with multistorey apartment blocks. It was inevitable that we would eventually give in and do the same. We decided to make plans to build.

Debbie and Zissis were aware of our plans to reconstruct, but they were content to let us handle the planning and research. In a high value area of Greece, it is common to make a deal with the architect. They would demolish and rebuild the property, covering all expenses, and in return they would receive half of the completed construction. We would receive three apartments and a new retail shop; our architect would receive the same. On paper, it was a good deal.

As Alex and I travelled more frequently, leaving Debbie and Zissis at home in Glyfada, we grappled with the reality of transforming our family home. After weeks of negotiations over the telephone from England, we finally decided on an architect. But convincing Debbie to take the final step would be the real challenge. The house was not just a structure of bricks and mortar; it was the keeper of cherished memories, laughter echoing through its walls, and the smell of home-cooked meals wafting through the air.

Yet Debbie had already realised, deep down, that she could not halt progress. She understood that our house was the only one left standing in the shadows of the new tower blocks surrounding it, and it was only a matter of time before she would need to comply. She could see that the quaint neighbourhood she once knew was transforming into a modern skyline, and her beloved home now seemed like an island amidst the sea of change. Despite her reluctance, she knew that embracing the future was necessary to preserve a piece of it.

Landing in Athens, we picked up Alex's family and headed to Castella for lunch to break the news. I had always had a close relationship with her parents. Debbie was generous and loving, while Zissis was formal and principled. They had welcomed me into their lives, and I hoped they would support our plan.

We chose a charming taverna by the harbour, and as Zissis ordered, I broached the subject. Debbie sipped her wine, considering our proposal to replace the old house with a new development. Her father had built the house when Glyfada was still a fishing village. It held many memories, but she saw the potential for a better future.

Reaching across the table, I took Debbie's hand. Tears ran down her cheeks, but she smiled. "Are you sure this is what you want?" she asked. Alex nodded.

"We can delay this for a few more years," I said.

Debbie shook her head. "You are my son and the husband of my daughter. If you think it's the right thing to do, you have my blessing. Let's do it now."

But at that time we had no idea of the drastic changes that had already begun to affect our village. We didn't realise that it would prove to be the beginning of the end for our neighbourhood. The friendly and open society would change forever in the name of progress. Glyfada would soon become a city in its own right.

Even as our multilevel apartment block was being completed, Glyfada was already becoming impersonal. In the old days, it had taken an entire morning to walk to the square. Every few metres, we would meet friends and neighbours on the street, catch up on local gossip and have coffee together. But now when we went out on errands, faceless strangers would rush by without a second glance. The cosy charm of the familiar coffee shops we used to go to had been lost, as corporate chains with modern decor had taken over, offering free Wi-Fi and serving mediocre coffee in disposable cups. The sense of community felt distant as we walked through the busy streets. City life was quickly replacing the warmth and familiarity of the village. The sleek storefronts and trendy cafes were replacing the traditional old establishments.

We were becoming nostalgic for simpler times. We longed for the days when every corner had a story and every face had a connection.

CHAPTER 3

Meet the Barbers

Every heart sings a song, incomplete, until another heart whispers back.

– Plato

Since we became a couple, it was important for us to embrace both of our cultures and become a genuine Anglo-Greek couple. Therefore, I made it a point to introduce Alex to my culture too. This meant a visit to England to meet my family.

Alex is no stranger to England. She studied at college, gained a degree. As a student, she had few English friends, however. Her life comprised hard study and being at home with her Greek family, with no socialising in between, so she missed any absorption into the culture. Although she was in England, she still lived the Greek life.

But this was about to change. She had agreed to marry me, for better or worse. She also needed to adapt to English culture This was going to be fun.

Marrying into a typical English family presented its own unique problems for Alex.

Since her days at university, Alex had rarely visited England. When she came, it was usually alone and for brief visits, such as the one when we had first reunited. But when we became a couple, our visits became more frequent. The first time travelling together was certainly fun.

Alex has an informality with everyone she meets. Sometimes I watch as she speaks to tax inspectors, police officers or the local mayor. She speaks using the same tone and Greek slang as she uses with her friends while enjoying a coffee. This is one thing I love about her. Her effortless style is charming, which puts people at their ease.

But, to Alex's surprise, it is a little different at Heathrow.

On our first visit to England as a couple, we approached passport control. Alex looked up and saw a Union Jack flag sticker pasted on a sign which read "Welcome to Border Control". Under this was a sour-looking, uniformed Home Office official ready to check our passports. Alex pulled her phone out of her bag to take a photograph.

"Stop!" the official yelled, and pointed to a "No Photographs" sign. Alex was undeterred. She continued to fiddle with her phone.

"Madam. It is against the law to take photographs here. This is border control. You will be arrested."

Whereas in Greece, the immigration officer would probably join you in a nice selfie and ask you to send them a copy on WhatsApp, here you are likely to be handcuffed and dragged away for interrogation, including an intimate body search and large quantities of Vaseline.

Alex was not impressed. I could feel her frustration growing. She was gearing up for a fight she couldn't possibly win. I gripped her arm tightly to keep her from confronting the situation head-on. Alex is reasonable and will follow rules, but only if they make sense. Not driving through a red light makes sense; it prevents accidents. Not stuffing fifty kilos of olive oil into your luggage makes sense too, given that it's a highly flammable liquid and we're already on a plane filled with jet fuel. But not being allowed to take a simple photo of a flag made no sense at all.

"Please don't make a fuss," I pleaded. "Things are different here. You may get away with this in Greece, but here you must follow the rules. No photographs."

Alex nodded and put her phone away, but she was still sulking as we went to collect our bags.

In Greece, a strong sense of formality persists within the family unit. Greeks hold a great deal of respect for their older family members. When conversing with these relatives, it is customary to address them in the plural form as a sign of respect. This practice is somewhat like the use of the royal "we". Instead of directly asking them a question, which is considered impolite, one would speak as if addressing a group of people. For example, one might say, "How are they feeling today?" or

"Have they eaten lunch today?" This is how Alex addresses her aunts, uncles and father. However, things were different with her mother. They shared a close bond and considered each other more like friends than mother and daughter. Therefore, she never used the plural form when speaking to her mother, and this arrangement suited them both.

Alex has a wonderful command of the English language. She is almost without an accent. Sometimes, when she speaks on the phone, she sounds as though she was born in a castle from royal stock. Her cut-glass accent is perfect. So when she first came with me to our family home in England and met my father, she clicked out of her usual accent mode and into her English telephone voice, complete with the plural form of address.

My dear cockney father looked most confused. He was expecting to meet the daughter of Zorba the Greek, complete with a hairy upper lip and an incomprehensible accent. Instead, standing before him was a glamorous, immaculately presented beauty who used English words he had never heard of.

She held out her hand and said, "It is so good to meet you, Mr Barber. How are they?"

My dad whispered to me, "I thought you were bringing your Greek girlfriend to meet me. Who's this one?"

"Dad, meet Alex. She is Greek, from Athens. That's in Greece."

I had to emphasise that he was talking to the right person. He had decided she could not possibly be Greek, not with that appearance and accent. He had already convinced himself I had been dumped by the Greek one and found an upgrade.

"Who is she talking to?" he said, looking around the room in case someone else had entered.

"She's talking to you in the plural as a mark of respect," I told him. This made no sense to my dad, who just nodded and smiled. But Alex charmed him, and like everyone who meets her for the first time, he was soon in love.

Next was the visit to my brother and sister. As soon as we arrived, Alex's Greek accent was back in full swing. She laughed and joked with them as if they were lifelong friends, effortlessly bridging the cultural gap. My brother and sister were instantly charmed by her warmth and energy.

My brother Jon was just about to leave for a holiday in Corfu.

"Come on, Alex, give us a quick Greek lesson," he asked.

I buried my head in my hands. I knew what was coming. Whatever she was going to teach them would certainly not be Greek found in any phrase book. I made a mental note to warn them against using Alex's teachings in polite company. I had already been a victim of her jokes when I thought I was learning formal Greek, only to find out by bitter experience that I should never repeat anything she taught me.

But they were grown adults, so be it on their heads.

"Okay, let's start with some basics," Alex said, grinning. "You should say 'Kaliméra' for good morning and 'Efharisto' for thank you."

"Kaliméra," my brother repeated, trying to mimic her accent. "Ef-hari-sto," he added, stumbling a bit over the unfamiliar sounds.

"That's great!" Alex encouraged, her eyes twinkling with amusement. "Next is 'Malaka' – it's a very useful word."

"What does 'Malaka' mean?" my sister asked, pen poised over her notepad.

Alex chuckled. "It has many uses. It's a nice way of telling someone they are a little bit of an idiot. But we use it informally to greet friends."

"Alex, don't tell them to use that word. It will get them in so much trouble." I turned to my sister. "It's a rude word. It's best to avoid that one."

My brother laughed out loud. "I know lots of malakas. This will be fun. They won't even know they've been insulted."

"Unless they are Greek," I told him. "Then you would probably get attacked. Just stick to kaliméra and efharisto and you'll be fine."

But Alex was just getting going.

"If you really want to impress your friends, there are a few other phrases," she said with a mischievous grin.

"Oh, great." My brother leaned in eagerly.

"Alright," Alex said, lowering her voice as if sharing a secret. "If someone's annoying you, you can say 'Gamísou!' It's like saying 'go away.'"

"Gamísou!" my brother repeated. "I'll remember that one." He still had no idea it meant "fuck off", but I was sure he would find out the hard way.

"And then there's 'pousti', which is a nice word to use in the police station. I use it quite a lot."

"No, don't," I told them, "unless you want to be arrested."

I looked at Alex. "You are going to get them into so much trouble. Stop it now."

Alex giggled. She was really enjoying herself.

"And what about something a little less insulting?" my brother asked.

"Well, you could say 'Se écho grápsei sta balákia mou.'" Alex paused just long enough for dramatic effect before adding, "It means 'I have written you on my balls.'"

"It's not too harsh," she added with a shrug.

As the lesson continued, Alex seamlessly blended rude language instruction with obscene anecdotes. By the time she was finished, we were all red-faced with tears running down our cheeks.

She shared stories about Greek traditions, making my brother and sister laugh with tales of her childhood. It was clear they were enthralled, not just by the unfamiliar words they were learning but by the way Alex made everything come alive.

"And if you want to impress someone, say 'S'agapo' – it means 'I love you,'" Alex said with a warm smile.

"S'agapo," my sister repeated shyly.

Alex nodded approvingly. "That's right. And 'Yamas' is a useful one too – it means 'Cheers!'"

"Yamas!" my brother and sister echoed, raising imaginary glasses.

"Okay, I think she's got you into enough trouble now," I said.

"Remember," Alex added, "any other Greek words you would like to know, just ask. Next time, I will teach you a few

Greek expressions."

"Never use those either," I said.

"Noted," my sister said, giggling. "But it's fun to learn. Thanks for the lesson, Alex."

By the time we left, my brother and sister were eagerly planning how they'd use their new language skills on their upcoming trips. They hugged Alex, thanking her for the lesson, and she promised to teach them more before they left.

In the car, I looked at Alex with admiration. "You really have a gift for making people feel comfortable," I said.

She smiled, her eyes sparkling. "It's easy when you meet such wonderful people."

Alex's ability to merge her Greek roots with British customs wasn't just about language or traditions; it was about her genuine interest in people and their stories. She took the time to understand my family's history, their quirks and their ways of life, just as she cherished her own family's background. Her adaptability and respect for both cultures allowed her to create connections and build bridges, making everyone around her feel valued and understood.

As we were planning to spend a few months in the UK, Alex faced the daunting task of adapting to British culture beyond the comfort of our family. As a foreigner in an unfamiliar land, she knew it would be challenging to find her place and feel at home.

In Greece, a friendly chat with a stranger can quickly turn into an invitation for coffee or a shared meal. But in Britain, she noticed that people tended to keep more to themselves. The contrast was noticeable when she visited a local coffee shop.

Alex was stood next to a woman at the counter. "It's a lovely day, isn't it?" she said, smiling warmly.

The woman looked up from her newspaper, a bit surprised by the sudden interaction. "Oh, yes," she replied politely but briefly, returning her attention to the paper.

Everywhere she went, Alex received the same reaction: polite, but distanced.

Later, Alex discussed the experience with me. "What's wrong with people here?" she fumed. "They are half dead. I can't figure it out. In Greece, we'd be chatting away like old friends by now. Here, it feels like I'm bothering them by just saying hello."

I tried to explain things are a little different here. "Don't worry," I reassured her. "People here just take a little longer to warm up. They're not unfriendly; it's just a different way of connecting."

Alex was beginning to understand why I had arrived in Greece with so much emotional baggage. "People don't want to talk to each other. They all have their heads down trying to hide."

If she was going to live here, England needed to change. Even Alex realised it would be difficult to change the entire country, but she had to start somewhere. She would start with our neighbourhood and build from there.

Our house in England is located in a cul-de-sac, with about thirty houses encircling it. Each of these houses has a small front garden. In England, it's not uncommon for people to live in their homes for years without ever getting to know their neighbours. The tendency to maintain a respectful distance seems to be a hallmark of British culture, where privacy is valued and personal space is respected. Alex, however, was determined to break through this cultural barrier and get to know everybody. She was ready to bring a touch of Greece to our corner of England.

"Why don't we know our neighbours yet?" she asked me one evening, a hint of challenge in her voice. "We've been here a week. Back home, we would have known everyone in the area by now."

"People here just take a little longer to open up," I replied, smiling at her persistence.

"Well, I'm going to change that," she declared, as she rolled up her sleeves like she was preparing for a new project.

The next day, Alex baked a batch of baklava, her signature Greek pastry, to share with the neighbours. Armed with her sweet offerings, she set out to introduce herself to each household on our street.

Her first stop was an elderly woman who lived two doors down. Alex knocked on the door. After a moment, the door creaked open, and eyes peered out cautiously.

"Hello!" Alex greeted her warmly. "I'm Alex, your new neighbour. I brought you some home-made baklava. I'm from Greece."

The lady's eyes widened in surprise, her cautious demeanour softening. "Well, isn't that lovely," she said, accepting the plate with a tentative smile. "Thank you, dear. My name is

Daisy. Would you like a cup of tea?"

Encouraged by her small victory, Alex continued her rounds, visiting each house and sharing her home-made treats. Some neighbours were reserved, while others were more welcoming, intrigued by Alex's friendly nature and the delicious pastries she brought.

When she returned home later that day, she was beaming with a sense of accomplishment. "I think I made a good start," she said, her eyes shining with satisfaction. "People here may be more reserved, but they're not unfriendly."

Over the next few weeks, Alex's efforts began to bear fruit. She started receiving invitations for coffee and found herself slowly being included in the community. She discovered that while British culture valued privacy, people were also curious and open to building relationships once the initial barrier was breached.

One evening, as we walked down the street, Alex waved to a man pruning roses in his front garden. "Good evening, Fred. How's Dorothy?" she asked.

Fred waved back from his garden. "Hi Alex! Would you and your husband like to join us for a barbecue this weekend?"

Alex smiled brightly, nudging me with her elbow. "See? It just takes a little kindness to get things started."

By embracing her natural warmth and friendliness, Alex was able to build bridges in her new environment. Her determination to start with the neighbours had not only helped her feel more at home but also brought a touch of Greek hospitality to our British street. But Alex wasn't finished there. Her next target was the local Zumba class, where she hoped to continue her quest to break down more barriers. Alex loved dancing, and she knew that music and movement were universal languages that could connect people.

When she joined her first class, she danced enthusiastically to the lively music, moving alongside the thirty or so women in attendance. At the end of the class, however, she noticed something peculiar. Despite the shared experience, most people gave only a few friendly waves before quietly leaving the room without engaging with one another.

Determined to change this, Alex devised a plan. The following day, she arrived at the class early and chatted with the instructor, who was delighted by Alex's interest and energy. "I just think it would be lovely if we all got to know each other a bit better," she explained with her characteristic enthusiasm.

As each person arrived, Alex made it a point to introduce herself personally. "Hi, I'm Alex! It's great to meet you," she would say, extending her hand and offering a genuine smile. Her openness and warmth quickly put people at ease, and they began to respond positively to her friendly approach.

During the class, Alex's spirited dance moves caught everyone's attention. People couldn't help but smile as they glanced over at her. Her infectious energy spread throughout the room, and some women gave her encouraging thumbs-ups and nodded in approval, clearly enjoying the presence of their lively new member.

When the music stopped, instead of rushing out like before, Alex took the opportunity to wander around the room, offering compliments and starting conversations. She approached one woman and said, "Wow, you're a great dancer! Are you a professional?"

The woman blushed at the unexpected praise. "Oh, no, I just enjoy dancing!"

The ice was broken, and soon others joined in, sharing stories about their love for dancing and how long they had been attending the class. Laughter and chatter filled the room and friendships began to form.

Alex had transformed the Zumba class from a mere exercise session into a social event. Her genuine interest in others and her natural ability to make people feel valued helped her turn strangers into friends. She was delighted to see the group slowly evolving into a fun place to be.

As the weeks passed, the Zumba class became a highlight for many of the women, who now stayed after class to chat, share stories, and even joined each other for coffee.

Alex had successfully turned the tide. She searched for other Zumba classes and promptly joined them. Within a few weeks, she found herself attending two sessions a day, each held at different locations.

Alex has always had a special place in her heart for older people. From a young age, she found herself drawn to the stories and wisdom that her grandparents and their friends shared. The warmth and kindness she received from them made her feel cherished, and she often sought their company for their comforting presence and invaluable life lessons. This affection naturally extended to the wider community, where she loved every opportunity to engage with the older generation.

One of Alex's favourite classes was Zumba Gold, a session specifically designed for older people who wanted to stay active during their golden years. Although Alex was younger than the rest of the group and an energetic, talented dancer, she deeply admired the determination these women showed in keeping fit.

She loved joining in with Zumba Gold, and it soon became her favourite group. Not just for the exercise but also for the fun and support that flowed through the room. When the original instructor announced she was leaving and that the gold class was going to end, Alex felt a strong calling to step up and fill the void. Her passion for helping others, combined with her respect and love for older people, inspired her.

"I've seen how much happiness this class brings to everyone, and I want to keep that going," Alex said to the group after a session. "I'm going to train as an instructor so we can keep dancing together." Her announcement was met with enthusiastic cheers and claps from the class, and the encouragement from her friends fuelled her determination. She studied an online course, and after a few days gained her qualification as a Zumba Gold instructor.

With her new qualification, Alex took over the Zumba Gold sessions, bringing her unique style and energy to each class. In taking on the role of instructor, Alex not only fulfilled a personal passion but also ensured that the older adults continued to have a space where they could enjoy fitness, friendship and fun. And with the new friendships she had cultivated, Alex realised that even though the approach was different, genuine connections could still be made. By embracing the differences and finding common ground, she slowly started feeling more comfortable in her new environment.

When it was time to return to Greece, Alex would be leaving behind a different culture in our small town, one that had been profoundly touched by her warmth and openness. Her presence had not only bridged cultural gaps but also inspired a sense of community that had long been missing.

Alex had managed to weave a tapestry of Greek hospitality into the fabric of our English neighbourhood. She had transformed our street into a place where neighbours greeted each other warmly, stopped to chat, and even organised occasional gatherings to share stories and laughter.

"Thank you for everything, Alex," said one of her students, hugging her tightly on the last day of class. "You've made such a difference here. We're going to miss you so much."

"You've taught us to dance, but more importantly, you've become a good friend," added another participant, wiping away tears.

When the day finally came to say goodbye, neighbours gathered to see us off. There were hugs and promises to stay in touch. Alex's departure was bittersweet, marked by gratitude for the memories created and the relationships forged.

"Don't forget to send us pictures from Greece," said one neighbour, waving as we drove away. "And come back soon!"

Alex smiled; she had certainly made a difference in the few short months. "We will," she promised, blowing kisses from the car window. "And remember, you're all welcome to visit us in Greece any time." And she meant it.

Returning to Greece felt like coming home, but the town she had left behind would always hold a special place in her heart. Alex had left behind more than just a different culture; she had left behind a legacy of friendship, acceptance and community spirit that would continue to inspire and thrive.

CHAPTER 4

Gossip and Intrigue in a Greek Village

Anybody can become angry – that is easy, but to be angry with the right person and to the right degree and at the right time and for the right purpose, and in the right way – that is not within everybody's power and is not easy.

– Aristotle

We arrived at Adonia's taverna, which she runs with her son Niko, just after it happened. The aftermath was quite evident, however. Coffee was dripping from the ceiling; the walls were freshly painted with splashes of sticky brown brew. We stepped over the puddles and took our seats. Adonia laughed as she told us the story.

Eleni, one of the oldest residents of the village, who was well into her nineties, had been chatting with Adonia, while Spiros, the eighty-eight-year-old gravedigger, was sitting at his regular table, enjoying his usual breakfast of two miniature bottles of the local firewater, tsipouro, goat's cheese and bread. It was an ordinary morning at the taverna. The fishermen had returned from their night of net dragging in the bay. They unloaded the fish onto the nearby harbour wall, packed them in ice, and prepared them for delivery to fish tavernas in the village. Any remaining fish would be sent to the market.

The conversation that day had been about Stavros, one of the older locals who had recently gone to meet his maker. He was over a hundred years old and died as he lived, with a glass of his beloved tsipouro in one hand and a cigarette in the other. The lifetime of heavy smoking and drinking had little effect. The old men of the village often tell me that smoke and alcohol are both preservatives, hence their long lives.

According to local gossip, his downfall had nothing to do with the smoke and booze but was attributed to his new young girlfriend. The villagers claimed that, at the age of seventy, she had placed unreasonable sexual expectations on him, ultimately leading to his demise.

The funeral would be in a couple of days. So, the subject of burial plots had come up.

We knew that Spiros and Eleni had had a tense relationship for a while. Spiros, while not digging graves, worked part-time tending them at a nearby cemetery. Eleni was particular about maintaining her husband's resting place there. Seven years earlier, when Spiros neglected her husband's plot, Eleni was furious. She confronted him, seeking an explanation and apology. However, Spiros, too proud to admit his mistake, dismissed her with a remark. Since then, tension had simmered between them.

Over time, what initially started as a simple disagreement transformed into a constant battle. Eleni would regularly visit the cemetery to check on her husband's plot, scrutinising every detail. If she noticed even the slightest imperfection, she would storm into the village, unleashing her anger with a barrage of complaints. Spiros, stubborn and resentful, would often respond with a defensive attitude, blaming Eleni for being overly demanding and nitpicky.

Their interactions became a spectacle for those who frequented the local tavernas. The villagers would whisper about the ongoing feud, while visitors would observe the tense exchanges from a distance. The air around Spiros and Eleni always seemed thick with animosity.

However, deep down, both Spiros and Eleni knew that the tension had long surpassed its original cause. It was no longer about a poorly cleaned grave. It had become a battle of wills, a clash between two individuals who refused to back down. They were trapped in a cycle of anger and resentment, unable to find a resolution or let go of their grievances.

They frequented the same cafes and restaurants, yet always sat apart. Eye contact and communication were absent. It reminded me of the relationship between the local cats and dogs who hung around the tavernas. They too would never look at each other or communicate if they could help it. When a piece of food dropped from the table, there would be a series of growls from the dogs and hisses from the cats, until one or the other won the battle and an uneasy peace was resumed. Eleni and Spiros just added to the rich variety of village wildlife. There was no affection, only tolerance of each other's presence. Occasionally, a spark ignited, leading to a swift explosion.

Eleni was known for her long memory and short fuse. Adonia shared a story from years ago when Eleni argued with her own father. Furious, she took his pickup truck and drove to the harbour wall. She then got out and pushed it with all her strength until it teetered over the edge and plunged into the water. She stood there watching as it sank below the surface, smiling with satisfaction as it disappeared into the depths.

The extent of her revenge had shocked the whole village. It required two JCB diggers and a fishing boat to retrieve the submerged car from the water. Spiros knew this story well and always kept his moped nearby, just in case she decided to throw that into the harbour, too.

With both Spiros and Eleni having strong personalities and history, it was only a matter of time before their clash reached its boiling point.

The day after Stavros died, Eleni spoke loudly, directing her criticism pointedly at Spiros.

"After Stavros's burial," she warned everyone, "do not let him get near the grave." She went on to blame him for ruining her husband's grave and not even apologising.

Anger flushed Spiros's face as he struggled to swallow a piece of goat's cheese.

"Your husband's fortunate to be underground. He doesn't care what his grave looks like. He's just happy to be free of you," he retorted.

The entire taverna held its breath.

Suddenly, the coffee Eleni held in her hand shot across the taverna, causing Spiros to quickly duck. Unfortunately it ended up hitting the back of Niko's head as he tried to escape. Coffee covered his hair and dripped down his face as he hurriedly sought cover. Eleni was furious with Niko becoming an unintended victim, but what angered her most was that Spiros had the audacity to dodge the coffee. As a result, she decided to take matters further.

With a burst of fury, she threw herself across the table, causing more coffee cups to fly and drenching nearby spectators. She grabbed hold of Spiros by the throat, attempting to throttle him.

Adonia quickly intervened, pulling Eleni away. Spiros took advantage of his adversary being restrained and lunged towards her with fists flying. He managed to give her a glancing blow to the top of her head, which infuriated her even more.

Eleni broke free from Adonia's grasp with a primal scream. She unleashed a flurry of punches, fuelled by pure rage. Her fists crashed into Spiros's face and he fought back with equal ferocity. Their bodies twisted and collided, crashing into tables and chairs. The taverna erupted into chaos as onlookers scattered in fear. Eventually, Spiros landed a devastating blow to Eleni's gut, knocking the wind out of her. Eleni gasped for air and watched him take advantage of the pause and run to his moped. She soon recovered and gave chase. But he escaped.

That was the point where we walked in. People were laughing and mopping coffee off their faces. Niko was sulking in the kitchen after his coffee bath.

Eleni returned, looking angry. She was tense and frustrated that Spiros had escaped. Her hate towards him was palpable. She sat between Adonia and Alex with the grace of a disgruntled cat, signalling her determination for vengeance. Alex tried to calm things down, but Eleni's hatred for Spiros was stubborn. She launched into a tirade, listing his sins with a voice quivering with rage. This was not just a spat; it was a vendetta. Sitting across from them, I tried to look concerned, but I couldn't help but admire Eleni's resolve. It was like watching a real-life soap opera. Eleni's quest for justice was far from over, and the conflict with Spiros loomed large, like a cliffhanger waiting for the next episode.

We really didn't want to discuss this. If we took sides, we would not only risk losing our neutrality but also become enemies with Spiros and half the village who supported him. We held back from expressing any opinions.

Soon, the rage subsided into a simmer. Eleni appeared to be calm now, but Niko hadn't come back from the kitchen yet. New guests took their seats at a table but weren't being served.

"Peter, go and get a nice cake for Niko," Alex said. "He needs cheering up."

I took the car and drove to the cake shop in the next village. While I was gone, Spiros remembered his unfinished breakfast and bravely came back for it. The unopened bottle of tsipouro had been calling him. He slunk in, aware that Eleni was sitting on the other side of the room. After the storm of earlier, they had both adopted their normal stance of not acknowledging each other's presence.

I returned from the cake shop to find the enemies back in their usual seats, the air thick with an unspoken truce. I walked over to Spiros first, smiling as I shook his hand. He eyed me warily, but when I placed the sticky cake in front of him, I caught a flicker of something that might have been a smile, quickly masked by his usual gruffness. He hesitated for a moment, then couldn't resist pinching off a corner and popping it into his mouth, the earlier coffee incident seemingly forgotten.

Next, I went to Eleni, who raised an eyebrow as I leaned in and kissed her on the cheek. I offered her a cake and she took it with a bemused look, a hint of surprise softening her stern features. "You know how to make peace," she said, breaking off a piece and nodding in approval.

Finally, I headed into the kitchen, where Niko was still sulking, arms crossed like a stubborn child. I placed the rest of the bag of goodies in front of him. He glared at me for a beat, but then his resolve cracked. With a sigh, he grabbed a cake, taking a big bite as if to show he wasn't impressed, but I caught the corners of his mouth twitching upwards in a reluctant grin. "You're lucky these are good," he muttered, crumbs already spilling onto his shirt.

Living in a small rural community has taught us the importance of staying true to ourselves, even in the face of gossip and pressure. It has shown us that true community is built on acceptance, empathy, and a willingness to understand different perspectives.

In Pefki we had become part of the village community. Instead of being treated as guests, people accepted us as locals. We had developed an easy relationship with most in the village and felt more than comfortable.

We were no longer the centre of attention in the village but a part of it. I was still known as "The Anglos" and Alex was called "Xeni", meaning "foreigner", because she came from Athens, which is two hundred kilometres from the village. But she was forgiven and accepted, even though she spoke a different type of Greek.

For years, I had dedicated myself to learning Greek. I tried various methods: books, tapes and downloaded language courses. Unfortunately, these only confused me more. I hired a professional Greek teacher for personalised one-on-one lessons. However, despite spending a month focusing on mastering upper and lower case characters and learning to count, I still found it difficult to hold a conversation. I felt useless. I was living in a beautiful country, but because of my lack of language skills I still felt like an outsider. I hated relying on Alex to translate conversations. To do that, she needed to break off from a chat to keep filling me in on the important bits, while I just sat and looked stupid. It felt like my goal of holding a coherent conversation was slipping further away with each passing day. As my long-suffering teacher tried to teach me grammar, I quickly realised that I was completely out of my depth. How could each word undergo such big changes? It seemed that depending on factors like gender, tense, or even the present versus the past, the words would take on entirely different forms.

Alex was no help at all. When we were first together, I asked her to teach me the language. But, after countless embarrassing experiences, I realised that Alex, rather than wanting to teach me Greek, found it much more fun to teach me phrases and words which would only embarrass me every time I tried to speak out loud. Ordering a one kilo penis in a bakery first led me to suspect her motives. My suspicions were confirmed when I asked a petrol pump assistant for sexual intercourse. I had asked him to fill me up rather than the tank. So, if I was going to learn Greek, I would need to do it alone.

Over the next few years, my language skills developed painfully slowly. I was still spending a lot of time away from Greece, so any acquired language skills were soon lost. When I returned, I discovered that I had forgotten most of what I had learned before I left and had no choice but to start over. Still, I had picked up useful words and sentences. I was getting proficient at shopping and found I could hold a basic conversation with a shop assistant. What's more, as we spent much of our time in tavernas, I became very good at ordering food and wine. Again, basic conversations were forming. Soon, Alex and I developed our own Greeklish language, a mixture of Greek and English, which became our normal method of communication.

This was not the first time I had experienced difficulties with language. As a child, I even had trouble learning my own language. I was often frustrated and embarrassed when asked to read aloud or complete writing assignments. While my classmates effortlessly composed coherent sentences, I struggled to even form legible letters. Teachers would often scold me for my sloppy handwriting and poor spelling, further diminishing my confidence. Despite my efforts, I always lagged in language-related tasks.

As I grew up, my lack of language skills began to impact daily life. Simple tasks like reading street signs or following written instructions were difficult. I would often avoid situations that required me to read or write. This constant struggle and feeling of inadequacy made me question my own intelligence and abilities.

I didn't learn about dyslexia until I was an adult. It was then that I realised it perfectly described my troubles.

Although dyslexia was not widely recognised in the nineteen sixties, I couldn't help but wonder how different my educational journey could have been if I had received support and understanding. I managed to excel in other subjects, particularly those that required more visual and hands-on learning. I developed a photographic memory. This gave me a glimmer of hope that I was not completely stupid.

In my late twenties I discovered word processing with spellcheckers. Something remarkable happened. It felt like a floodgate had been opened, releasing years of suppressed creativity. Instantly words I never realised were trapped in my mind burst out in an unstoppable stream. I could write. It was a life-changing experience. Finally, my dyslexia no longer held me back, thanks to this simple tool. I was free to express my innermost thoughts. Through writing, I discovered a world filled with colours and flavours. Writing became my sanctuary, my passion, and my way of connecting with the world.

Had I stumbled on the reason for my inability to learn Greek? Obviously my brain was wired differently. Dyslexia, being a language-processing disorder, made it difficult for me to learn basic comprehension skills in my native language. So how could I expect to excel in a foreign one? While that might explain everything, I refused to be beaten by it. Now that I had identified the problem, I could change my approach. Instead of following a formal learning structure, I would immerse myself in conversations with people and integrate at my own pace.

Once I had found the reason for my appalling Greek language skills, things began to improve. I was understanding more every day.

When I explained this to Alex, she made a concentrated effort to help as much as she could. She would explain difficult words and pronunciation. She would speak slowly, allowing me time to hear the full words rather than a jumble of incoherent phrases. She would break down the words into syllables, which I managed to follow and repeat. Together we were getting there. At last, I would speak Greek. Or that was the plan until we arrived in our Greek village.

The local dialect and village accents bore little relation to what I had been learning in Glyfada and Athens. This sounded like a different language completely. It reminded me of my Geordie grandfather, who would say things like "Howay ye canny bairn" (come here, child). I didn't understand a word he said to me until I was ten years old. I needed to almost begin from scratch, listen to the words and fill in the gaps. This was frustrating but necessary if we were going to be part of this charming village and communicate with its lovely inhabitants.

In cities and towns worldwide, we live our lives in obscurity. On the island, things are different. Everyone knows everyone. They know their names and have intimate knowledge of them. They know what they do for a living, what they like to eat, how often they go shopping, and numerous other personal details. If they don't know something about someone, they make it up. According to the villagers in Pefki, I'm a lord with a castle in England. They believe I'm rich because I don't rent my house to tourists. They also think I'm a nice guy, but because of my limited language skills I seem a little dim.

My brother-in-law, Christos, was recently visiting us and enjoying a coffee at the local kafenio. He couldn't wait to come home and tell me about the conversation he'd overheard. He laughed as he recounted it:

"Have you heard about that foreigner who moved here?"

"Yes, he's some kind of lord with a castle in England!"

"Well, he might be rich, but I heard he's not the brightest. They say he's a nice guy though."

"Oh, and did you hear about his fishing skills?"

"They say he's the worst fisherman they've ever known. Can't catch a thing. And have you seen the hats he wears?"

I loved this. Though I did take offence at the comment about my hats.

Living in small rural communities can be both rewarding and challenging. On the one hand, their tight-knit nature fosters a sense of belonging and friendliness. On the other, the close proximity of everyone makes even the most personal matters common knowledge. When Alex and I moved to Pefki, we were amazed by how swiftly gossip spread. It was quite amusing even for Alex, who grew up in a Greek village. She should have been used to it.

We spoke one day to the owner of a local seaside taverna about buying trees, then got into our car to drive home, where we were surprised to find Maria, our neighbour, waiting on our patio. She had a small pot with a sapling lemon tree.

"I heard you wanted to buy some trees," she told us. "You can start with that one."

However, we soon realised being included in the local gossip was a sign that we had truly become part of the community. It meant that people felt comfortable enough to share their thoughts and opinions with us.

But as time went on, we noticed that this new-found inclusion came with its own set of challenges.

We had liked everyone we met and were always treated with kindness and respect. However, we quickly learned that some of our neighbours had long-standing feuds or disagreements with people from nearby villages, and they often expected us to share their dislike for their rivals. Although Greeks are known for their hospitality and love of foreigners, they seem to harbour distrust towards people from neighbouring villages. To our villagers, the real "xenos", or foreigner, was not the tourist from another country but someone from the next town, who should never be trusted. We had to carefully choose our words and actions to avoid any hostility or jealousy. It felt like we were constantly walking on eggshells, trying to please everyone.

Stamos, our builder, was a prime example. He lived in the next village of Gouves. We did not realise at the time of employing him that he too was viewed as a xenos. Maria complained to us that we should have employed a builder who lived in our village. The fact that no builders lived in our village didn't seem to occur to her. But Maria made us promise that in future we would only employ local tradesmen. By local, I think she meant within shouting distance of our house. If they can't hear you, they must be foreign.

We found ourselves caught in the middle of arguments and expected to take sides. It became clear that we couldn't please everyone as it was exhausting and ultimately impossible. Instead, we made a conscious decision to focus on building genuine relationships with our neighbours. We chose not to get involved with gossip. By staying neutral and treating everyone with kindness, we hoped to create a harmonious environment within the community. But often we still found ourselves expected to take sides.

Although we did our best to remain neutral with the affairs of the village, bureaucracy was an issue where everyone could unite.

Greeks have always been subject to mind-bending and inexplicable bureaucracies. But the sheer stupidity of some government policies just serves to unite people. Without government assistance, we have learned to rely on each other.

From experience, we've realised that most decisions from the local government don't help us. Instead, they interfere with the harmony of our village. Slowly, we're being forced into the steamroller of progress. The village is a living, breathing entity. Like nature, we evolve at our own pace. External interference erodes our traditions and strips away our local culture, trying to make us into a perfect clone.

Our village used to have a mayor chosen from the residents. This mayor cared about our issues and listened to our concerns. They understood our unique challenges and made decisions that reflected our needs.

When we first built our house here, our mayor was the local chicken-and-egg supplier. He would arrive at our house on his old moped, wearing a grubby T-shirt and a wide smile. He would come after cleaning out his chicken coop, still smelling of its contents. He would sit with us, enjoy a coffee, then hop back on his moped and ride into the village to his small mayor's office. There, he would listen to complaints and local issues and do his best to help the people.

But then our village was merged into a larger region, and the local government said we didn't need individual mayors any more. They replaced them with one person holding the title of the mayor of North Evia. We were now ruled by professional politicians who cared more about their image and getting votes than our simple needs. They ignored our local issues, and problems that used to be resolved were now being ignored. The central government imposed their policies on our village without considering what we wanted. This top-down approach disregarded our unique characteristics and preferences, leaving us frustrated and disillusioned.

The new mayor's first decision left the entire village in shock and disbelief. For generations, the sea had been an integral part of daily life, providing not only sustenance through fishing but also serving as a gathering place for the community. Placing tables and chairs near the sea had been a cherished tradition, where families and friends would come together to enjoy meals, share stories, and watch the mesmerising waves.

However, with the stroke of a pen, the mayor declared this tradition against the law. The news spread like wildfire, igniting anger and confusion among the villagers. They couldn't fathom the reasoning behind such a drastic measure. The once lively and vibrant coastline now stood devoid of its usual charm, as tables and chairs were hastily removed, leaving behind an emptiness that would be difficult to fill.

This policy may seem well intentioned, aimed at preserving the natural beauty of our coastlines. However, implementing such a regulation had terrible consequences for our village, especially Adonia's seaside taverna. By forcing these establishments to move their tables five metres away from the shoreline, several of the most beautiful and traditional tavernas faced the kiss of death.

The strip of pavement along the bustling harbour wall was adorned with charming restaurants. Their tables were covered with crisp white paper, secured by clips to prevent them from blowing away in the light sea breeze. In their busy kitchens, cooks toiled away, creating mouthwatering aromas from sizzling delicacies.

Across the narrow road, servers gracefully navigated, balancing heavy trays filled with delectable Greek specialties. Hungry diners eagerly awaited their meals, eyes locked on the horizon of the sparkling sea below. The gentle sea breeze brought the briny scent of the ocean, making the dining experience more exciting. Servers came to the tables, and the clinking of cutlery blended with the sound of waves crashing against the harbour wall. However, everything changed because of the new law. This law threatened to shut down family businesses that had been started by their grandfathers long ago.

Overnight, JCB diggers arrived and dug up all the paving along the harbour wall, leaving a muddy strip all along the road. Adonia watched sadly as her livelihood was taken away. The attraction of her taverna was the proximity to the sea. Now she was left with only five tables squeezed together inside, instead of the fifteen tables on the harbour wall she would fill every day.

Rather than admit defeat, she and Niko spent a day levelling out the earth, placed a few flowerpots around her patch, and set up two tables. Within the hour, the police arrived and issued her with a one-thousand-euro fine and demanded they were removed. The next day, we drove past and saw she had indeed removed the offending tables, but being stubborn, had replaced them with a tiny table and chair that would have fitted quite nicely in a doll's house. The police arrived again and issued another fine notice. This time it was double the last. She finally admitted defeat and left the previously beautiful seating area to grow weeds.

Tourists would often drive into the village searching for a charming seaside taverna for lunch. However, now they often leave disappointed and continue on to another village without stopping. They can easily find another restaurant elsewhere. But for us, these tavernas hold great historical significance. It was at one of these tavernas that we first heard about the available land which we went on to buy. While enjoying lunch there, we sat and planned the construction of our house. Our best ideas came to us as we sat at a table on the harbour wall, gazing out to sea, savouring calamari and a glass of local wine.

Strangely, the new law didn't seem to affect other nearby villages. There, we could still find tavernas right on the beach, others spread in lines along the harbour wall. Our village seemed to be the only one affected; specifically, Adonia and her neighbours.

CHAPTER 5

The Tale of the Sneaky River

If you want rainbow, you have to deal with the rain.

– Augustus

We had settled into life in Pefki so well that I'd almost forgotten what real urgency felt like. The days had a way of blurring together, like a lazy watercolour painting, each brushstroke a little softer than the last. I'd become so comfortable that even the smallest tasks felt like monumental achievements. I remember one morning proudly declaring to Alex that I had accomplished my entire to-do list before lunch.

"What did you do?" she asked, eyebrows raised.

"Well, I bought bread and … had a coffee with the

fishermen," I admitted sheepishly. We both laughed, realising how our priorities had shifted.

It was easy to slip into this kind of rhythm – the kind where the highlight of your day is picking the ripest figs from the garden or deciding which taverna to visit for dinner. But as blissful as it was, a small part of me wondered if we were getting too relaxed, like a boat that's drifted into calm waters and forgotten it has a sail.

We mustn't get too comfortable. We must be sent challenges to keep us from drifting off into fantasy. They prevent us from becoming complacent in our comfort zones. When faced with challenges, we become better people and expand our capabilities; we learn to adapt to unforeseen circumstances. These obstacles force us to confront our limitations, question our beliefs, and push the boundaries of our potential. They serve as reality checks, reminding us that life is not always smooth sailing. In Greece, these challenges can include natural disasters like earthquakes and wildfires and floods.

But the gods had decided that our minds were more worthy of improvement than others. Either that, or the gods had it in for us.

So one day, Zeus, the god of thunder, came to visit, and with him he brought chaos.

When we were buying our land in Pefki, the owner had given us the ordnance plan during negotiations. It clearly marked our plot with a red perimeter. We didn't pay much attention to the thin blue dotted line at the rear of our land. We were too excited to study the map in detail. We only focused on our little part of the Greek island within the red box. We went ahead and built our dream home in the sun.

Getting the necessary permissions had been difficult. There were always bureaucrats doing their best to scupper our dreams by putting obstacles in our way at every turn. But Alex's charm usually won through. When smiles and sweetness failed, swearing and threats eventually worked, and our determination and patience paid off. Standing in front of our new home, pride washed over us, knowing we had created our own Aegean paradise.

"Kaliméra, welcome," came a voice from behind us.

Our neighbour, standing at his gate, introduced himself as George. He had been living in the village with his wife, Helen, for the past few years, having returned from Australia. In Athens, George used to own a karate and boxing school, but he decided to give it up to lead a peaceful life here. Though he was semi-retired, George still ran a small boxing school from his garage. Every Thursday evening, a few locals would gather to spend a couple of hours learning to take out their frustrations on each other in a controlled environment. They seemed to enjoy punching each other.

He was happily reminiscing about his life in Australia, his karate school in Athens and his move to this village, when his expression changed and a serious look spread across his face.

"You'll have to be careful of your river," he warned us. "In the wintertime, it floods and runs down the street and into my garden. There's water everywhere."

"We have a river?"

"Of course, it's right there, at the far end of your garden," he said, gesturing towards the wall of bamboo at the back of our property.

I had no clue that along with the land, we had also acquired a section of river. This was incredible news. Having a house by a river had always been a dream of mine.

Meanwhile Maria arrived, pulling a large shopping cage on wheels. The cage was filled with oranges and lemons, freshly picked from her trees. Whenever she dragged it over a bump, one or two fruits would jump out and roll down the road. She always brought a gift when she came to see us. She came most days. To her, we were exotic foreigners, constantly travelling. She knew we were likely to have much better-quality gossip than the meagre snippets of information from the rest of the village. She knew that a gift would buy her an hour or two to sit and drink coffee while we shared our stories about Athens and England. In turn, she was always happy to reveal the secrets of the village.

"Kaliméra Peter, yahsoo George," she said as she dragged her fully laden trolley up our driveway to find Alex.

I left George and followed her to the patio, where Alex was sipping a coffee.

"You didn't tell us about the river," I said to Maria.

"We have a river?" Alex asked. "Where?"

"Yes, the river runs through my village over there." She waved her hand in the direction of some escaped lemons. "But when it reaches here, it disappears. I'm not sure where it goes. It was at the end of your garden, but it was covered by bamboo years ago. Sometimes it flows on this road, sometimes on the road in the back. It happens most winters."

She didn't seem too concerned. She had more important things to talk about than a boring old river.

Maria was the village gossip. She knew everything about everyone. What she didn't know, she'd simply make up. Today, her subject was the scandal involving the local priest. She cast a suspicious glance around to make sure no one else was in earshot. Leaning in close, her eyes sparkled with excitement.

"I have to tell you something," she whispered, her voice oozing with intrigue. "The priest was seen in the sea … swimming."

She sat back, arms crossed, eagerly awaiting our reaction. We exchanged puzzled looks, trying to understand why this was a scandal.

"And he wasn't even wearing his robes!" Maria added, her voice a cocktail of shock and disapproval.

I tried to stifle a giggle. "Maria, priests need to cool off too. They can't always be sweating in those heavy robes."

Maria looked horrified, her hands flailing in exasperation. "But he's a priest! Aren't priests supposed to be … different?"

Alex, who had been quietly enjoying the show, decided to jump in. "In England, priests swim too, you know. They don't wear their uniforms all the time. They're just regular people."

Maria wasn't convinced. She took a thoughtful sip of her coffee. "But it's different," she insisted. "He's supposed to be holy!"

I couldn't help but tease her a little. "Maria, do you think he takes baths in his robes too? Or maybe sleeps in them?"

Alex burst out laughing, and Maria shot me a stern look. "Don't be ridiculous. Of course not. But seeing him in the sea like that … it's just not right."

I leaned in, trying to ease her mind. "Maria, he's still human. He needs to relax like the rest of us. Swimming is normal!"

She sighed, clearly torn between scandal and logic. "I suppose you're right. But it's going to be the talk of the village for weeks!"

"Maybe it'll blow over," Alex suggested with a grin. "Soon enough, the village will find something else to gossip about. Then the poor priest will be left alone."

Maria nodded, though her eyes were still full of uncertainty. "I hope so. I don't want him to get into trouble over something so silly."

With that, Maria relaxed a little, though I knew she'd be the first to spread the next juicy titbit that crossed her path.

As Maria left, Alex nudged me. "You handled that well," she said. "Who knew gossiping about priests could be so complicated?"

I laughed. "Welcome to village life. There's never a dull moment."

We had initially only cleared a small corner of our huge plot of land to build the house. The rest was unknown, hidden by gigantic walls of bamboo and head-high barriers of prickly brambles. Although we were given a photocopied plan of our new domain, Greek maps were not very accurate, so we still didn't really know how much of this village we owned.

Walking through the impenetrable jungle was inconceivable. Untouched for years, it was a chaotic mix of weeds and shrubs, making it impossible to see any sign of the river we had now been warned about.

We set out on a mission to reclaim our land and find a hidden waterway. With a JCB excavator and obliging driver, who Alex found drinking coffee at the local kafenio, we got to work. The machine effortlessly cleared the overgrown vegetation, breaking branches and tearing through thorny vines. Dust filled the air as the JCB rumbled through the garden, leaving destruction in its path. The once lush landscape was now barren as the undergrowth was mercilessly hacked away, but our determination grew with each passing hour, fuelled by the excitement of rediscovering the long-lost river. George had never seen the river itself. The only sign of its presence was the occasional occurrence of water gushing out from the undergrowth, causing the road to flood.

I watched as the JCB, having bulldozed all the brambles and wild plants together with tons of earth, old metal frames and rusty feta cheese tins, finished its work.

Suddenly, Alex waved at me from the end of the garden.

'I've found it!' she yelled over the noise of the digger.

I rushed to where she was standing, then looked down. This was disappointing. The "river" was a small ditch, about two metres wide. There was no water, just a few dry stones and weeds sporadically growing at the base, and a large frog watching me suspiciously.

Despite the lack of water, there was still an air of mystery surrounding the hidden river. I couldn't help but wonder where it came from, and where it went. I was determined to follow the dry riverbed towards the nearby village of Artemision, where Maria had told me it came from. Unknown to us when we purchased our land, it was on the border between two villages. Our house was in Pefki, but our back garden was in Artemision, a stone's throw from the end of our garden. We did find that rather nice as we could boast that we had land in two villages.

As I ducked under the branches and continued walking in what I believed to be the upstream direction, away from our land, the ditch underwent a remarkable transformation right before my eyes. It quickly became more impressive, although it remained dry. Instead of being overrun with wild plants, it now boasted a captivating array of smooth pebbles and glistening shingle. The earth banks on both sides grew higher as I approached the nearby centre of Artemision. As I turned a corner, a bridge came into view. Passing beneath it, I noticed that the river had expanded even further. Earth banks were replaced with sturdy stone walls on both sides. I looked up at the buildings of the village towering above me, searching for a way to scale the steep walls. But I was too far down, and the walls had been smoothed by the passage of water. Clear evidence of a recent flood remained visible in the tide mark etched onto the stones above me. This was clearly a serious river.

I was getting worried as I retraced my steps to the end of our garden. Instead of leaping out of the shallow ditch, I was curious to see where it went after it passed us. I traced its path a few metres beyond the boundary of our property. Then, to my surprise, the ditch vanished, giving way to a stretch of level ground. The river had ended abruptly at the end of my garden.

It finally dawned on me why our neighbour George had been so concerned. The river that ran through the neighbouring village flowed freely and deeply under the bridge, then gradually narrowed as it approached our garden, until it eventually disappeared completely at the end of our land.

From there, it could flow no further. I assumed it must just come to the end and run wherever it could. From the look of it, our garden was the only logical path. Clearly, before our house was constructed, the river would have used our land as a run-off. Now our home would be used instead when the river flooded.

Our home faced a real threat. We had never been told about any incidents of flooding when we purchased the land. Our building permission had been granted. The only stipulations were that we needed to get an archaeologist report to make sure there were no buried monuments, and a forestry survey to ensure we didn't have any protected trees on our land. The river was never mentioned.

We had already owned the land for two years. We had seen intense rain during some winter months but had never seen any sign of flooding. Perhaps I was overreacting. Maybe it would never become a problem?

It was still early summer, and even if the river was going to fill up, it was not likely to bother us for a few months, so we decided to improve our garden before dealing with it. The JCB had made our land look like the moon's surface but with more craters. We immediately started working on the garden. As the summer progressed, we were feeling less concerned about the river. I still hadn't seen any water, so maybe it would never come. The bamboo grew and covered the river completely. We focused on other things. I was determined to create a comfortable outdoor space, and we built a patio and added a roof to shade us from the scorching sun.

When Maria suggested her neighbour Dimitri as our gardener, we were thrilled. He lived just a short distance away, making him the perfect choice. Maria's recommendations always seemed to involve locals, leading us to joke that she must be earning a commission for each one. But honestly, we didn't mind her potential side hustle. We were grateful for the tip-off.

According to Maria, Dimitri was the village odd-job man. Leaky tap? Call Dimitri. Fence needs mending? Garden needs planting? Dimitri's got you covered. He had a magic touch for fixing things and was always willing to help.

But Dimitri's talents didn't end there. When he wasn't repairing something, you could find him stalking wild boars through the mountains with his trusty 12-bore shotgun, or out on the sea in his small boat, catching fish for the local tavernas. His method for fishing was different to most. He preferred the old ways. He always went out at night, heading towards the nearby fish farm. Instead of using a rod and line or a net, Dimitri would wield a trident. He claimed to have a special trick: a bucket of sand mixed with olive oil. To cut the water's glare and spot the fish more clearly, he would toss a handful of the mixture across the surface. Unlike divers, Dimitri always came back dry, having speared his catch from the comfort of his boat. The taverna owners, appreciating the fresh fish and good price, never asked too many questions.

Our first meeting was interesting. He was looking for blood, literally.

Dimitri was a man in his forties, fit and tanned from years of working under the Greek sun. His arrival was announced by the sound of his battered old pickup truck, the engine coughing and sputtering like an old friend with a persistent cold. A fishing trident jutted out of one window and the barrel of a 12-bore shotgun poked out of the other, hinting at a life filled with tales of both land and sea.

The truck bed was a hodgepodge of old boat motor parts, shovels, and a petrol-driven chainsaw, all rattling like an impromptu orchestra as he parked. As Dimitri climbed out of the truck, his boots crunched on the gravel. Approaching the house, he extended a calloused hand for a firm handshake, his grip strong and steady – a testament to his hard-working nature.

"I'm Dimitri," he said, offering a friendly grin that revealed the crinkles at the corners of his eyes, etched by years of laughter and squinting into the sun.

"Nice to meet you, Dimitri," I replied. "Can I offer you a coffee?"

"That sounds great," he said, his eyes lighting up at the prospect of a break. It was clear that for Dimitri, life was a balance of work and simple pleasures, his demeanour reflecting the easy-going charm that seemed to be woven into the very fabric of the Greek village. I liked him immediately.

We headed to the back of the house, where the garden stretched out before us in a mess of muddy soil and uprooted weeds. As we sipped our coffees, I could see Dimitri surveying the chaos with a practised eye, mentally cataloguing what needed to be done. His presence felt reassuring, like he was already forming a plan to bring some order to our swamp-like garden. We sat at the patio table and Alex came to join us. We agreed on a daily rate which was more than reasonable, and he agreed to start work in a few days. As he got up to leave, he suddenly remembered something.

"Can I have some of your blood?" He looked nervous, almost embarrassed about the question.

"Dimitri, if you help me get my garden sorted out, I'll give you anything, but don't you think asking for my blood is going a little far?" I replied.

Dimitri laughed and stared back at his empty coffee cup. "I need an operation," he mumbled. "I've had this pain in my side for a while. The doctor says it's a grumbling appendix, and it needs to come out."

In Greece, if you need an operation, the hospital asks for a donation of blood from family members or friends. It doesn't have to match your blood type; it's to keep the blood banks stocked.

I had come across this before. A few years ago, Zissis, Alex's father, needed surgery. A scan had revealed a tumour on one of his kidneys. According to the doctors, it was likely to be a cancer, so we couldn't wait too long. He came back from the hospital with a request for five pints of blood, and vouchers for each relative to fill out as proof. This seemed easy; we had lots of friends and cousins who would certainly be happy to help. But when we started to ask around, it became clear it was going to be a challenge. Alex and I agreed to give some, but Debbie wasn't eligible. Unfortunately, if you are over sixty-five years old, or take blood pressure or cholesterol-reducing tablets, you are banned from donating. Since most of our friends and cousins were either too old or taking medication, they were also ruled out. We had managed to find two more donors, but we were still going to be short. But then one of our neighbours, who had been on a trip, returned and heard about our shortage and agreed to provide the last pint.

Alex and I went to the local hospital in Voula to donate our share. The blood clinic was bustling with people. When it was our turn, we went behind the curtain together. Alex volunteered to go first. She sat down and the nurse, reading from a clipboard, started to ask questions.

"Have you ever had an AIDS test?"

"No."

"Have you been to Africa or been diagnosed with West Nile fever?"

"No."

"Do you plan to drive any heavy vehicles, emergency response vehicles, or climb ladders in the next thirty-six hours?"

"No."

"Have you recently had sex with someone who had been diagnosed with or was being treated for a sexually transmitted disease (excluding chlamydia, genital herpes or genital warts)?"

Alex raised an eyebrow and looked at me. "Well, have I?"

"No!" I replied.

The nurse blinked, surprised. "I'm just asking the questions here."

"Good, because the answer to that question might have caused a divorce," Alex said, smiling.

The nurse chuckled and continued. "Just a few more questions."

"Oh, there's more?" Alex said, pretending to faint. "Is this an interrogation or a blood donation?"

"Okay, last one, I promise," the nurse reassured her. "Have you ever been banned from donating blood for any reason?"

"No," Alex replied, "but I might be after this if you keep asking personal questions."

The nurse laughed as she finished up, and Alex finally donated her pint of blood. When it was my turn, I already knew the questions, so it went quicker.

After Alex's and my donation, our cousin Bia and her husband gave their share, but when our neighbour tried to give his contribution, he was found to be diabetic and therefore his blood was not accepted. We were still one pint short. Without the full quota, the hospital would deny him the operation.

This was getting urgent. We had already assumed we had enough blood to ensure Zissis's admission, and the hospital appointment was booked for the next day. We had exhausted every possibility other than accosting strangers on the street. Alex was up for that idea, but I did caution her that approaching complete strangers and asking for a pint of their blood would likely not end well.

Then Alex heard about a priest in the next village who donated blood to people in need, especially those who didn't have any relatives to help them. Intrigued and hopeful, we decided to visit his church and ask for his help.

The priest's church was a modest building, nestled among olive trees and blooming wildflowers. The interior was simple but warm, with rows of wooden pews and an altar adorned with fresh flowers and candles. The air was filled with the faint scent of incense, adding a sense of tranquillity to the space. We found the priest in his small office, a cluttered room filled with books, religious icons and a few personal mementos.

He greeted us with a kind smile, his eyes twinkling with genuine warmth. "Welcome, my children," he said, gesturing for us to sit down. "How can I help you today?"

Alex explained our situation. The priest listened attentively. When she finished, he leaned back in his chair, his expression thoughtful.

"I'm more than happy to help," he said after a moment. "Let us go to the hospital immediately and see what we can do."

A wave of relief washed over us. The priest's willingness to assist us without hesitation was an incredible gesture. Alex took his hand and kissed it. He simply smiled, waving away our gratitude as if it were nothing.

At the hospital, the staff greeted the priest with respect and familiarity; they clearly knew him well. I wondered how many times a week he did this for people. He rolled up his sleeve without a second thought, chatting cheerfully with the nurses as they prepared the equipment. Alex and I watched, feeling a profound sense of gratitude for this man who had been a stranger to us just hours before.

As the priest donated his blood, he told us stories of others he had helped, each tale filled with hope and kindness. His words were a reminder of the goodness that still existed in the world, even in the most challenging times.

Once the donation was complete, the nurse handed us the final voucher, completing the set needed for Alex's father's surgery. We thanked the priest again, wishing there was something we could do for him.

In England, when I gave blood I got a cup of tea and a biscuit. But I didn't think this was enough for this great guy. I asked him if he would join us for lunch as a thank you. "You've done so much for us," Alex said. "It's the least we can do to show our gratitude."

The priest smiled warmly. "I would be honoured," he replied. "But only if you let me buy the wine. It's my favourite part of the meal."

"We will see about that," I said, and the three of us made our way to a nearby taverna. The afternoon sun was warm, and the scent of grilling meat and fresh herbs filled the air as we found a table outside. The taverna was a charming place, with vines draped over the pergola and colourful flowers in pots around the patio.

Over lunch, we learned more about the priest. He had grown up in a small village much like Alex's early Glyfada, and had always felt a calling to help those in need. His stories were filled with humour and wisdom, and we found ourselves laughing and nodding along, feeling a deep connection to this kind and generous man.

The meal was a feast of local dishes – grilled lamb, fresh salads, and warm bread straight from the oven. The priest ordered a bottle of his favourite wine, and we toasted to new friendships and the kindness that had brought us together.

As the afternoon turned into evening, we knew we had made a friend for life. The priest's selflessness and warmth had touched our hearts, and we promised to keep in touch and help him in any way we could in the future.

When it was time to leave, the priest gave us a blessing, wishing us health and happiness. We walked back to our car, feeling lighter and more hopeful than we had in days. The world seemed a little brighter, thanks to the kindness of one man who had gone out of his way to help us in our time of need.

Zissis had his surgery. It was indeed an early cancer growth, but still encapsulated, so his kidney was removed with the offending growth just in time.

Back in the present, Dimitri looked relieved I hadn't refused him outright.

"It's not just about the blood type," he explained. "Hospitals here want to make sure they have enough blood for everyone. It's a precaution. If I can provide a few donors, they feel more secure about going ahead with the operation. But I'm having trouble finding donors."

"I know," I assured him. "It's more about maintaining the blood supply than matching types. We've done this before."

"Exactly," Dimitri said. "It's a common practice here. They just want to make sure there's enough for emergencies and other patients."

We both agreed to give a share, and he went on to have his operation. Since then, he always introduced me to his pals as "my xenos blood brother"

Combining his handyman prowess with his patience from fishing, Dimitri was a gardening guru. His meticulous attention to detail and dedication meant that our garden would be in the best possible hands. He selected the best trees that would grow well in our type of soil. He planted fast-growing plants that wouldn't need too much watering. Slowly, our decimated land began to look like a garden.

Dimitri warned me about the challenges of planting a lawn in this area. He mentioned the risk of attracting mosquitoes and providing hiding spots for snakes. But I couldn't think of a better way to add some much-needed cover over our bare earth. So I decided to plant a lawn anyway, hoping to bring some greenery and a touch of nature to the garden. I still had over four hundred square metres of land to cover – a daunting task. The trees looked majestic, their leaves swaying gently in the breeze, and the new plants added splashes of intense colour. Yet, the majority of the land still consisted of dry, compacted earth, cracked and parched under the relentless sun.

I was determined to transform this barren expanse. I set to work. I could almost feel the heat radiating from the ground as Dimitri and I began to prepare the soil. It was back-breaking work, loosening up the compacted dirt and enriching it with compost. Sweat trickled down my back and my muscles ached, but I pressed on, driven by the vision of a lush green lawn.

After days of preparing the soil, I spread the grass seeds with care. I imagined the green blades that would soon cover the ground. Each seed held a promise of beauty. I watered the area thoroughly, hoping the seeds would take root and flourish.

Dimitri's warnings echoed in my mind, but I pushed them aside. I focused on the potential transformation ahead. I envisioned our garden as a vibrant oasis, a stark contrast to the dry, dusty landscape it once was.

However, my hopes were dashed when the ants arrived. They stole every single seed. For the next few weeks, I battled with the ants. I would plant new seeds, only to have them stolen at night. I resorted to sitting in the darkness, armed with a hosepipe, spraying the garden. I hoped that the ants would be deterred by the water. But instead, the ants seemed to enjoy a shower; it seemed to give them an appetite. And they were not the only insect keen on water. My actions attracted mosquitoes. They feasted on every exposed part of my body.

In the morning, Dimitri would arrive and witness the sight of a swollen Englishman with reddened flesh covered in mosquito bites.

"Been watering the garden at night again?" he teased.

But I was winning. The days turned into weeks, and I

began to see small green shoots emerging from the soil. Each sprout filled me with a sense of accomplishment and victory. The barren earth was slowly being replaced by a soft carpet of grass. The ants seemed to have lost interest. Next door's fig tree had come into fruit, and this was a far tastier alternative for the ants than boring grass seeds.

Despite Dimitri's warnings, I was happy with my new lawn. The snakes, if they were there, stayed out of sight, and the occasional loss of a pint or two of blood from the ferocious mosquitoes was a small price to pay for the beauty of my new lawn.

I was also delighted to discover that one of Dimitri's skills was fishing. Coincidentally, I had recently purchased a small motorboat with the intention of improving my angling abilities. Spearfishing didn't interest me; I wanted to catch fish with honour, using a fishing rod and line. Dimitri proved to be a wealth of knowledge. He guided me on where to launch the boat safely, which areas of the coastline to avoid, and provided general information about the sea conditions throughout the year. "The sea loves heroes," he would often say.

One day, we were both out on my boat. Despite fishing for an hour, we hadn't caught anything. Dimitri seemed preoccupied and wore a worried expression as he gazed at the horizon. "Pull up the anchor and start the motor, Peter," he instructed. Confused, I inquired why. He informed me that a storm was approaching and suggested we return to the harbour. I glanced around, puzzled. The sun still shone brightly, the sky was devoid of clouds, and the water remained eerily calm. However, I respected Dimitri's expertise as an experienced sailor, so I took his advice seriously.

As we steered away from our fishing spot, the wind gradually picked up. The tranquil sea transformed into powerful waves that grew in size, crashing over the boat and drenching us. Once we reached the safety of the sheltered harbour, I glanced back at the sea. It had erupted into a chaotic maelstrom of white water and tumultuous waves. Dimitri had accurately interpreted the signs and wasn't willing to take any chances.

"What did you see that alerted you to the coming storm?" I asked.

"In the distance, I saw a black line in the sea coming from the east. When you see that, it's a sure sign that a storm is coming."

By the end of the summer, our garden was complete. Although freshly planted and still juveniles, the branches of our new pomegranate and fig trees were heavy with fruit. The scent of freshly bloomed roses, daisies and sunflowers filled the air, attracting butterflies and bees. The vibrant colours of petunias, marigolds and lilies added an enchanting touch to the landscape. As we walked through our garden, the soft blades of grass brushed against our feet, inviting us to sit and enjoy the tranquillity. Our once barren land had transformed into a picturesque oasis where nature's beauty thrived in abundance.

Autumn slowly replaced summer, and the colours of the

landscape transformed from shades of green to warm hues of red, orange and yellow. As the days grew shorter, the sunlight filtered through the canopy of the trees, casting a golden glow over the surroundings. The sound of the summer symphonies of continuous tzz-tzz-tzz, the song of the cicadas, gradually faded, replaced by the gentle rustling of leaves being carried by the wind. The garden now wore a carpet of fallen leaves from the abundant platanus trees on the land next door. With each passing day, the crispness in the air grew more pronounced, reminding us that winter was fast approaching. The mornings greeted me with a chill, and the misty raindrops on my window hinted at the arrival of the frosty days which would soon be with us, Despite the task of raking leaves becoming a never-ending chore, there was a certain charm in watching the season's transition.

The long summer days were gone. Alex began to wear a coat when we went out. Compared to an English autumn, I found the weather was positively warm. November in England is one of the most depressing months and usually comprises dull, grey drizzly days interspersed with storms. Here, despite a slight chill in the air, the sun kept shining.

But in central Greece, I'd learned the weather can change from a warm, calm day to a severe storm in a few moments.

We had decided to take our small boat out for a last fishing trip before the winter finally arrived. Wearing my usual T-shirt and floppy straw hat, I hooked the trailer to the back of my car. Alex came out and joined me, wearing two woolly jumpers, a heavy coat, wellington boots, a scarf around her neck and a bright orange life jacket. She was also qualified to drive our little boat, but never did. She would just watch every move I made, then tell me how many things I got wrong. She is the ultimate back-seat driver.

We felt the excitement as we got into the car. The drive to where we launch the boat was only five minutes. It took us through narrow village streets and past seafront tavernas. The sea was right in front of us, a vast expanse of shimmering blue. It looked inviting and calm.

Arriving at the slipway, we stepped out of the car and were greeted by the scent of saltwater and the sound of gentle waves lapping against the dock. We were ready for another adventure. Launching the boat was always a stressful routine for me: untying ropes, checking the engine and making sure everything was in place, and most importantly, checking the plugs were rammed into the drain holes. I had forgotten these several times, and it always resulted in a near sinking – and once or twice, real sinking. Alex watched with a scrutinising eye as I navigated these tasks. Her presence always added to my pressure.

Once aboard, we set off from the harbour, the engine purring as we glided away from the shore. The picturesque village slowly shrank behind us, replaced by the open sea. The water was a mirror, reflecting the clear sky and surrounding landscape with an almost surreal stillness.

"Watch the harbour wall!" Alex called out as I steered the boat. I veered away, feeling her eyes on me. A container ship was just a blur on the horizon, but to Alex, it was a looming threat. "Keep an eye out for that seagull," she added, pointing to a lone bird bobbing in our path. Despite my recent improvements, she still saw me as a novice in need of constant supervision.

As we moved further out, the sea remained eerily calm, not a single ripple disturbing its surface. It was as if nature itself had paused, holding its breath. The peace was unnerving, a stark contrast to the usual rhythm of the sea. Alex's silence was even more unusual. She hadn't instructed me to adjust our speed or course. She seemed distracted, her gaze fixed on the horizon behind us.

Curious and a bit concerned, I glanced back to see what had captured her attention. Dark, ominous clouds were gathering, spreading like ink across the sky. They grew more menacing with each passing minute, the air thick with an electric tension. The realisation hit me hard – a storm was coming, and it was coming fast.

We were in the middle of the sea, with nowhere to go but forward. The calm water now felt like the calm before the storm, and I could sense the shift in the atmosphere. Alex's usual criticisms were absent, replaced by a shared understanding of the impending danger. The sea, once our serene escape, was about to test us in ways we hadn't expected.

"Turn around, we have to go back!" Alex shouted over the noise of the engine.

I put the motor into neutral and looked up at the roiling mass of black cloud which was now above our heads. Then, with a deafening crack of thunder accompanied by a flash of lightning, the floodgates of the sky opened. A deluge of large, heavy raindrops pounded the deck with an unyielding force. The downpour was relentless, as if the sky had finally found an outlet for its pent-up anger. Rain cascaded from the heavens. The once calm sea had transformed into a tumultuous and treacherous body of water. The wind howled and whipped through the air. Waves crashed against the boat, each one seemingly larger than the last, threatening to engulf us at any moment. Intense rain pelted down, making it difficult to see more than a few feet ahead.

The boat was rocked violently by the relentless force of the waves. Despite our best efforts to navigate back towards the safety of our harbour, it felt as though we were at the mercy of the tempestuous elements. The adrenaline surged through my veins as I negotiated each wave, desperately hoping to reach shelter before the storm's fury overpowered us. Alex stood beside me with a look of grim determination. She said nothing, just looked ahead until the harbour finally came into view. We had escaped, I thought, but the boat was full of water and leaning to one side. The small bilge pump had no effect on the quantity of water on the deck that was sloshing around our legs. We were sinking fast as we entered the harbour just in time. If Alex hadn't told me to go back when she did … I shudder to think of the consequences of staying out there a moment longer.

We were drenched, but we had to get our waterlogged boat onto the trailer. I released the bungs to drain the water, but the rain was filling it faster than it could flow out. It was too heavy to winch onto the trailer, so we dragged it as far as we could out of the water and secured it to a tree. We would have to come back to retrieve it when the storm had passed.

The storm was in full flow as we climbed into the car. The streets had turned into rivers, making it challenging to navigate, windscreen wipers doing nothing to improve our vision ahead. I drove carefully, manoeuvring through the flooded roads as best as I could. The sound of rain pounding on the roof of the car added to the tense atmosphere. We could feel the tyres splashing through the water, creating ripples that seemed to stretch endlessly. Our home, which was just a short distance away, felt like a distant haven in the midst of this watery chaos.

When we arrived home, we stepped out of the car into an ankle-deep river running past our home. Our peaceful garden was now a chaotic scene. The heavy downpour had intensified, transforming the garden into a waterlogged terrain. The vibrant flowers and lush greenery were now submerged, leaves barely visible beneath the murky water. The sound of the rain was deafening, and was now accompanied by the loud rushing sound of a river. That innocent ditch at the end of our garden was a raging torrent. The force of the water was so strong that it carried with it uprooted trees and debris. The garden now resembled a wild riverbed, with swirling eddies and frothy rapids. It was a surreal sight.

With nowhere to go, the river had broken up into several tributaries. One cut across our garden, undoing all our hard work and changing it back into an untamed wilderness, while others formed raging rivers on the surrounding roads and pathways. The air was filled with a damp, earthy scent as the rain mixed with the soil and vegetation.

A few hours later, the storm had passed. Half of our newly planted garden was gone, replaced by a murky lake. Although the deluge didn't come too close to the house, it would certainly be a risk in the future. We needed to take action.

We called Stamos, the local builder.

"We need to talk about the river," Alex said. "It floods, and our garden turns into a lake when we get heavy rain."

"Yes, I know about that. Someone over there built his house in the river. That's why."

"Why did someone build a house in the river?" I asked incredulously.

"Perhaps the land was cheap," Stamos replied. "People do strange things here."

We respected our neighbour's privacy and never enquired why he chose to build a house right on the river. However, the signs were clear – his construction had altered the river's natural flow. As newcomers, we decided to keep our opinions to ourselves and concentrate on safeguarding our own property. Our plan was to build a small wall along our side of the riverbank to prevent flooding in our garden. Stamos would handle the construction while we took a trip to England.

CHAPTER 6

The Calm Before the Chaos

Wise men speak because they have something to say; fools because they have to say something.

– Plato

Although we were in England for work, we took the opportunity to visit family and catch up with some old friends. We were a bit worried about our home in Pefki after the recent flooding in our garden, but Stamos was handling the construction of new walls to protect us. So, we began to relax and enjoy ourselves.

One day, we decided to play tourist and explore some of London's famous landmarks. We strolled along the Thames, looking at iconic sights like Tower Bridge and the London Eye.

I deliberately avoided the subject of museums. I was still licking my wounds after our last, and only, visit to the British

Museum. Alex held strong opinions about the Parthenon Marbles, viewing it as a stash of stolen treasures.

That experience was enough to last a lifetime. As we walked through the halls, Alex's eyes narrowed in anger, and I could almost feel the heat of her indignation radiating off her. She stopped in front of the Marbles, arms crossed with a dramatic flair that could rival any Greek tragedy.

"This is disgusting," she said loudly, her voice echoing in the grand hall. "Look what you have done. They belong in Greece, not some old building thousands of miles away."

People in the hall looked around at Alex, but she didn't care.

"Please keep your voice down," I pleaded.

She cut me off with a sharp look. "Why, do you think they will be offended? You lot are no better than pirates," she said, her voice dripping with disdain. "Stealing treasures and hiding them away. You should feel ashamed of yourselves."

By now, everyone around us had stopped looking at the displays and turned their attention to Alex, who was just getting started. Her anger was palpable, and she seemed unfazed by the growing audience.

"Imagine if they took the Tower of London to Athens. How would you feel then?" Her voice rang out louder now, echoing through the grand hall. People began to drift in from other parts of the museum, drawn by the commotion and intrigued by her passionate outburst.

A buzz of agreement spread around the hall as people began to understand her point. Murmurs of "She's right" and

"It's unfair" rippled through the crowd, which now numbered in the dozens.

A guard, looking slightly uncomfortable, approached her cautiously. "Madam, could you please keep your voice down?" he whispered, trying to defuse the situation.

"No, I won't," Alex replied defiantly, her volume rising even more. "These people are looking at stolen property. They have a right to know."

The guard hesitated, glancing around at the crowd, which was clearly captivated by Alex's words. Her passion and conviction were undeniable, and it was clear that many in the audience were beginning to see the Marbles in a new light.

Alex continued, gesturing towards the Marbles with a sweeping hand. "These sculptures were crafted by our ancestors, meant to be seen in the sunlight of Greece, not trapped in this dim hall. They are pieces of our history, our culture, and they deserve to be returned to their rightful place."

The crowd murmured in agreement, some nodding, others whispering to each other about the injustice of it all. A few people even began to join in, calling out in support of Alex's cause.

"I know you're just doing your job," Alex said, addressing the guard with a touch of empathy in her voice. "But this isn't only about art; it's about respect and justice. These Marbles are not just stones – they are symbols of our identity and our history."

The guard stepped back, seemingly unsure of how to handle the situation as more visitors joined the gathering crowd, curious to hear what had stirred such emotion. Alex's message had resonated, sparking a discussion among the museum-goers about cultural heritage and the ethics of historical artefacts in museums.

As we left the museum, she sulked for a moment before saying, "It's not just about the Marbles, you know. It's about respect for history and culture. These pieces are part of our identity, our story."

I placed a reassuring hand on her shoulder, acknowledging her frustration. "I get it, Alex. I really do. Maybe one day they will find their way back home."

She sighed, her anger slowly giving way to a weary hopefulness. "I just wish people understood what they mean to us. They're more than just art; they are a piece of who we are."

So, on this visit, instead of going anywhere that might get me into trouble, we wandered through Hyde Park, where Alex insisted on feeding the pigeons. This quickly turned into a scene from Alfred Hitchcock's *The Birds*. "I think they like me!" She smiled as a particularly bold pigeon tried to make a nest in her hair. I, on the other hand, was frantically waving my arms to fend off the feathery onslaught.

Despite our worries, we managed to spend a relaxing week enjoying ourselves, confident that Stamos was holding down the fort back home. But then came the phone call.

It was Maria. Her voice blasted out of the phone. "Where are you? We have a big problem," she shouted, her voice crackling through the line. "You have to come back! Your garden is swarming with yelling people. There are three police cars and six police officers. They're searching for you. Stamos has run away, and the police have issued an arrest warrant for him." She paused for breath. "And you're under arrest as well."

Stamos had disappeared and was avoiding our calls. We were clueless about the laws we had violated, but it seemed like a grave matter. In Greece, the police handle cases related to planning offences. So, if you construct something on your property without obtaining the necessary permission, you could find yourself surviving on bread and water while peering through prison bars. Stamos had been so eager to secure a lucrative construction project that he conveniently neglected to inform us about the requirement of obtaining approval from the planning office before commencing any work. We found out later that Stamos was well known for this. He always worked on the premise that "In Greece, it's better to ask for forgiveness than permission". But he didn't tell us that.

We had never needed to be involved in the bureaucracy of obtaining building permission. When we built our home in Glyfada, this was all done for us. The land in Pefki came with building consent, so our architect only needed to submit plans. As far as we were aware, we had the right to build a wall around our property. We really couldn't see the problem. But in Greece, nothing is ever straightforward.

Our new wall had been spotted by someone, and the news spread quickly. Flooding was apparently common in the houses near the river; their owners assumed that our wall would worsen their problem and reported us to the police, who were taking it very seriously.

We immediately left our home in England to return to our exploding Greek village.

After a short flight, we arrived at Athens airport. I nervously shuffled my feet as the immigration officer took longer than usual to inspect our passports. I worried that mugshots of us had flashed up on his screen, showing that we were wanted by the Greek equivalent of the FBI. Alex, on the other hand, was completely unperturbed. She just stared at her phone, checking her Facebook page. The officer passed back our passports and waved the next passenger in the queue to his desk.

The drive north to Evia felt longer than normal. I imagined being confronted by an angry lynch mob on arrival, complete with pitchforks, the smell of burning effigies overpowering the usual scent of mountain herbs.

In fact, I should come clean here: we had been arrested before, for building a Parthenon on our rooftop in Glyfada. Some locals didn't like it and reported us to the police. Luckily, we evaded Greek justice by making some adjustments to comply with the planning regulations. But this new offence seemed to have been taken much more seriously. We were in big trouble.

It was only ten days since we left. How could so much trouble occur in such a short time? We nervously turned into our street, but it was strangely quiet. There were no mobs screaming or police cars with flashing lights. Instead, there was a massive wall surrounding our garden. It was enormous, much taller than the waist-height barrier we had asked for to protect against the river. Stamos had gone above and beyond by constructing a concrete wall over two metres high, blocking out the sun. It was definitely not what we had asked for, but Stamos, being a conscientious builder and eager to please us, had given us a sturdy defence against tsunamis along with protection from the river. We could now see what the fuss was all about.

Within a few moments of our arrival, Maria had picked us up on her radar and appeared. There is no line of sight from her house, but she always somehow knows when we are home.

"It was terrible," she cried. "There were police everywhere. Stamos has run away, and I didn't know what to do."

Alex put her arms around Maria and reassured her. "It's fine, we're here now, we will sort it out. Please don't worry."

Rather than wait at the house to be arrested by a passing police car, we decided to get it over with. We got into our car and nervously drove the ten kilometres to the police station to turn ourselves in. My stomach churned with anxiety, and my knuckles were white as I gripped the steering wheel. Neither of us had ever been in any real trouble with the law before, and the prospect of facing the police was daunting.

Our village had no police station, so we had to drive to the nearby market town of Istiea to give our confession. The drive felt like an eternity. The beautiful countryside, with its rolling hills and olive groves, now seemed foreboding under the circumstances. I kept glancing at the rear-view mirror, half expecting a police car to appear, lights flashing, to drag us to the police station. At least if we got there first, it would look like we were taking it seriously.

"Do you think they'll arrest us right away?" Alex asked, her voice wavering.

"I don't know," I replied, my voice just as shaky. "I guess it depends on how serious they think this is."

Alex let out a nervous laugh. "Well, we've always wanted adventures. Be careful what you wish for, right?"

As we approached Istiea, the market town's bustling streets were a stark contrast to the quiet tension in our car. People went about their day, oblivious to the turmoil we were experiencing. We parked near the police station, taking a moment to gather ourselves before stepping out of the car. The station loomed ahead, a stark and intimidating building.

Inside, the air was thick with the scent of disinfectant and a sense of bureaucratic indifference. A stern-looking officer sat behind a desk, glancing up as we approached. My heart pounded in my chest, and I could hear Alex's rapid breathing beside me.

"We need to speak with someone about … a building issue," I said, my voice barely above a whisper.

The officer raised an eyebrow. "What kind of issue?"

"We, uh, we built a wall without the proper permits," Alex admitted, her voice trembling.

The officer's expression didn't change, but he motioned for us to sit. "Wait here," he said before disappearing into a back room.

Minutes ticked by like hours as we sat on the hard wooden bench. The tension was almost unbearable. I kept imagining the worst-case scenarios: fines, court dates, possibly even jail time. Alex reached for my hand, her grip tight and reassuring.

Finally, the officer returned with a colleague, a slightly older man with a tired look in his eyes. "You're the ones with the wall?" he asked.

We nodded, explaining the whole situation – how we thought we had the right to build it, the confusing bureaucracy, Stamos starting construction without telling us we needed approval. The officers listened patiently, occasionally jotting down notes.

When we finished, there was a long silence. The second officer finally spoke. "You should have got a permit." He sighed and looked at us with a degree of pity. "But this happens more often than you think. Let's see how we can resolve this."

Relief washed over us like a wave. It wasn't a free pass, but it wasn't the end of the world either. The officers explained the steps we needed to take to rectify the situation, including fines and additional paperwork. We would have to tear down the wall immediately. But we wouldn't be facing any criminal charges.

"Off you go then," the policeman said. "Take this paper to the planning office, and have a nice day."

We strolled across the busy square to submit our papers to the planning office. As we approached the Perspex window, a young lady greeted us with a warm smile.

She explained that if we had constructed the wall in a different area of our garden, we might have faced a minor penalty but we could have retained it. However, our offence was more severe. We had erected a wall near the river, which is strictly prohibited under Greek law. It had to be dismantled immediately. We would still be subject to a fine, and the penalty would double for each week the wall remained standing.

As we left, the tension began to dissipate, replaced by a sense of cautious optimism. We had a plan to fix our mistake, and more importantly, we weren't going to jail. The drive back to our village felt lighter, the countryside once again beautiful and inviting. Alex squeezed my hand. "Looks like our Greek adventure continues," she said with a smile.

I nodded, feeling a new-found appreciation for the complexity of Greek bureaucracy and the importance of patience. "Let's just be careful in the future," I said. "We don't want to come to the police station again."

I wondered what would have happened if we had been arrested. As a foreigner, would my lack of knowledge about local rules be an advantage? However, Alex, being Greek, should have been more aware. While a foreigner might be forgiven, a Greek should have known better. Maybe we were not properly arrested because they wanted to avoid potential diplomatic issues and the overwhelming paperwork.

We had been searching for Stamos for days, determined to have him return and demolish the wall that had caused us so much trouble. After finally tracking him down, we told him he was in the clear – provided the wall was removed immediately. Just an hour later, a large yellow bulldozer made its way into our garden, ready to take on the task at hand. With determination and precision, the crew worked tirelessly, and within a mere two hours, our once imposing wall was reduced to a mere pile of rubble scattered across the lawn. It was a sight to behold as a lorry arrived, equipped with a grab to swiftly remove the debris. As the remnants of the wall were hauled away, the riverbank was left untouched, effortlessly blending back into its original state. It was as if the wall had never even existed, leaving us with a renewed sense of space and a huge feeling of relief.

In Greece, being the home of democracy, if someone makes a complaint, you have a right to know who reported you, and where they live. Ironically, it turned out that the person who reported us was the old lady who had built her house in the river, causing all the problems in the first place.

That was our first experience with the results of flooding in Pefki, and it was a nightmare. We had poured so much love and effort into our garden, only to see it ravaged by the relentless waters. The lush greenery we had cultivated was turned into a soggy mess, with plants uprooted and soil eroded. We hoped this would never happen again, but the worry was always at the back of our minds.

Determined to prevent a repeat of this disaster, we tried to go through the correct channels. We spent months navigating the labyrinthine bureaucracy, desperately seeking permission to rebuild the wall we'd been ordered to remove. Each day was filled with phone calls, meetings and piles of paperwork. It was exhausting and incredibly frustrating. Every time we thought we were making progress, we hit another roadblock.

The Greek law was clear: no building of anything less than forty-five metres from a river. This meant that if we wanted to build a wall, it would cut our garden down to a tiny fraction of its original size. Instead of a sprawling spacious oasis, we would be left with a small patio hemmed in by a stone wall. The thought was disheartening.

We sat on our porch, looking out at the remnants of our once beautiful garden. The idea of losing it all was painful. "I can't believe this," Alex said, her voice tinged with frustration. "All this effort, and now we're supposed to be happy with a tiny patio and a wall right in front of us?"

"I know," I said. "It's like we're being punished for trying to protect our home."

"How can we enjoy our garden when all we'll see is a wall?" she continued, her anger rising. "We might as well not have a garden at all."

We spent countless evenings discussing possible solutions, brainstorming ideas that might satisfy the strict regulations without sacrificing our garden. But each idea seemed more impractical than the last. The rules were inflexible, and we were left feeling helpless.

One day, as we surveyed the wreckage, Alex turned to me with a purposeful look. "We can't let this beat us," she said. "We'll find another way. Maybe we can't build a wall, but there has to be something else we can do."

Her resolve sparked a renewed sense of determination in me. "You're right. We won't give up. We'll protect our land somehow."

Despite the setbacks, we refused to let our dreams die. Our garden was more than just a piece of land; it was a symbol of our life here in Pefki, a testament to our hard work and love. We knew we had to fight for it, no matter how long it took or how many obstacles we faced.

And so, our battle continued. The frustration of losing most of our garden was a heavy burden, but it also fuelled our strength of will and single-mindedness. We would find a way to keep it thriving, even if it meant bending the rules or finding creative solutions.

This was our home, and we were not ready to give it up.

CHAPTER 7

Celebrating a Life of Greatness

The fear of death is only natural to humans, but death should be viewed as the achievement of life.

– Plato

Winter in our village is always surprisingly cold. The mountainous terrain of Evia often transforms into a snow-covered wonderland extending all the way down to our village at sea level, making it a picturesque but chilly place to live. Snow is a frequent visitor, and it's not unusual for us to have to fit chains to our car wheels just to drive short distances. The icy roads and heavy snowfall turn even the simplest errands into small adventures.

Alex loves this time of the year. I'm always a little wary of stepping out into the garden when there's fresh snow. Her aim with a snowball is incredible. She can hit the back of my head from twenty metres away, and often does. Alex grew up near Athens, where snow was rare, and when it did fall, it would melt in a few hours, leaving little opportunity for making snowmen. Here in Pefki, she can relive her childhood, but this time with snow as her toy.

One of her favourite pastimes is sneaking up behind me when I'm least expecting it and launching a perfectly aimed snowball at the back of my head. There I am, minding my own business, perhaps contemplating the beauty of our winter wonderland, when – thwack! A snowball explodes against my neck. I soon became used to the cold trickle down my spine from melting ice.

Despite the snowy fun, there's something magical about winter in Pefki. The village, which bustles with activity in the summer, becomes peaceful and quiet under a blanket of snow. The houses look like they belong on the front of Christmas cards, with smoke gently curling from the chimneys and the scent of wood smoke mingling with the crisp, cold air.

We often send photos to our friends in other parts of the world, capturing the serene beauty of our winter scenes. These images feature snow-laden trees, rooftops blanketed in white, and people bundled up in heavy coats and bobble hats, exhaling puffs of breath into the frosty air. The response is almost always one of disbelief. Many have trouble recognising that these scenes are from Greece. They have a preconceived image of Greece as a land of perpetual sunshine, sandy beaches and open-air tavernas.

However, like many other European countries, Greece gets its fair share of snow and ice. The contrast between the sun-drenched summers and the frosty winters is stark, and it's one of the many charms of living here. Our village feels worlds away from the sun-baked islands and coastal towns that most people associate with Greece. We've come to appreciate the quiet, introspective charm of Greek winters. It's a time to slow down, to enjoy the simple pleasures of a warm home and good company. The local taverna, with its roaring fire and hearty stews, becomes a cosy refuge from the chill outside. And while it might not fit the postcard image of Greece, it's a side of the country that we love.

As winter transitioned into spring, the cold and grey days gradually gave way to vibrant bursts of colour and warmth. The platanus and fig trees began to bud, their delicate new leaves casting a stunning array of pastel hues against the clear blue sky. The fields, once blanketed in snow, now bloomed with wildflowers. The air was filled with the sweet scent of blossoms, and the harmonious chirping of birds signalled the arrival of a new season. Villagers emerged from their homes, shedding their heavy coats and embracing the new-found energy that spring brought. Laughter and chatter filled the streets as people gathered at outdoor cafes. The deserted village square once again became a hub of activity, with locals and visitors alike savouring the lively atmosphere and celebrating the beauty of nature's rebirth. The transition from winter to spring was not just a change in the weather, but a renewal of spirit for everyone in the village. There was anticipation of sunny days ahead, with gardens and fields that had lain dormant during the winter months now bursting into life. Villagers tended to their plants and flowers with renewed vigour. Local bars and hotels were bustling with activity as they prepared sunbeds and straw parasols on the beach, eagerly awaiting the arrival of the first tourists.

During the winter months, we couldn't do much with the garden. It remained a barren wasteland after the flooding. The bulldozer tracks from our aborted wall project still crisscrossed the land like scars, and the lawn we had tended so carefully was now just a memory. With spring finally here, we decided to make a fresh start. It was time to level the ground and plant some grass seeds. If I was lucky, I might even get the lawn growing before the ants woke up for the summer.

We'd decided not to build another wall close to the house. Sacrificing so much of the garden felt like admitting defeat. Besides, we'd made it through a wet winter without flooding, and for the first time in months, we were starting to feel a little safer. Even so, the sight of the river still made my stomach tighten. The law meant we couldn't construct any kind of flood barrier, and the only person with the authority to override it was the mayor – a man I'd yet to meet. I'd been mentally rehearsing how to approach him, how to plead our case. I wasn't optimistic, but it felt like our last chance for some protection.

That's when Dimitri arrived.

He strolled in, sleeves rolled up, ready to help with the

clean-up as he always did. But there was something different about him today. An unmistakable energy. Before we even had a chance to hand him a rake, he grinned and said, "I have good news."

I stopped in my tracks. "Good news?" I asked cautiously. "About the river?"

Dimitri's grin widened. "You no longer have problems with the river. It's taken care of itself. Come on, I'll show you."

Alex and I exchanged a glance, a flicker of disbelief passing between us. "Taken care of itself?" she repeated. Her voice was sceptical, but her eyes betrayed a glimmer of hope. Without hesitating, we followed Dimitri as he led us out of the garden, down the road and towards the small village of Artemision.

We stopped at the bridge, and my breath caught in my throat. The once raging river, the source of so many sleepless nights and frantic calculations, had transformed into a gentle, murmuring stream. It meandered calmly beneath the bridge, no longer the monster that had roared through our land and threatened to swallow our home.

"Come, there's more," Dimitri urged, waving us onward.

We walked down the road that bordered our property, the familiar route taking on a new, almost magical quality. As we approached the end of our garden, we noticed something extraordinary. Water trickled from the undergrowth, carving a new path through the sandy soil, far away from our land. The river had shifted, rerouting itself naturally towards the beach.

I stared at the scene. "It's ... it's gone," I said, the words barely audible. Alex clutched my arm, her grip tight, and I turned to see her eyes shimmering with tears. For months, the river had loomed over us like a shadow, a constant reminder of nature's unpredictable power. Now, that shadow had lifted.

Dimitri beamed with pride, as if he had orchestrated the river's new course himself. "You see?" he said. "No wall, no mayor, no problem. The river won't bother you any more."

For a moment, none of us spoke. We just stood there, watching the water flow gently past as if it had always belonged there. The weight that had pressed on my chest for so long began to lift, replaced by a lightness I hadn't felt in months.

Alex broke the silence. "It's like the land is healing itself," she said softly. I nodded, unable to find the right words. This wasn't just good news – it was a gift; one we hadn't dared to hope for.

As we walked back home, the world felt different. Brighter. Safer. The problems that once seemed insurmountable had, in the end, resolved themselves. The river had made its choice, and for the first time in what felt like forever, we could truly exhale.

But now we had other things to worry about. It was clear from our daily phone calls that Debbie's health was failing fast. She looked poorly during our last visit a few short weeks ago, but now things seemed to be getting worse. We were increasingly worried about her well-being. We couldn't provide the care she needed from far away, so we decided to spend some time in Glyfada. Alex could then help take care of her. After all, Debbie had always taken care of everyone else, so it was time to give something back.

From the moment I met Debbie, I could sense her warmth and genuine kindness. Her infectious laughter and comforting hugs created an instant connection, making me feel like a part of the family. She possessed a unique ability to make everyone around her feel seen and valued, effortlessly bringing out the best in everyone who knew her. Whether it was through her thoughtful gestures or heartfelt conversations, Debbie had an uncanny knack for knowing exactly what someone needed at any given moment. Her support and encouragement became a pillar of strength during challenging times, reminding me of my potential and pushing me to reach for my dreams. It was through her unwavering belief in me that I found the courage to take risks and embrace personal growth. Debbie's presence was not just a beacon of light in my life, but a constant reminder of the power of love, compassion and selflessness. She taught me the importance of cherishing relationships, valuing the small moments, and finding joy in the simplest of things. In her own subtle way, Debbie became a mentor, guiding me towards becoming a better version of myself.

People often see adversity as a negative aspect of life, something they would prefer to avoid. However, it is through facing challenges and overcoming obstacles that heroes are formed. Smooth seas may provide comfort and ease, but they do not require us to push beyond our limits or tap into our potential. It is during the stormy days, when the waves crash against our ship, that we discover our true strengths and resilience. Where would we be without heroes? Adversity teaches us valuable life lessons, such as perseverance, adaptability, and problem-solving skills. It forces us to step out of our comfort zones and confront our fears. Through adversity, we learn to navigate through the unpredictable waters of life, becoming skilful sailors who can weather any storm that comes our way.

Debbie, as a young girl, lived through the Second World War and the Nazi occupation of Greece. She experienced firsthand the Great Famine (also known as the Grand Famine in Greek: Μεγάλος Λιμός). By the end of the winter of 1941–1942, the famine had resulted in between one hundred thousand and two hundred thousand deaths and left many Greeks facing starvation. She remembers visiting the market and the only edible thing available was a donkey's head.

Germany occupied Greece in April 1941 after a successful campaign in the Balkans. They established a fascist regime and looted the country. Foodstuffs were exported to meet the needs of the German and Italian armies. The remaining food was used to feed the occupiers, leaving little for the Greek people.

Debbie vividly remembered the suffering of her friends and neighbours. Cries of hunger filled her village, where many people were dying. Initially, Debbie's family was better off because her father, a respected ship captain, provided well for them. However, the Nazis arrested him for being a member of the Greek resistance, working for the allies by aiding the escape of British soldiers and airmen. He escaped from the clutches of the SS, leaving his wife and children to fend for themselves. Yet, from his forced exile, he managed to smuggle gold sovereigns to his wife through resistance channels. This allowed her to buy whatever food was available, in a futile attempt to alleviate the suffering of her starving neighbours.

Debbie was deeply affected by this experience. It stayed with her throughout her life. When she became a mother, she spent most of her time in her small kitchen. She created huge quantities of the most delicious food. It was always far too much for the family, so her home became a local kitchen. Anyone could arrive and eat. Debbie would ensure nobody ever went hungry again.

Word quickly spread in the village that Debbie's house always had a meal available. Many less fortunate people would come to eat and share their stories. Debbie would listen to their troubles and help them as much as she could.

Among the daily visitors there was a young boy, his useless legs dragging him around the village. Debbie managed to convince her doctor friend in England to perform a life-changing operation. She raised enough money for the airfare and his family's stay. Thanks to Debbie's relentless efforts, the boy was able to walk confidently, and, now a grown man, has risen to a prominent position in a nearby government office.

When Alex and her brother received offers from British universities, Debbie made it clear that she had no intention of letting them go alone. Her children were her top priority, and she couldn't bear the thought of them going their separate ways without a mother's care. As a result, she decided to rent a house in England and accompany them on their journey.

Alex and Christos brought home new friends from their university, and they became part of her growing family. Their living conditions in student halls and meagre diet surprised her. They mainly ate pasta and Pot Noodles. Whenever they visited, they left with generous bags of deliciously prepared food to ensure they ate properly. Debbie invited some of them to stay in the house so she could take care of them.

Debbie was a cherished matriarch, always caring and nurturing. Over the years, her influence echoed in the hearts of those she touched. They would always remember her warm smile and encouraging words. Some became doctors, lawyers or accomplished professionals, but they stayed connected through phone calls, letters and reunions. Debbie's impact was etched deep in their hearts, ensuring she would never be forgotten.

After finishing their university education, Alex and Christos returned to Greece. Debbie was thrilled to continue her life in the village. Alex pursued her passion for beauty therapy and started her own business at home. With her expertise and new university degree, she became renowned for offering outstanding beauty treatments and personalised care. Christos used his new engineering skills to create automation systems for Greek factories. His solutions enhanced production processes, efficiency, and cost reduction across various industries.

Greece has faced a significant amount of turmoil throughout its long history. However, after the Second World War, the Greek Civil War, and the military junta of the nineteen seventies, Greece began to recover. People were becoming richer. Athens had become an overcrowded capital city, so eyes began to turn towards the suburbs. As the economy stabilised, foreign investment started pouring into the country. This new-found prosperity was particularly evident in Glyfada. The once sleepy village was now booming with new developments, luxurious villas and upscale shopping centres. As people's disposable income increased, they began to indulge in a more lavish lifestyle. The streets were lined with expensive cars, and the marina was filled with yachts owned by affluent residents and foreigners. With its beautiful beaches and proximity to Athens, Glyfada became a sought-after destination for both locals and tourists alike.

The transformation of Glyfada came with a price for the original residents who had been living there for generations. The once quiet and close-knit community saw its cultural way of life disrupted as modernisation took over. Trendy cafes, boutiques and upscale restaurants, catering to the influx of tourists and wealthy Athenians, replaced traditional shops and businesses. The neighbourhood underwent significant changes, losing its original charm.

We were the last ones in our street to give in to the overwhelming force of progress. As the only house left, surrounded by towering apartment buildings, we finally gave in.

The construction of our new apartment block signalled the end of our village way of life. It changed the landscape of the street and replaced our tight community with a disconnected group of new neighbours. The sense of friendship and shared values slowly faded as people from different backgrounds moved in. The once peaceful and quiet streets became crowded and noisy with constant traffic and city hustle. The charm and simplicity of village life were lost, replaced by an impersonal and fast-paced urban environment.

Debbie had recently settled into her new apartment on the first floor. Standing on her balcony, she could see the changes on the street below, which teemed with hurried individuals navigating towards their destinations. The allure of her former street had vanished. Before, each house had possessed its own unique character, with no need for doorbells or knockers. Debbie yearned for the familiarity of those neighbourly customs she had grown used to. The impersonal atmosphere of the new building lacked the warmth and connection she had previously cherished.

Most of her friends had departed, leaving behind a void. They embraced their new-found prosperity and retreated to islands or ancestral villages. Glyfada lost its uniqueness with their departure, leaving Debbie with fading dreams.

Debbie felt the weight of this isolation, and it took a toll on her health. The twinkle in her eyes began to fade, and her once energetic spirit grew weary. She longed for the days when the village was alive with joy and friendship. Debbie knew deep down that things would never be the same again, and as her health declined, it became a painful reminder of the irreversible changes that had taken place in her beloved community.

Upon our arrival, it was clear that she had drastically changed in a short time. We had only been away for a few weeks. She was a shadow of her previous self. Gone were the days when her eyes gleamed with mischief and vitality. Her once rosy, cherubic face now appeared pallid and lacklustre, reflecting an overwhelming sense of surrender and sorrow. We did everything in our power to lift her spirits, to bring back the sound of her laughter that once filled our lives. We held on to the belief that this would have a positive impact on her deteriorating health. Despite it all, she still found moments of joy in our jokes, but behind that smile, we could sense the deep-rooted pain and despair. She was aware that her time on this earth was coming to an end. The realisation weighed heavily on her, knowing that her future would burden her family. The simplest of tasks became insurmountable, and she relied on others for help. Cooking, something she once enjoyed, was now impossible. Basic daily activities, like washing and using the toilet, required someone's aid. She felt utterly useless. Debbie had always been a pillar of strength. She had never relied on anyone before. Yet now, her very survival depended on the support of others.

Debbie loved us all deeply and showed it by always being warm and affectionate. She wanted to protect us and carefully planned her departure to spare us the pain of a heartbreaking goodbye. But fate had different plans.

She had waited until we went back to Pefki after our last visit. While we were away, she simply gave up. We were packing, ready to go to catch the ferry, when Alex received a call from the hospital in Athens. Debbie had been admitted and was not expected to last the night. Her beautiful heart, once so full of life and love, was now surrendering.

Though we had witnessed Debbie's decline, the reality of losing her hit us with an unexpected force. We had expected a few more years, more moments to cherish. But now, we had to face the truth. We had to be there. We had to be with her. It was the least we could do. We wanted to honour her beautiful spirit until the very end. We wanted to make sure she left this world surrounded by those she loved and who loved her.

We hurriedly made our way to the ferry. Three agonising hours later, we finally navigated through the congested early evening Athens traffic and arrived at the hospital. The rain fell steadily, creating a soft pitter-patter as we stepped out of the car. The sterile scent of antiseptic filled the air, mingling with the scent of rain. Our hearts raced with hope and apprehension as we stepped out of the elevator.

As we entered the ward, the soft hum of machines and hushed whispers enveloped the room. The machines beeped rhythmically, creating a melodic backdrop to the tension in the air. And there she lay, Debbie, poised and tranquil, her presence casting a calming aura over the room. With trembling hands, we settled ourselves by her bedside, feeling the coolness of the sheets against our skin, a comforting touch amidst the anxiety.

The rest of the family had already gathered, their faces etched with anxiety mirroring our own fears. Zissis sat on one side, his face lined with worry. On the other side was Christos, who had just arrived from Holland. Other family members had received the news and were sitting on chairs slightly back from the bed, all showing exhaustion and concern on their faces. At the foot of her bed, a priest stood, his voice gentle and soothing as he recited the last rites. The solemn words hung in the air, adding an air of finality to the room.

With every word uttered, the gravity of the moment intensified, and a bittersweet stillness settled upon us. Debbie's once darkened eyes now sparkled with a glimmer of light, a serene smile gracing her lips. In that moment, it was clear she had accepted her impending journey, unburdened by fear. Her unwavering faith illuminated her spirit, infusing the room with an indescribable sense of peace. However, amidst her acceptance, a tinge of sadness remained. With great effort, she lifted one frail hand, beckoning me closer.

"Peteraki," she said, her voice filled with tenderness. The sound of her voice always brought me comfort. It was a term of endearment, a nickname that meant "small Peter". The familiar scent of her perfume lingered in the air, a delicate floral fragrance that reminded me of our shared memories. As she prepared to leave, her words resonated in my heart. "I entrust my family to you," she whispered. The weight of her trust settled upon my shoulders, a responsibility I willingly accepted. "Take care of my daughter," she pleaded, her eyes filled with a mix of love and concern. At that moment, I felt the strength she saw in me. "Keep my family safe," she urged, her voice filled with determination. Her words became a solemn promise, a vow to protect those she held dear. And as she uttered the words, "I love you," I could feel the depth of her affection enveloping me like a warm embrace.

Alex leaned over the bed and held onto her mother tightly, feeling the warmth of her body and the rise and fall of her chest. Debbie's vibrant and energetic spirit had gradually faded, her illness taking its toll. But in this moment, as they lay together in the calm and quiet room, Alex could still feel the connection between them, the bond of love that had always been unbreakable.

The room was dimly lit, with soft sunlight filtering through the window. A bouquet of fresh flowers sat on the bedside table, their sweet fragrance blending with the sterile scent of the hospital. Outside, the world continued to spin, oblivious to the profound moment unfolding within these four walls.

Alex whispered soothing words into her mother's ear, her voice filled with tenderness and sadness. She gently brushed her fingers through Debbie's hair, remembering the countless times her mother had done the same for her when she was a child. It was a bittersweet moment, knowing that this would be their final embrace before Debbie's journey came to an end.

As the minutes turned into hours, the room remained still, the only sound the soft rhythm of their breathing. Alex could hear the steady beat of her own heart, a reminder of the life she still had to live without her mother by her side. She tried to hold on to every detail, etching it into her memory, knowing that these precious moments would sustain her in the days, months and years to come.

And then, with a peaceful sigh, Debbie's breathing slowed until it became almost imperceptible. Alex watched as her mother's features relaxed, the lines of pain and worry smoothing away. Debbie's face appeared composed, as if she had finally found solace in her slumber.

Tears welled up in Alex's eyes as she whispered a final goodbye, her voice choked with emotion. She pressed her lips gently against her mother's forehead, feeling the coolness of her skin. In that moment, Alex knew that Debbie had found peace, her journey complete.

Debbie was an incredible woman who always went out of her way to help others. Whether it was lending a listening ear, offering a helping hand, or simply spreading kindness, she had a remarkable impact on those around her. Her genuine spirit and compassionate nature touched the lives of many, leaving a lasting impression on everyone she encountered. Now, her legacy lives on through her daughter, who shares the same values and carries forward the torch of her mother's love and kindness. I am incredibly proud to call her my wife, as she continues to touch the lives of others and make the world a better place, just like her mother always did.

CHAPTER 8

The Day the Gods Came to Visit

The worst of all deceptions is self-deception.

– Plato

Three months after Debbie passed away, we finally returned to Pefki. Both Alex and I had changed profoundly. The loss of Debbie was a devastating blow to us both, leaving a void that seemed impossible to fill. The previous few weeks had flown by in a whirlwind of funeral arrangements, dealing with her affairs, and generally making sure everything was settled.

During that time, we had barely had a moment to process our grief. Every day brought a new task, a new responsibility, that kept us moving forward even when all we wanted to do was pause and remember her. Organising the funeral was an emotionally exhausting process. We wanted it to be a celebration of her life, filled with the love and warmth she had always given so freely. Friends and family gathered, sharing stories and memories, their laughter mingling with tears. It was a bittersweet tribute to a woman who had touched so many lives.

Sorting through Debbie's affairs was equally challenging. Her home, once filled with her vivacious presence, now felt eerily quiet. Every item we came across was a reminder of her – a piece of jewellery, a favourite book, a handwritten recipe. Each discovery brought a fresh wave of grief, but also a sense of connection, as if she were still there with us, guiding us through the process.

Alex, who had always been the rock in our relationship, found herself struggling to cope with the loss. She had been incredibly close to her mother, and losing Debbie felt like losing a part of herself. Her usual spark seemed dimmed, replaced by a quiet sadness that she tried hard to hide.

When we finally returned to Pefki it felt like stepping into a different world. The familiar sights and sounds of our village were comforting. The villagers, with their sense of community and compassion, welcomed us back with open arms. They brought food and offered their condolences, their kindness a reminder that we were not alone in our sorrow.

We began to find a new rhythm in our lives. We spent hours in our garden, finding solace in the simple act of tending to the plants. Each day, we nurtured the flowers and shrubs, feeling a sense of accomplishment as they flourished under our care. The garden became a sanctuary where we could escape our grief, losing ourselves in the comforting routines of watering, pruning and planting.

We also took comfort in the routines of village life. The familiar rituals – morning coffee at the local taverna, evening walks along the beach, chatting with our neighbours – provided a sense of normalcy and continuity. Each interaction slowly stitched the fabric of our lives back together.

Our garden, which had suffered so much during the floods, became our main project for the summer. The bare and battered plot of land gradually transformed once more into a vibrant oasis. The lawn, which had initially seemed an impossible dream, grew lush and green. The flowers that had been damaged in the flood started to bloom again, their bright colours a testament to resilience and renewal.

We worked tirelessly, adding new plants and nurturing the old ones back to health. Dimitri had taken the damage to our garden to heart and spent most days with us helping the garden to recover. Slowly we managed to coax life back into even the most forlorn corners of the garden.

Dimitri was spending most of his time in our garden, and looked tired. He was beginning to neglect his other work in the village, and continually refused payment.

"Look, Dimitri," I told him one day. "You are working so hard here. You need money. How will you live if you insist on helping me without payment?"

"You helped me when I needed you. You now need me. You are my friend and in need. It's the least I can do."

By September, our garden was fully restored to its previous glory. We sat back one evening, the cool breeze of early autumn rustling the leaves, and admired our creation. The lawn was a perfect green carpet, the flower beds bursting with colour. The trees stood tall and proud, their branches swaying gently.

Sipping our wine, we watched the sun set over Pefki. The sky turned shades of pink and orange, casting a warm glow over our garden. We felt a deep sense of peace and accomplishment, knowing that we had created something beautiful out of our pain. The garden was not just a testament to our resilience, but also to the enduring power of love and memory.

Living in Greece comes with its fair share of risks. We have the usual culprits like mosquitoes, which love feasting on exposed skin during the night. There are sneaky, gnat-sized mosquitoes that are practically invisible and operate in stealth mode. Occasionally, I see a giant centipede chasing after the cats in our garden. And believe it or not, I was stung by a small scorpion once. But what I never considered was that some of the plants in my garden could be deadly. Maybe I'm being a bit dramatic, but as a child in England, I learned about most dangerous things through personal experience. Thorny bushes and brambles made it challenging to reach juicy blackberries, and I often ended up with puncture wounds in exchange for sweet fruit. Falling into a patch of stinging nettles was no laughing matter. We were well aware never to eat unknown berries, no matter how tempting they looked. But I never encountered anything that posed a serious threat to my well-being.

One day, I was wandering around my Pefki garden and found a patch of bushes with pretty white flowers and spiky green fruit. They didn't look ripe, so I decided to keep an eye on them. Perhaps they may be edible, I thought.

Living in Greece, I still like to keep informed on news events back in England. Most mornings, I sit on my patio, check world news on my laptop and drink my first coffee of the day. One day, I came across an article on the BBC page with the headline "Highly Poisonous Plant Found in English Garden". There on the screen was a picture of my plant, showing the spiky green fruit. The garden where it was discovered had been closed off with red tape. Four people in hazmat chemical protection suits were carefully removing the offensive plant and stuffing it into big yellow bags marked "Hazardous".

I took my laptop up the garden and compared the picture on the screen to the plant in front of me. They were certainly making a fuss, ensuring no part of the plant touched their skin. They wore gas masks so none of the supposed toxic pollen could be inhaled. There it was, growing next to my geraniums. It was a plant called datura, and according to Google, it was highly poisonous. Commonly known as thorn apples or jimson weeds, they are also called devil's trumpets or mad apples, or in our Greek village, a weed.

Other English names include moonflower, devil's weed, and hell's bells. All species of datura are extremely poisonous and psychoactive, especially their seeds and flowers. They can cause respiratory depression, arrhythmias, fever, delirium, hallucinations, anticholinergic syndrome, psychosis, and death if taken internally. It has occasionally been used not only as a poison but also as a hallucinogen for centuries. Traditionally, its psychoactive properties have been associated with witchcraft and sorcery. It had to be removed. I called Dimitri to ask if he knew where I could get a chemical protection suit.

When he arrived, he asked why I needed one. I pointed at the clump of poison. He walked over to the toxic plants, hit them with a stick, stuffed them in a bag and threw them in the back of his truck. Problem solved.

Danger is a way of life in our Greek village. It's common to see a moped whizzing by with the driver, his wife and a couple of kids all crammed onto the seat. Once, I even spotted a moped with a goat perched on the back. But this is part of the relaxed lifestyle here, and nobody gives it a second glance.

Other common hazards include devastating wildfires, which almost wiped out some villages. In August 2021, a heatwave caused a wildfire that consumed over four hundred square kilometres of northern Evia before being halted on the other side of the main road running through our village. Our region is prone to earthquakes because it sits on a major fault line. We have had several earthquakes in the past, causing some destruction but no loss of life. The nearby port town of Edipsos is built on a volcanic vent, which provides hot water and thermal baths to hotels and tourists.

In the town where I was born in England, we never had

to worry about earthquakes. Forest fires were unknown, and flooding was limited to a few puddles after a strong thunderstorm. The extent of what we've experienced here is unlike anything I had ever seen before.

But no one had ever experienced a storm as fierce as the one approaching us. It started with gossip in the local tavernas. People discussed the storm causing havoc in nearby Volos. The worst flooding ever recorded was washing away homes. Fields and crops were completely submerged. Local radio and TV issued warnings that the storm was heading our way. A few hours later, a loud noise emanated from our phones, followed by a text message advising us of a life-threatening weather event. We had never received a text message like this before. It was in both Greek and English and demanded we take cover immediately from the impending storm.

The sky was still blue and cloudless; the sun was beating down on the beach, the last of the season's tourists getting their final dose of sunshine before the end of their holidays. There was no wind, and the day was warm.

As the evening unfolded, we sat in the calm atmosphere of our garden, enjoying the refreshing taste of ouzo in our glasses. The night sky shimmered with bright stars, while a gentle stillness filled the air. There was no sign of the storm that had been predicted. Hours had passed since we received the text message, leaving us to wonder if the "life-threatening event" had veered off its projected path. We were due to fly to the UK the next day, and we had already packed our bags ready for the trip. We needed to get up early to catch the ferry as we wanted to spend a few hours in Glyfada before heading to the airport. So, we finished our ouzo and went to bed.

The sound of crashing thunder woke me up the next morning. Rain was lashing onto the patio and running in trickles down our driveway. I opened the front door to find a large frog sheltering from the monsoon under our overhanging porch roof. What had he known that we didn't?

I stepped over the frog and looked down the road. Muddy water was gushing from the land next door, flowing towards the sea in a torrent. The road had disappeared under the river. I went around our house to check the garden. Despite the heavy rain, the seating area looked intact. There were water pools near the willow tree by the river, but this wasn't a cause for concern. We'd seen this before during heavy rain and minor flooding. My biggest worry was the roads in the village. Mudslides and water running off the mountains often make them impassable at certain times of the year. During the forest fires on Evia two years ago, we lost four hundred square kilometres of dense pines that used to prevent mud from flowing down the mountains. Without the trees, stormwater now flowed freely towards our village, causing raging torrents that had the potential to destroy everything in its path.

Today brought more concern, as we had a booking for the evening flight from Athens to Heathrow. We had to leave immediately to avoid getting stranded on the island. We urgently needed to get ahead of this weather and catch the ferry.

As I woke Alex, the car was already submerged up to its wheel trims in the rapidly rising deluge. Quickly, we locked up the house, waded through the water towards the car and tossed our suitcases into the boot. However, the roads had vanished, replaced by muddy rivers where smooth tarmac used to lie. The situation was deteriorating rapidly. The sky was intermittently illuminated by lightning, and the rain poured down in sheets rather than drops. The feeble attempts of the windscreen wipers did little to improve our visibility. With caution, we inched forward along the watery current until we reached the next village. We could hear the rumble of thunder in the distance, adding to the intensity of the storm. The rain seemed never-ending. The roads had turned into treacherous obstacles, with deep ravines forming from the force of the water. These mini rivers rushed across the path, adding to the main torrent running along the road. Men wearing dayglow jackets, their clothing drenched and faces determined, stood tall in their wellington boots and oilskins. Their red flags caught our attention, signalling the safest route through the chaos. We relied on their expertise as they skilfully directed vehicles through the maze of broken roads and fallen trees. It was a comforting sight, witnessing the resilience of these men and the power of nature colliding in this harsh and unforgiving storm.

The air was heavy with a sense of anticipation as we arrived at the port. Travellers waiting to board the ferry sheltered from the rain under the canopies and tin roofs of the ticket offices spread along the harbour wall. They had obviously suffered too with their journeys here, negotiating the broken roads and fallen trees. The raindrops fell relentlessly, adding to the gloomy atmosphere. The ferry's horn echoed through the misty harbour, signalling its imminent departure. Undeterred by the raging storm, the crew members bustled about, securing the vehicles and directing passengers to their designated areas.

As we drove slowly up the ferry ramp onto the car deck, the sound of the rain intensified, the droplets splashing against the metal surface. The grey waters of the Aegean Sea blended seamlessly with the dark sky, creating an eerie and mysterious ambiance.

Then my phone rang. It was Helen, our neighbour.

"Where are you?" she shouted down the phone. "Your house is under water. You must come back now. We are all drowning here!"

Since we left, things had worsened, she explained. The river at the end of our garden had transformed into a raging maelstrom, changed direction, and was now flowing around our house. Water from the mountain had arrived in our village.

I stopped and put our car into reverse, intending to leave the ferry and return to Pefki.

"Where are you going?" Alex said.

"We need to get back to Pefki and save our house," I told her.

"Look. Even if we manage to make it through the flooded roads, what can we really do?" Alex calmly replied. "We're here now. No matter what happens, we can always find a way to fix it. The most important thing is that we're safe. Let's just keep going and head to Athens without worrying too much for now."

She was speaking sensibly. We had only just negotiated the floods and broken roads. The rain had shown no sign of easing; it was heavier. Our chances of getting back to Pefki were slim. Even if we did manage to return home, what could we do? If, as Helen had told us, our house was in a river, there was not much we could do apart from helplessly watch the drama unfold.

As the ferry ramp lifted, we followed instructions and backed into our designated parking bay, the rain intensifying. We chose to remain in our car for the short crossing. I took out my phone to check the security cameras which monitored our home. It was a blank screen; they were offline.

This was really frustrating. The cameras happily warn me of a bumblebee buzzing about or a trespassing cat wandering around the garden, and I even saw an owl peering into the lens once. But they always seemed to fail when we really needed them.

During the forest fire a couple of years earlier, when we'd really wanted to see if the house was okay, the flames had melted the electrical lines in our village as the fire approached, rendering the cameras useless. This time, we were anxiously wondering if our house was now floating towards Skiathos.

We left the ferry and joined the motorway towards Athens. The rain eased from torrents to fat drops. By the time we reached our home in Glyfada, patches of blue sky had begun to appear.

We began to relax a little. Clearly we had problems at our home in Pefki, but the weather seemed to be easing. As the sun came out from behind the clouds, it brought with it a feeling of relief. It was a wise decision to continue our journey. We would come back in a couple of weeks and deal with any minor damage, mop up any spillage.

But we were very wrong to be optimistic. Although we didn't know it at the time, the most severe storm in the region's history was continuing to batter Pefki and northern Evia.

In Glyfada, we brewed coffee. We sat on the balcony and tried to call our neighbour in Pefki for an update. The call wouldn't connect. We tried another neighbour but had the same result. We opened the app on my phone to check the security cameras at our home, but they were still offline, so no help there. While I was holding the phone, a message appeared. It was a video, sent by Dimitri, who had taken the time to go and check our house.

I clicked on the video to see what it was about. As it started, we were shocked. It was a shaky film of a fast-running river. In its current, a small car was being dragged sideways along the road. The camera panned to the right, and we saw it – our beautiful home was in the middle of the raging river. The water had reached the windowsills on the side of the house, meaning it was now over one metre deep. It had washed away the gates. The camera then zoomed towards our front door. Water was spurting from the frame and around the windows. The water had entered the back of the house and was now finding its way through the front door frame, adding to the deepening floods. Our cherished home was being destroyed by the unrelenting deluge, and there was nothing we could do. The sight was both horrifying and terrifying.

We immediately tried our neighbours again, but the calls still wouldn't connect. Panic set in as we frantically searched for any news or updates online. However, there seemed to be no information available regarding the incident. Desperate for answers, we tried calling more of our friends, hoping they could provide some insight into what was happening. The phones didn't connect, so we sent text messages. We anxiously awaited their responses. The unsettling feeling of uncertainty loomed over us. We worried about the safety of our neighbours and the unfolding disaster. We couldn't go to England now. We had to return to Pefki.

Finally, a text message popped through. It was our friend Marily, who owned a small luxury hotel in the village. We immediately called her back, and this time the phone connected. Marily explained that the entire region was in turmoil. Fire trucks were parked around the village, pumping water out of homes. JCB diggers were cutting trenches to let the rivers flow into the sea. She switched her phone to video mode, and we were shocked by what we saw. The water was flowing from the land and rushing into the bay, turning the sea into a canvas of swirling brown mud, a stark contrast to its usual Aegean blue. In the background, we heard the gushing water and regular claps of thunder as the storm continued.

Alex asked if there was any further news about our home. We still hadn't been able to contact any of our neighbours and didn't even know if they were okay. We were anxious about George and Helen, who lived opposite. Their home would be in a similar situation to ours.

"You need to come back," said Marily. "You obviously can't go anywhere near your house, but you can stay at my hotel as long as you want. The flooding hasn't affected us yet. I'll check the ferries to make sure they're running. Stand by. I'll call you back."

She quickly confirmed that the ferries were running despite the storm. "I'll prepare a room for you. Take your time to sort things out, and remember, we're here to support you." Marily's genuine concern and offer of help comforted us. We gratefully accepted.

"But be careful," she said. "If you miss the ferry, don't even consider driving through from Chalkida. The storm washed away the roads on the island. But the roads from the port are passable if you're cautious. The last ferry departs from Arkitsa at nine this evening, so you should arrive here around eleven. I'll wait for you."

We thought about staying the night in Glyfada and making our way back in the morning. It seemed like the practical thing to do. After all, there was probably nothing we could do when we did arrive other than watch as our village submerged further under the relentless floodwaters. But at least we would be there to assess the damage for ourselves, to see with our own eyes what had become of our beloved home.

The decision to head back immediately, though fraught with uncertainty, was driven by an overwhelming need to be present, to face the devastation head-on. Marily's report and the shaky video had painted a grim picture of our village's fate. We couldn't just sit in the relative comfort of Glyfada, surrounded by dry streets and functioning utilities, while our home and community were being ravaged by nature's fury. We needed to be there, not just for ourselves but for our friends, who were undoubtedly facing the same struggles.

The port was just over three hours away from Athens, and the clock was ticking. We jumped into the car with our suitcases already packed for our aborted trip to London and made our way towards the national road. As we reached the port, the ferry awaited our arrival, its presence creating a sense of urgency. We desperately wanted to see our house for ourselves, hoping it was not as bad as the video had shown. With mere moments to spare, we successfully boarded the vessel for the second time today. The ramp was lifted, and the ferry, emitting a thunderous roar from its engines, skilfully reversed away from the dock.

Forty-five minutes later, we were back in Evia. The rain had stopped, but the roads were still partially flooded, and navigating the treacherous route proved challenging. Our headlights struggled to pierce through the darkness, revealing standing water and scattered rocks and trees strewn across the roads. Eventually, we arrived in our village, an eerie silence enveloping the deserted streets. Every bar and restaurant was shut, devoid of any signs of life. Amidst this stillness, a solitary fire engine stood parked, its blue lights flashing and hoses extending into a nearby house. We drove through the main street, only to find a deep, water-filled trench blocking our path home. We retraced our way through the village, hoping to access our home from an alternative route, but another raging river cut us off. Even though Marily had warned us, we had to try. But she had been correct. There was no conceivable way to reach our precious house.

We turned and drove through rivers up to our wheel arches back into the centre of the village. We stopped on a part of an elevated road which was above the flooding, behind the fire engine, and spoke to the crew busy pumping floodwater out of a house.

"Do you know when the road will open?" Alex asked one of the firemen.

"No," he replied. "There's no way out of the village in that direction." He waved his hand towards Artemision, where our home was now cut off from the village. "There's no power up there. The electrical cables are down, nobody can get there to fix them. Mobile phones aren't working there either; probably the towers have gone too."

The devastating storm had left our small community in a state of chaos and uncertainty. The sight that greeted us as we returned was heart-wrenching. The streets were littered with debris and fallen trees. Looking at the surrounding devastation, our hearts sank with the fear that our own home might have been completely destroyed. We had no means of communication to check on our neighbours, leaving us feeling helpless and anxious. The lack of information only intensified our worry for their safety and well-being.

"Have you had any reports of casualties?" Alex asked the fire crew.

"Not yet. But you need to take shelter somewhere. There's

an even bigger storm coming tonight. We're expecting things to get much worse."

By now it was almost midnight, and Marily was expecting us. We were exhausted and famished as we returned to the village where we had started out earlier that day. It felt like we had driven through half the country, even though it was only a seven-hour drive to Athens and back. The journey had taken its toll on us, and every mile seemed to stretch on endlessly.

We drove the short distance to her hotel, parked the car on a raised area of ground above the floodwater and rang her bell. Marily greeted us warmly and invited us inside. She hugged Alex first, then me. We followed her upstairs and entered the hotel suite. Compared to the chaos unfolding on the streets outside, the room felt cosy and inviting. The king-size bed glowed under blue and mauve lights. Spotlights were tastefully positioned. The balcony overlooked the beach and distant islands, and there was a glass table with four metal chairs. It was the perfect sanctuary to sit and reflect on the day's events.

Marily left us to unpack while she went downstairs to prepare some food. Alex and I sat on the balcony and looked across the dark sea towards Volos, where the sky was flashing with lightning. We could hear the distant rumbling of thunder, and the air felt unnaturally calm. The storm was coming back to torment us further. It was going to be a big one, and by all accounts it would be much worse than the last.

CHAPTER 9

The Gods Hadn't Finished with Us Yet

Nothing in life is more necessary than friendship.

– Aristotle

Marily arrived with a tray laden with food and iced glasses of beer, and joined us on the balcony just as the storm clouds began to gather ominously on the horizon. She settled into a chair, ready to share the latest updates.

"Pefki is the last accessible village in North Evia," she began, her tone serious. "The main road to the next village has been washed away. There's talk of a giant mudslide in Gouves, but no one can get there to confirm." Her words hung heavy in the air as we tried to process the extent of the devastation. "We have no idea what's going on there or how they're coping."

She went on to explain that the small village of Artemision was also cut off, which meant our own neighbourhood was isolated as well. We would have to wait until morning for more news.

As Marily got up to leave, Alex hugged her tightly. "Thank you so much for everything," I said, genuinely grateful. "You are a lifesaver. I don't know what we would have done without you."

Marily waved her hand dismissively, a modest smile on her face. "Don't even think about it," she replied. "We're all in this together."

As we lay down to sleep, the noise began. First, it was the wind. Windows rattled. The canopy over the balcony flapped uncontrollably until we heard a loud ripping sound as the canvas parted from the frame and flew away. The sound of the sea went from a gentle lapping onto the shingle beach to a systematic roar as each wave increased in size and hit the shore, then a sound of scraping as it retreated, dragging huge amounts of shingle and large stones with it. Then the lightning came. Each bolt of lightning was accompanied by an explosion of deafening sound, nothing like the rumbling of normal thunder. The rain beat down so hard that we lost the sound of the roaring waves. All we could hear now were torrents of water and booming from the sky. It sounded like someone directing a powerful hose on the window while setting off sticks of dynamite. There was no way we could sleep through this maelstrom, so we pulled our chairs up to the glass door and watched. Lightning illuminated the dark sky as Pefki sunk below us into the deepening flood of water.

We had given up trying to sleep. As the morning sky lightened, we could make out the damage. The road below us was a fast-flowing river. Our car, parked opposite on the high ground, was now in the middle of a lake, with water up to the wheel hubs. A JCB had arrived and was busy digging a trench from the road to the sea to ease the flood and direct it across the beach and away from the road. The shoreline was no longer visible. It was covered with fallen trees, masses of driftwood piled high on top of brown seaweed ripped from the seabed.

There was a knock at the door and Marily arrived with a Primus stove to make coffee; the storm had knocked out the power. She looked tired. She had not slept either and had black rings around her eyes, but with a warm smile she announced that breakfast was on the way.

A few moments later, she returned holding a large tray and placed it on the balcony table. There were glasses of freshly squeezed orange juice, bread, slices of cake, jam and honey. A selection of cold meats and finely sliced fruit. A big pot of coffee, cream, and bowls of fresh yogurt.

The three of us sat and ate breakfast while looking through the glass doors at the increasing activity below us. The storm had passed, but light rain was still splashing onto the passing river. Across the sea, the sky was becoming blue, and clouds were thinning as the sun emerged from behind them. Soon, the light of the sun was shining onto the river below us, which had reduced from a foaming torrent to a gentle flow. More JCBs had arrived to cut trenches, and the water was flowing away from the road into the sea.

With a dry area now stretching from the hotel entrance to the car, we quickly finished the rest of our breakfast and decided to attempt to reach our house.

We left Marily at the hotel entrance and got into our car. The carpets were wet, and my feet splashed in a pool of water near the pedals. Alex slid into the seat beside me. The road at the end of the village was still closed, but we were determined to find a way through, so we headed back past the harbour and joined the main road. We waited in a small queue of cars as the bulldozers buzzed around, scooping mud and earth from the road, and soon a small section became passable. We followed the pickup truck in front and slowly drove along the road towards home. Eventually, we turned into our street. Mud and silt covered the tarmac. A vehicle must have passed shortly before, as deep furrows resembling bulldozer tracks had been left in the goo. We followed the tracks towards home and ensured we lined up our wheels in the furrows to avoid getting bogged down as we arrived outside our house.

Thick, squelching mud and silt now concealed our once pristine front garden wall. The elegant wrought-iron fence was now a chaotic collage of debris, with fragments of wood, tangled vegetation, and remnants of our air conditioning unit. As I surveyed the scene, the pungent smell of damp earth filled the air, mingling with the faint scent of decay. Against the twisted railings, my inflatable boat and a garden chair had become lodged, forming a makeshift dam trapping even more debris and mire.

To our great relief, our house was still here. We noticed muddy streaks, evidence of water forcefully escaping through the windows, but from our vantage point, the walls appeared to be intact.

We exited the car and stepped into deep mud. As I tried to walk up the driveway, my foot sank to my thighs. I pulled my foot out, but the mud clung to my shoe and sucked it off. I tried again, but the mud was getting deeper. Walking or wading through it was impossible. Looking for a solution, I spotted a small plank of wood wedged against the wall. I retrieved it and placed it on the muddy driveway. It served as a bridge to reach the front patio. Alex followed, and we stood by the front door with the key in hand, nervous about entering.

Upon opening the door, the first thing we saw was mud – an overwhelming amount of it. As we surveyed the room, the unmistakable smell of damp earth filled our nostrils. The plasterboard coverings had been violently torn away, leaving behind large holes and exposing the rough walls and torn yellow insulation underneath. The remaining walls were streaked with muddy trails, giving them an eerie, ghostly appearance. The furniture, once a symbol of luxury and comfort, now resembled ancient relics buried beneath a thick layer of muck. The beds were completely covered in sludge. Black dirt seemed to cling to everything it touched. It was a scene of utter devastation.

The water had rushed in through the windows with an overwhelming roar, obliterating everything in its path.

Furniture and cherished belongings had been tossed about as if they were mere debris in a violent storm. The relentless force of the current had torn through our home, leaving behind shattered remnants of the life we once knew. Kitchen units and appliances were completely hidden beneath layers of mud, and the house itself groaned under the weight of the damage. Two back windows had shattered under the force of the floodwaters, allowing chaos to flood into every room. The memories we had created within these walls had been dismantled in a matter of minutes. The kitchen cabinets hung precariously at odd angles, their doors gaping open like the mouths of shipwrecked sailors. Plates and glassware were scattered across the floor, shattered and mixed with the slurry of sludge. The dining table, once a place of joyful meals and lively conversations, now stood alone like a melancholic island in a sea of brown.

However, amidst the chaos, there was a glimmer of hope. The glass doors at the back of the room, barely visible through the towering piles of mud, remained miraculously unscathed. It was as if the house had waged a fierce battle against nature and, though battered, had managed to remain standing. The floor tiles squelched beneath our feet as we carefully navigated through the wreckage. Despite the extensive cleaning and restoration that lay ahead, there was a strange sense of relief. The structure itself seemed to have survived mostly unscathed. The structural walls, although dirty and damaged, were still largely intact. We had lost all our furniture, clothing and possessions, but the foundations of the house remained strong.

We didn't want to risk opening the back doors. A huge pile

of mud, over a metre high, had accumulated against the glass. The weight hadn't broken the glass, which was astonishing. We decided to take the alternative route to the back garden using the driveway beside the house.

We carefully walked through the thick, sticky mud on the front terrace. Amongst the debris, I found another plank and placed it adjacent to the one we used to enter the house. This created a walkway. Slowly, we moved towards the back of our house, alternating the planks as we squelched through the mud. With each cautious step, we hoped that the makeshift walkway would hold and not sink into the mire.

But our garden had gone, vanished, replaced by a thick layer of mud and silt. The entire plot had been elevated by over a metre.

The scene before us was truly heart-wrenching. Everything we had worked for had gone. The neatly arranged pathways, stone borders, and the lush lawn I had worked so hard to grow had all disappeared, their former beauty now lost to the chaotic aftermath of the flood.

Our beloved garden furniture, which had provided us with countless moments of relaxation and enjoyment, had been swept away. The cosy wicker chairs where we had sipped morning coffee, the sturdy wooden bench where we had shared quiet conversations, and the colourful parasol that had shaded us from the sun – all were gone. In their place was a scene of total devastation, a testament to the power of nature's fury.

Our outdoor dining tables and the stone barbecue, where we had cooked our evening meals under the starry sky, lay buried under a mound of earth. The pergola, which had been draped with roses, was swallowed by the mud. The sense of loss was overwhelming. Each corner of the garden had held a memory, a moment of happiness now replaced by a stark reminder of the storm's destructive force. The giant stone arch we had so much fun building stood as a silent sentinel in the middle of the garden, half-submerged in the muck.

The flood was incredibly powerful, and our small ditch at the end of our garden couldn't handle the heavy rainfall. The water changed its path, cutting a new riverbed through our garden and flooding our house. As the flood reached its peak, the new river course couldn't contain the water and burst again. With nowhere for the water to flow, water levels kept rising. Silt and mud accumulated, causing the land to elevate. Eventually, the land rose so high that the river could no longer flow towards our submerged house and had to find an alternative route.

This new route took the water through the land next to us, discharging onto the road and engulfing more gardens as it forced its way towards the sea. The resulting cascade of water formed a magnificent waterfall, splashing and spraying as it rushed past our house and flowed down the road.

Standing amidst the ruins of what had once been our beautiful garden, I felt hollow. The devastation was almost too much to take in. I tried to summon some sense of determination, but instead, a wave of despair swept over me. How could we possibly begin again? The enormity of the task ahead felt overwhelming, like trying to rebuild a cathedral from a pile of rubble. As I looked around, all I could see was destruction. I didn't even know where to start.

Alex, however, was already moving. She stood beside me, hands on her hips, surveying the scene. For a moment, she said nothing. Then, with a small shrug and a smile that carried more reassurance than words ever could, she turned to me. "It's not so bad," she said, her tone light, almost playful. "We'll fix it. You'll see."

I stared at her in disbelief. How could she be so calm? So practical? I wanted to say something, to challenge her optimism, but the words stuck in my throat. In that moment, I envied her ability to find hope amid the chaos. While I was sinking into the enormity of what we'd lost, she was already imagining what we could create in its place.

Her confidence sparked something in me, though I couldn't quite name it. Admiration, perhaps, or maybe just the faintest glimmer of hope. As she bent down to pick up a broken branch and tossed it onto the pile of debris, I realised that this was Alex's way. She didn't waste time mourning what couldn't be changed. Instead, she focused on what could be rebuilt, even if it was from nothing.

I wasn't there yet. My mind kept circling back to the effort it would take, the setbacks we'd face. But as I watched Alex work, her resilience became a quiet anchor. I didn't have to feel hopeful right now; she had enough for both of us.

"The house is still standing. It just needs a good clean-up, but we can handle it. We'll start by using shovels to dig out the mud. Then we'll clean the floors, walls and every surface until they shine. It might take some time and effort, but with a little elbow grease it can be even better than before. We needed new furniture anyway, so let's get started."

The flooding felt like a cruel twist of fate. Pefki had already endured so much and was still reeling from the devastating wildfires of August 2021. Nature had already dealt its worst, and we were only just beginning to recover.

The wildfires had been catastrophic, destroying hundreds of square miles of pine forests and reducing homes to ashes. Even two years later, the air still carried faint traces of smoke, and the hillsides were marked with blackened scars. Livelihoods had been lost, and the community was left grappling with the enormity of what had been taken from us.

But amidst the destruction, there had been hope. Volunteers from all over Greece and beyond had arrived, bringing supplies, clearing debris and helping rebuild homes. Slowly but surely, we began to piece our village back together. It had been a long and painful process, but it felt as though we were finally turning a corner.

And now this. Standing in the garden, I couldn't help but feel the weight of it all pressing down. Just as we'd begun to heal, another blow had come to knock us down again. It felt unfair, almost unbearable.

It felt as though the gods were testing our resilience. If there were any lingering doubts about climate change, this recent catastrophe only solidified our conviction.

We had to make sure George and Helen were okay. We didn't know if they had stayed through the whole storm or if they had left to find safety somewhere else. I called over their wall, my voice echoing in the eerie silence after the storm. Soon, George stepped out of his house, looking tired but relieved.

His home, built on a raised concrete platform, had stayed dry and untouched by the floodwaters. But everything around it was destroyed. His outbuildings and garden walls, which were right in the path of the water, were completely ruined. His garden, once filled with lush greenery and blooming flowers, was now a muddy mess. The sturdy trees that had stood tall for years were uprooted and scattered like matchsticks.

As we walked closer, I saw that all of his outbuildings were filled with silt and mud. Their doors hung open, and the contents were strewn about in a muddy mess.

Despite all this destruction, George and Helen were safe. They had taken shelter in their raised home and watched in horror as the storm tore through everything around them. George told us about the terrifying experience, describing how they had watched the water rise and sweep away everything in its path. He talked about the sound of the rushing water, the crashing debris, and the overwhelming fear they had felt.

Yet despite the devastation, there was a sense of gratitude. Their home, their sanctuary, had withstood the storm. George and Helen were unharmed, and their spirits, though shaken, remained strong. They were relieved that the worst was over and determined to rebuild and restore what had been lost.

As we stood there looking at the damage, we knew that the road to recovery would be long and difficult. But in that moment, the safety of George and Helen was a beacon of hope amidst the ruins. It reminded us of the resilience of the human spirit in the face of nature's fury.

The rest of the day was spent assessing the damage and beginning the massive clean-up. Faced with so much destruction, we had no idea where to start. I decided to clear a pathway from the road to our front door. But when I tried to lift a shovel full of the sticky mass, it was like trying to lift treacle. I was wasting my time. Even mechanical diggers would have been useless as they would have sunk into the muck. There was nothing that could be done outdoors until the mud and silt started to dry and become firm enough to at least walk on without sinking to our thighs. Any further attempt at cleaning was pointless. We were just spreading muck from one place to another. It was all far too wet and sticky to make any difference.

By evening, exhausted and covered in mud, we returned to Marily's hotel. She welcomed us back with warm food and a comforting smile, providing a much-needed respite from the day's labour. We sat on the balcony, watching the sun set over the now calm sea, and reflected on the challenges ahead.

CHAPTER 10

A New Beginning

Helpfulness towards someone in need, not in return for anything, nor for the advantage of the helper himself, but for that of the person helped.

– Aristotle

The next day, the Greek sun bathed the surroundings in a warm glow. The roads still had a gentle flow of water covering the tarmac but had transformed from yesterday's furious torrents. After breakfast, we left the hotel and drove the short distance to our house. Already, the mud was beginning to dry, and the surface was baking to a crust. It would soon be ready to move and for the real work to begin.

We were thinking about where to begin our mammoth task when a van stopped outside. Four women got out. We recognised one as Theodora. She was the mother of Mary, the waitress who worked at Manya's taverna during the summer. Theodora, Mary and two aunties jumped out of the van, ready for action. Mary was holding a mop and bucket. Her mother had a spade. The others carried an assortment of cleaning materials and rubbish bags.

"We've come to clean your house," Theodora announced with a bright smile. Her voice was firm but friendly. "We kindly ask you to step outside and not worry about a thing. This is routine for us. We've handled many floods in the village over the years. Although this one is a bit more challenging, it just needs a little extra work. So please, let us take care of it."

As Theodora spoke, her warm smile made us feel reassured. She gently guided us towards the exit, encouraging us to take a well-deserved rest. "Enjoy some fresh air and relax," she said. "We've got everything under control here. Your home will be back to normal in no time."

Reluctantly, Alex relented and allowed the determined ladies to take charge of cleaning the house. They scurried around in a flurry of activity, shovelling mud, dragging furniture outside and scrubbing surfaces with vigour. It was clear they were not going to take no for an answer. Their sense of community and camaraderie was inspiring as they worked together with unwavering determination to lighten Alex's load.

Despite their insistence, Alex couldn't help but feel a pang of guilt for not tackling the cleaning tasks herself. She watched them work tirelessly, their faces etched with resolve and empathy. However, their kindness and genuine concern for her well-being began to ease her worries.

It was a humbling experience for Alex, realising that sometimes, accepting help is not a sign of weakness but rather a testament to the strength of a supportive community. As she saw the ladies work with such dedication, she understood that their actions were not just about cleaning the house, but about showing solidarity and love in a time of need.

Theodora wiped a streak of mud from her forehead and grinned at Alex. "What do you foreigners know about cleaning?" she teased, her eyes sparkling with mischief. "We are used to this. You will just get under our feet."

Alex couldn't help but laugh at Theodora's playful jab. She knew there was truth in her words. These women had likely weathered many storms in their lives, and their resilience showed in their swift and efficient movements.

Mary continued. "Besides, we can have this place looking like new in no time. You just relax and let us handle it."

Another woman chimed in. "Yes, Alex, leave it to us. We've got this!"

This was a typical gesture I had seen so many times during my time as part of a Greek family. Now, in the village, we had found another family, just as loving as the first. It wasn't only my immediate family who displayed such kindness. I quickly discovered that kindness was a common trait among Greek people. Whether it was a neighbour bringing fresh oranges from their tree, delivering freshly laid eggs from their own hens, or a stranger gladly offering directions when I was lost, I was constantly amazed by the generosity and warmth of the Greek people. Even in situations where there was a language barrier, someone would go out of their way to assist me. This unwavering kindness truly astounded me.

Over the years, I have come to realise that this inherent kindness is deeply ingrained in Greek culture. The concept of "philoxenia", which translates to "love of strangers", is highly valued in Greek society. Greeks believe in treating others with respect and compassion, regardless of their background or circumstances. This philosophy extends beyond family and friends; it is woven into the very fabric of Greek society.

The kindness of the Greek people has not only made me feel welcomed and loved, but it has also taught me the importance of extending kindness to others. It has inspired me to be more compassionate, understanding, and willing to lend a helping hand, just as the Greek people have been for me. Their acts of kindness have left an indelible mark on my life, and I will forever be grateful for the love and warmth I have always received.

The unexpected assistance from the women in our village left Alex and me with some free time on our hands. Instead of shovelling mud out of our home as we had anticipated, we found ourselves at a loose end. Grateful for their help, we now needed to figure out how to make the most of this unexpected break. So, after being banned from our own house, Alex and I decided to drive around the area in the hope of offering assistance elsewhere.

We had heard that the neighbouring village of Gouves was the most severely affected. As we made our way towards the car, Marily pulled up next to us, with a variety of brooms, shovels and mops sticking out of the back window.

"I've come to help," she called out of her open car window. Alex thanked her but pointed to the flurry of activity in our house.

"I don't think they will let you in. They've already thrown us out," Alex told her.

"Okay, where are you going?" She didn't wait for an answer. "It doesn't matter. I will come with you anyway." She left her car parked, still with the brooms and shovels sticking out of the window, and climbed into the back seat of ours, and we set off.

As we drove over the silt-covered roads, we entered the neighbouring village of Gouves. The once charming village now appeared desolate and gloomy. The pretty houses were coated in mud, their bright colours muted. Streets that had been lively with activity were eerily quiet, with debris scattered everywhere. The air was thick with the smell of damp earth. Trees and plants, weighed down by silt, stood as sombre reminders of the recent devastation. The air was filled with the sound of shovels scraping against the ground. The roads were difficult to manoeuvre; we had to follow the tyre tracks from previous vehicles, creating a treacherous path. It felt like driving in snow. If we veered away from the tracks, we would get stuck in the mud. The main street was a chaotic scene of JCBs working to clear the mud banks.

We could drive no further. We parked our car on the outskirts, its tyres sinking slightly into the muck as we stepped out and began our slow walk towards the centre of the village.

With each step, our shoes became caked with mud, making

the trudge through the thick sludge even more difficult. The squelching sound accompanied us as we moved forward, each step feeling heavier than the last. As we approached the heart of the village, we were shocked by the sight of the gardens overwhelmed by mudslides. The disaster, triggered by the heavy rainfall and the steep slopes of the mountains, had left a devastating impact on the community.

Ankle-deep mud had infiltrated everywhere, seeping into homes, shops and public spaces. It was a grim reminder of the destructive force that had swept through.

The storm had caused terrible damage to the infrastructure. Trees that had stood tall for decades were uprooted, their roots exposed and tangled like forgotten relics. Power lines lay scattered across the streets, some hanging precariously from broken poles. The lack of electricity also meant that the water pumps were not functioning, leaving the taps dry and the villagers without access to clean water.

We made our way to the village centre, where a small group of residents had gathered to discuss the next steps. Their conversations were hushed and serious, punctuated by the occasional sigh or shake of the head. An elderly man leaned on his cane, staring at the devastation with a look of profound sadness.

The road to recovery was daunting. People began to organise themselves, forming groups to tackle different tasks. Some focused on clearing the mud from homes and streets, while others worked to restore the water supply.

Alex looked around, trying to assess how we could help.

People were busy cleaning mud away from homes, but they could only go so far. Without water to wash away the remnants, it would still be a sticky mess.

As far as Alex could see, the most immediate need was drinking water. The only supermarket in the village was closed, banks of mud and silt piled up against the door. The nearest shop selling bottled water was in Pefki.

"Let's go and get some water for these people," Alex suggested. "We can load up the car. At least they will have something to drink."

Leaving Marily behind, we hurried back to our car and embarked on our short journey. We wanted to contribute in some small measure to help in any way we could.

At the supermarket, Alex approached the owner. "How many bottles of water do you have in stock?" The owner guided us to the back of the shop. In the dimly lit storage area were three towering pallets, each stacked with five hundred bottles of water.

"That will do for a start," Alex told the owner. "Can you deliver now?"

The owner's eyes widened in surprise. "All of it?"

Alex explained the reason for wanting all of his stock.

"Sure, no problem. I have a pickup truck, though it might take three or four trips. And don't worry about any extra charges – I'll only charge you the cost price for the water and I'll deliver everything for free."

We paid him and helped to load the heavy six-packs of water onto his truck. We used our back seat and boot to load a few more before setting off.

As we followed him back to Gouves, the weight of the loaded truck seemed to have a noticeable effect on its bodywork. The tyres appeared slightly compressed under the immense load. Every bump on the road caused the truck to bounce, and the bodywork even seemed to brush against the ground at times. Despite this, he skilfully manoeuvred the truck, ensuring the precious cargo remained secure.

The square was bustling with activity as the truck pulled in. A sense of urgency filled the air as people quickly gathered around to lend a hand. Men and women of all ages, from the strong and able-bodied to the frail and elderly, came together to unload the truck. People worked together, forming an assembly line to pass the bottles from person to person and carefully placing them in small piles.

As the last bottle was unloaded, I sat on a wall with a sigh of relief. But there was no time for celebration or rest. Almost immediately, the water was in high demand. The elderly ladies, some with walking canes and others with shopping baskets on wheels, quickly took charge. Each collected as many bottles as they could, making sure not to drop a single one. With a strength that belied their age, they pushed their loaded shopping baskets towards their sodden homes.

I was so proud of Alex. It was evident that the water had brought not just physical relief but also a sense of hope to these individuals who had faced such hardship. But we didn't have time to enjoy the moment. We had a few more bottles to collect.

By midday, all the water had been delivered. Everyone who needed some had taken their share, leaving a small pile untouched. I was happy about having some left over as it meant we had satisfied the immediate needs for today, and hopefully, the water supply would be restored by tomorrow.

After our morning of activity, I was getting hungry and suggested we head back to Pefki for lunch at Adonia's taverna. Alex and Marily agreed, but Marily suggested I might first want to meet her uncle, who lived nearby. She told us he was a shipowner with over thirty ships. Alex, whose own family were seafarers and captains, liked the idea of meeting him. "Okay," I agreed. "Perhaps he would like to join us for lunch."

Marily led us along the muddy road and stopped outside a small derelict house with one window boarded up. If this guy was a shipowner, he must be rather eccentric to live in a place like this, I thought. I have always liked eccentric people, so was keen to meet him.

Marily tapped on the door. The creaking door swung open, revealing darkness that seemed to swallow the room. A silhouette emerged, taking the shape of a stout man. As he stepped into the sunlight, a warm glow enveloped his figure, casting a soft radiance upon his features. A gentle smile spread across his face, reaching his eyes, and a sense of familiarity washed over us. He wore a dirty blue T-shirt with a faded Greek flag printed on the front. His eyes twinkled with mirth and his weathered face showed the signs of a life spent at sea. Despite the rundown exterior of his home, there was an air of mystery and intrigue surrounding him. As he greeted us warmly, his voice carried the deep resonance of someone who had commanded respect in the open waters. It was clear that beneath his humble exterior, this man held a wealth of stories and experiences.

Marily introduced us to her uncle Stavros, and he eagerly accepted our invitation to join us for lunch at Adonia's taverna. I was interested to hear about his life as a shipowner and the adventures he had encountered with his fleet.

"Would you like to see my ships first?" he asked.

I was surprised at this offer. There are a few large ports in Greece capable of mooring thirty ships, but as far as I knew, there were none nearby. I asked where they were moored, expecting the answer to be Piraeus or another large shipyard.

He waved his hand towards the sea and said, "Not far, just a few minutes' drive."

I was familiar with North Evia and I'm certain I would have noticed a fleet of thirty ships aside from the fishing boats and pleasure yachts in the small bays and local harbours.

We all piled into the car to see his ships. We drove out of the village, avoiding the fire trucks and bulldozers cleaning mud off the roads, but instead of heading towards the sea, Stavros directed us in the other direction, up the mountain.

After a mile or two, he asked us to stop near a dirt track leading away from the road. We left the car and followed the path. It led through a brook and into a field with a concrete shed in the middle.

"Alex, what are we doing here?" I asked as I batted away the midges trying to feast on me.

"We have come to see his ships," Alex replied.

Suddenly, Stavros began to make strange noises and whistling sounds. He led us towards the shed and proudly showed us his ships.

Alex and Marily were in on the joke and fell about laughing as the reality dawned on me. He was not a shipowner; he was a sheep owner. Being proud of his flock, he was determined to show them off.

As I stroked the sheep, a small puppy approached. He was the trainee ship dog.

"What's his name?" I asked Stavros.

"Anonymous," he replied. Was this his real name, or was he just anonymous? In Greece, you never really know.

After meeting the woolly "ships", we got back in the car and headed back through Gouves, towards Pefki and lunch. As we entered Gouves, we saw a small huddle of people standing next to a bulldozer. A TV news camera was pointing towards one man dressed immaculately in a snow-white, open-necked silk shirt and slacks. He seemed so out of place in the muddy village. We were dirty after our morning's exertions, and I was scratching insect bites from walking through a midge-infested field. A young reporter from a local news station was holding a microphone towards the well-dressed individual, eager to capture his words. Surrounding them were curious villagers, their faces smudged with dirt, their clothes caked in mud.

He was the only person in the village not covered in mud. It was our mayor, Athanasios. He stood on the silt-covered street, his confident demeanour and polished appearance contrasting sharply with the others. Alex yelled for me to stop. She threw open the car door, sprang out, and interrupted the mayor's interview.

"Hey, Athanasios! There are people here suffering. There's no water, no power. Everyone is walking around in mud. Here you are, looking pretty doing nothing."

Athanasios, taken aback by her directness, paused for a moment before responding. "I understand your frustration, Alex," he said, his voice filled with sincerity. "But please believe me when I say that we are working tirelessly to address the water and electricity issues. We have teams on the ground doing their best to restore services as quickly as possible."

He glanced at the camera briefly, then turned his attention back to Alex. "I know it may seem like I'm avoiding the problem by appearing on TV, but raising awareness is crucial in situations like these. It helps us gather support and resources to aid in the recovery efforts."

Alex crossed her arms, clearly still not convinced. "Well, the people here need more than just awareness. They need immediate action," she retorted.

Athanasios sighed. "You're right, Alex. The public meeting tonight in Pefki is an opportunity for the community to voice their concerns and for us to discuss potential solutions together. I genuinely want to hear from the residents and work together to find the best way forward. Please come, and encourage others to join as well. We need everyone's input to make a difference."

The mayor knew that he had been losing support in our village. During the devastating fires in 2021, he and the council were absent. The villagers united and saved our homes without any assistance from politicians. We doubted that the situation would change now.

We left the village behind us as we drove back towards Pefki. It was long past lunchtime, but we knew that Adonia's would still be open. On the way, we stopped at our house to check the progress. The road outside our home was littered with damaged furniture, tables, chairs and mattresses. These were the items damaged beyond repair or cleaning. Our prized possessions were piled up in a jumble of discarded rubbish. It was sad to see, but necessary for our ultimate recovery.

We stepped out of the car and surveyed the scene. Our once cosy and welcoming home now looked like a disaster zone. The sight of our belongings, items that had held so many memories, reduced to a heap of debris was heart-wrenching. But we knew that holding on to these things was pointless. A tear ran down Alex's face. The feeling of helplessness was intense, but amidst the sorrow we also felt a flicker of resolve to rebuild and move forward. It was a painful but essential step in our recovery.

Inside, the tenacious ladies were still hard at work. They greeted us with warm smiles, their faces streaked with dirt and sweat but shining with determination. The living room was now looking much cleaner. The floors were scrubbed, and the air, though still damp, smelled of fresh cleaning supplies rather than stagnant muck.

"Theodora and the others have done an amazing job," Alex said, her voice filled with gratitude.

"Yes, they have," I agreed. I turned to Theodora. "Come on,

you have all done enough today. Come with us for lunch. The least we can do is feed you."

The ladies climbed into their van and followed us towards the harbour and the waiting taverna.

As we arrived at Adonia's, the familiar aroma of grilled fish and herbs greeted us, bringing a sense of comfort. Despite the new regulations pushing tables further from the shore, Adonia had managed to maintain the warm and inviting atmosphere that her taverna was known for. The tables were still adorned with bright tablecloths and fresh flowers, and the sound of the waves crashing in the distance provided a soothing background.

"Welcome back," Adonia called out as we walked in. She was behind the counter, her hands busy, but her face lit up with a welcoming smile. "I saved you a table. I thought you might need a good meal after everything." She saw we had company and called Niko to bring another table and join them together.

"Thank you, Adonia," Alex replied, her voice filled with appreciation. "You always know just what we need."

We settled at the table and looked out across the muddy strip of land where Adonia's tables used to stand. The distant waves sparkled under the afternoon sun, and for a moment, we allowed ourselves to relax and take in the beauty around us. It was a reminder that despite the chaos and destruction, some things remained unchanged.

As we enjoyed our meal, Adonia joined us, bringing four bottles of her home-made wine. "This is on the house," she said with a wink. "You all need it."

We laughed and thanked her, raising our glasses in a silent

toast to resilience and community.

"How are things at the house?" Adonia asked, her tone turning serious.

"We're making progress," I replied, "thanks to Theodora and the others. They've been incredible."

Adonia nodded. "We take care of our own here. That's how it's always been. And we'll get through this, too."

Her words were reassuring, a reminder of the strength and solidarity that defined our village. We spent the rest of the afternoon talking and sharing stories, finding solace in each other's company.

As the sun began to set, painting the sky in hues of orange and pink, we felt a renewed sense of hope. The road ahead was still long and uncertain, but with the support of our friends and neighbours, we knew we could face whatever challenges lay ahead.

When we finally left our friends at Adonia's, the evening air was cool and refreshing. We walked hand in hand along the shoreline, the distant lights of the village twinkling like stars.

"It's getting late," Alex said. "We should get some rest."

She was right. Tomorrow would bring more challenges, but for now, we had each other and the unwavering support of our community.

As we lay in bed in Marily's hotel that night, the sound of the waves lulling us to sleep, I couldn't help but feel optimistic. We had a long way to go, but with the resilience of our village and the strength of our bonds, I knew we would rebuild and emerge stronger than ever.

CHAPTER 11

Life in the Pokey

Opinion is the lowest form of knowledge, lying between knowledge and ignorance.

– **Plato**

The next evening, we arrived at the town meeting held at Kostas's bar and saw crowds spilling out onto the road. The cosy bar, usually a place for laughter and casual chats, was now packed with people, every chair and table occupied. The buzz of conversation filled the warm evening air, a blend of urgent whispers and concerned murmurings. Friends and neighbours stood in small clusters, their faces a mix of concern and curiosity. Familiar faces greeted us with nods and brief smiles, reflecting our shared worries.

The dim glow of the streetlights cast long shadows as people jostled for a better view. There was standing room only as the mayor took his microphone and began to speak. The atmosphere was charged with anticipation, everyone eager to hear what would be discussed. The weight of the recent events hung heavily in the air, binding us together in a moment of collective hope and uncertainty.

The mayor made a promise to enhance flood protection measures and provide assistance to all those affected by the floods, assuring us that such a disaster would never occur again. However, his speech was greeted with a considerable amount of scepticism. We had heard similar promises before, following the devastating fires that nearly decimated the island's economy, and now we found ourselves starting from scratch once again.

As I looked around, I saw heads shaking and murmurs of doubt spreading through the crowd. The memory of those fires was still fresh, and the pain of rebuilding was a shared experience. The road to recovery for our village would be long and arduous, and we were not inclined to accept this seemingly comforting speech at face value. The mayor's words felt hollow against the backdrop of our collective suffering and resilience. We knew better than to rely solely on promises. Our strength lay in our community, in the hands of our friends and neighbours who stood beside us, ready to face whatever challenges lay ahead.

Once the mayor had finished his speech, he opened the floor to questions. Alex manoeuvred through the bustling crowd, pushing her way towards the centre. The air in the bar was filled with anticipation as she firmly grasped the microphone. As she spoke, her voice reverberated through the room, capturing everyone's attention.

I set my phone to record and positioned the camera to show both Alex and the mayor, and recorded the full exchange.

"As you know, Mr Mayor, our house was the worst affected in Pefki," Alex told him.

The mayor nodded and acknowledged this.

"So what I want to know is, when are you going to fix the river so it never happens again?"

The mayor was ready for this. "We are preparing a study to redirect the river, but we need to secure funds from the government."

"So you will not help?"

"Of course we will, but in time." It was clear he was using those weasel words to pacify the community, while the government had no intention of taking any action. It was frustrating to see our pleas for help falling on deaf ears. But unknown to the mayor, Alex was setting a trap.

"But when we built a wall to protect ourselves against the river before, we were arrested by the police and forced to remove it." A mumble of approval rose from the assembled crowd. "The police accused us of obstructing the natural flow, which was not true. They forced us to tear it down."

The murmurs of agreement grew louder, echoing the shared dissatisfaction of the villagers. The mayor was falling into Alex's trap.

"Yes, I am aware of what happened to you before. It was wrong for you to be victimised for just trying to protect yourself," he told Alex, but continued to make empty promises about government plans for the river. "Today I spoke with officials in Athens to discuss plans for reinforcing the riverbanks and improving our drainage systems," the mayor said, trying to sound convincing. "These projects are top priority, and I will personally oversee their implementation."

Alex pushed him harder. "In view of our recent catastrophe, will you now let us build a barrier to protect ourselves while the government is pissing around?"

"Alexandra, I am telling you in front of all these witnesses that I give my full permission to do anything you think will protect your property."

She had him! Alex thanked the mayor and handed the microphone to the next in line, and came back to me.

"Everyone heard that," she said. "We can now build a bank or a wall to protect ourselves. The mayor has given his permission. Let's get a bulldozer and start the clean-up."

The next day, we discovered Ilias, a local bulldozer driver. He owned a small rusty machine with a plough on one end for pushing soil and a digger on the other for lifting debris. Ilias was eager for work and agreed to tackle the huge task of moving the hundreds of tons of silt that the river had deposited in our garden. Removing the vast amount of soil and mud was impractical. It would have required a fleet of enormous trucks to transport it, and we didn't know where to take it. Instead, we chose to clear around the house, patio, and some of the garden where trees were planted. But we would leave the silt in place for the rest of the garden and have some parts elevated. We would now need to walk uphill to access some parts, but it was better to leave the earth where it been deposited near the river as removing it might enable the water to come back. However, we didn't mind as long as it was smooth and green once more. The earth moving cost would be high but manageable. Instead of immediately building a wall, we decided we would pile up some of the silt ploughed from the land to create a barrier along the riverbank. After all, we had been given permission to do this by the mayor himself. This would give us temporary protection against the river until we finished the clean-up and could afford to construct something permanent. A makeshift barrier would give us some safety from future flooding, and we could even plant flowers in the future to make it look nice.

The following day, the bulldozers arrived. The silt had dried to a crust in the hot Greek sun, so we could walk on it without sinking. The excavator began the huge task of removing the tons of silt piled against the house walls, then attacking the accumulation in the garden, which was over a metre deep. It slowly revealed the base of the trees, unveiling our magnificent stone arch. Also, it skilfully bulldozed the earth to form a two-metre-high bank along the river. By the close of the initial day, we were able to freely walk around our house without the unpleasant sludge clinging to our shoes. Moreover, the new earth dyke effectively prevented the river from coming near our house again.

The next day, we woke early and left our comfortable room in Marily's hotel. It was around seven when we arrived at our house. We were keen to check the progress and be here when the bulldozer driver arrived to start his work.

We were about to enter when a police car arrived outside our gate.

A young policeman stepped out of the patrol car and approached the house. He was wearing a pressed uniform, and his police-issued shoes were shining with a high gloss. Around his waist, he had a belt with a brand-new gun holstered.

"You are under arrest," he confidently told Alex.

"Why?" Alex asked.

"You have piled earth in the river and interrupted its flow. That is against the law."

"No, we haven't. We just made a bank on our side; we haven't touched the river. Come and look for yourself. We have been given permission by the mayor himself to build a bank. We have it on video as proof. We can show you."

The young policeman, however, was not interested in checking to see if his information was correct and refused to accompany us to the riverbank to see for himself, or look at any video. He had instructions to arrest us, not to confirm we had committed an offence. Investigating the alleged offence was not his job. That was up to someone else.

"You are still under arrest," he repeated. "You have to accompany me to the police station."

"No, we have done nothing wrong. You need to check your facts before arresting us. Now bugger off, we're busy."

The young, spotty policeman shuffled his feet on our doorstep, unsure of what to do next. He wasn't expecting Alex to make a fuss. They had sent him to escort us to the police station to answer a complaint made by one of our neighbours. Seeing that Alex was in no mood to comply with his order, he changed tack.

"Please come with me," he pleaded. "They've never sent me alone to arrest someone before. It's a big deal for me. If you don't come, I might get in trouble and lose my authority to make arrests."

"I don't care," replied Alex. "Look at the state of the place, we're far too busy to be arrested. Now bugger off."

So he buggered off, but only as far as his police car parked outside. We heard a faint radio crackle and an unclear conversation from our door. But he didn't get out of his car. He just sat there looking sheepish. A few moments later, another police car arrived. It was the local police chief. He looked angry as he stepped out of his car, slamming the door. He marched over to the young, spotty officer, who had by now left his own car. We heard shouting as the chief poked the youth in the chest and commanded him to go back and arrest us. The youth hesitated. He was clearly considering who he was most frightened of. Alex did look fierce and was certainly in no mood to comply. But his boss had ordered him to complete his task and arrest us. So, under the watchful eye of his superior, he returned to our doorstep.

By now, the neighbours had seen the police cars outside our house and came to investigate. Our neighbours George and Helen came out of their gate, Maria had appeared with Dimitri, and along with the police chief, all watched as the youngster nervously climbed the steps to our door.

"I told you to bugger off," Alex told him. "We have done nothing wrong. I'm not coming to the police station to waste my time over some stupid, unfounded complaint. I will come when I'm good and ready."

He turned to the fast-growing audience, lifted both hands in a sign of surrender, and looked at his boss.

"She won't come," he whined.

This was too much for the chief of police. He marched up to our door and confronted Alex.

"Madam. We have received a serious complaint that you have interfered with the river. I am placing you under arrest, and you will both get into my car and accompany me to the police station to give your statement."

"Look," Alex said. "Our house and garden are in ruins; we have a bulldozer in the garden. We have mud on our floor, all our furniture is piled up in the street, and you want to waste our time answering a complaint made by some idiot? You can bugger off too."

More neighbours had arrived to watch the show. He couldn't really snap us in handcuffs and physically drag us away with everyone watching. And by the expression on Alex's face, it was unlikely he would win a physical struggle.

Then Ilias, the bulldozer driver, arrived to continue his work in our garden. He looked unfazed to see two police cars and a growing crowd outside. He walked past, climbed into his digger and started it up. Suddenly, the police chief realised he had an easier target.

"Are you the bulldozer driver?" he asked.

"Good detective work. I can see why you're the chief of police. Nothing gets past you," he replied from the cab of his machine.

A roar of laughter erupted from our neighbours as the policeman's face reddened. "You are under arrest too!" he yelled over the sound of the motor. "Switch it off and come with me."

The driver switched his machine off, dropped the keys in his pocket and came to join us on the step.

"Ready when you are, officer," he said.

"Where are you going?" Alex asked Ilias.

"I'm under arrest. I need to accompany these gentlemen now."

"Well, I'm not going," Alex pouted. "Nor should you. Get back on the bulldozer and keep digging."

"Look," he said, "the police are here to arrest us. They're not going away. Let's just get it over with – it's only a formality. We just need to make a statement. It shouldn't take long, and we'll be back in an hour."

"He's right, they're not going away," I told Alex. "Let's confront the situation, make our statement, and get it over and done with."

Realising she wasn't going to win this battle, she wavered a little. However, she wasn't pleased about the arrest bit.

"I'm not getting in that police car," she insisted. "We will come to make our statement on the condition that we are not arrested and can use our own car." The chief and the spotty youth shared a smile. They could sense victory.

"Okay," the chief said. "I agree you are not under arrest. I have only invited you to the station to make a statement, and it's fine to come in your own car."

Alex and I got into our car with the bulldozer driver in the back seat. The police chief instructed us to follow. The young officer fell in behind us as we left home in a convoy, sandwiched between two police cars, each with flashing blue lights.

As we drove along the seafront flanked by the officials, we felt rather important. To get a police escort in Greece, you have to be a high-ranking politician or royalty. We were neither. We had just piled a little earth along our riverbank. Alex waved as she passed groups of tourists who were keen to peer into our window to identify which celebrity had blessed them with their presence.

We arrived at the harbour, and Alex told me to stop outside the cafe.

"I want a coffee," she said.

The police car in front realised we had stopped and screeched to a halt. The other pulled up behind us. Alex jumped out of the passenger seat.

"We are going to grab a coffee. Do you want one?" Alex asked the young officer in the squad car behind.

"Yes, a frappe for me." His face lit up.

She went to the convoy's leader. By now, he had reversed and got out of his car, wondering why we had stopped.

"We are going to get a coffee," she informed him. "Do you want one?"

He frowned. "Get back in the car! You can't stop for a coffee, you're under arrest."

"No, we're not," Alex replied. "You have invited us to the police station. We agreed to come, but I want a coffee first. Do you want one or not?"

"I'll have an espresso then," he mumbled, "no sugar."

A few moments later, Alex emerged from the cafe holding a cardboard tray containing five coffees. She passed one to each of the officers, one to Ilias sitting in the back seat, then got back into the car. We recommenced the convoy out of Pefki into the countryside, heading for the market town of Istiea.

I took my phone and called the mayor's number. He didn't answer, so I left a message.

"Hi, Athanasios. Do you remember saying at the public meeting that we have the right to protect our property however we want? Well, we've been arrested. Can you come to the police station and tell them that we had your permission to do it?"

By the time we arrived at the police station, he hadn't returned my call.

Outside the building, our accusers confronted us. There was an elderly woman, her face twisted in a vile scowl, eyes burning with rage. Her hands were clenched into tight fists, her bony frame trembling with anger. A sneer etched across her lips, and her cold stare pierced through us, filled with disdain and resentment. It was clear she held a deep grudge against us, but the reason remained speculation. The tension in the air was palpable.

Beside her was an even older man, dishevelled in

appearance, sporting a torn T-shirt and wellington boots. As the police chief entered, the dreadful woman and the old man followed suit. We trailed behind, ascending the dingy staircase towards the reception. Halfway up, the old man in wellies began to pant, struggling with the climb. Alex placed her hand on his shoulder and kindly enquired, "Are you feeling alright? You appear unwell. Would you like me to hold your hand as we ascend together?"

Despite his being one of our accusers, Alex's caring nature surpassed any anger towards the old man. She felt sorry for him and wanted to help. But when it came to our other accuser, the elderly woman, things took a different turn. She looked unpleasant and vindictive, seemingly finding pleasure in the fact that she had successfully deceived the police into getting involved. Alex felt no sympathy for her.

We had never knowingly crossed paths with her until now. We knew most of our neighbours and felt part of the village. Everyone we had met over the last few years we liked. There had been no real animosity in the village. Squabbles were common, raised voices often heard, but nobody ever took offence. People swearing at each other yesterday were the best of friends today. Apart from the long-running feud between Eleni and Spiros, people rarely held onto anything and they harboured no grudges. But this person was out to get us. We had no idea why. But soon we would find out.

We climbed up the dark stairwell and reached the top. The police station door was right there, level with the top step and without a landing. Peering through the bars of the open hatch, we had to squeeze onto the top step. We stood a few steps back down, patiently waiting for the door to open. Finally, in single file, we entered the station. Inside, there was a small waiting area with a few plastic chairs placed on a bare concrete floor. Directly ahead, an open door led to the chief's office, and on the left was a general office, with three desks occupied. We were instructed to sit in the reception area and wait. Meanwhile, they took the horrible-looking old lady into the chief's office to formalise her complaint against us.

I sat beside Ilias, while Alex sat next to the old man. "Are you feeling better now?" she asked him with concern.

He nodded and told her he did, then looked Alex in the eye and smiled apologetically. "I didn't want to report you, but she made me complain." He waved his hand in the direction of the office where she was giving her statement. "She can be a bit of a handful, so I usually agree to do what she wants. She said you blocked the river. You shouldn't have done that," he added.

"We did not block the river," Alex told him. "We just asked our bulldozer driver to form a bank on our land to protect ourselves while he was cleaning the mud from our garden. The river is still flowing."

The old man looked uncertain. "But she said you caused the flooding."

"How could we possibly have caused the flooding?" Alex said. "The riverbed comes from Artemision, under the bridge, past our garden and then ends. It doesn't go anywhere. There are houses built on the old riverbed further down which stopped the river. But where do you live?" she asked. "How did the flooding affect you?"

Suddenly, the old man became evasive. He was not ready for questions from Alex. He had no intention of telling her where he lived and which was his house. "Oh, I live up in the mountains. Well away from the river." This was clearly a lie, but we had no way of proving it. If he did indeed live in the mountains, then whatever we did with our riverbank could not have possibly affected him.

Alex pressed him further. "So why have you reported us?"

The old man shifted uncomfortably and looked away. The door to the chief's office opened and the horrible old lady emerged with a victorious smile on her face. She swept past us and out of the door. It was the old man's turn to give his evidence. He stood up, went to the office door and whispered to the officer. Then he turned and left, following the horrible lady down the stairs. He had withdrawn his complaint and wanted to go home.

So, Alex, Ilias and I found ourselves alone in the waiting room, waiting for our turn.

"Okay, lock them in," came the call from the police chief. A young officer appeared with the keys and locked the main door. Then it was clear we were under arrest. They had lied to us. This was no polite invitation to the police station. This was full-blown custody.

Now, because the police station contained us, apparently serious criminals, it was in full lockdown. If anyone wanted to enter the police station, they would first have to knock on the door. An officer would open a small hatch with bars to see who it was before letting them in or turning them away.

Alex got up to find the toilet.

"Sit down," the policeman barked.

Alex refused. "I want to go to the toilet!" she yelled.

"Okay, wait," he commanded. He talked into the intercom on his desk. A policewoman appeared and stood beside Alex. "Now you can go to the toilet, but this officer will come with you."

If we needed to be escorted to the toilet and could not leave, this was getting serious.

Alex returned and sat down. I moved from my chair next to Ilias and took the seat next to Alex vacated by the old man. I whispered to her, "I think we're in big trouble."

"I don't care. We didn't do anything wrong, so they can't detain us," she replied.

However, the police had different plans. We were called in for our interview. When we entered the office, we saw a series of photographs on the desk. The photos brought back memories of the wall we had once built in our garden, a misguided attempt to protect ourselves from the river. At the time, we hadn't realised it was against the law, even on our own land. That mistake had led to legal trouble, forcing us to dismantle it and leave the river's course untouched. Unfortunately, this record of illegal construction made it easy for the authorities to accuse us again. We were in for a tough time.

The horrible old lady had been keeping these photos for years. The realisation hit us like a ton of bricks. She was the one who built the house in the river. Her motives were clear now; she had been lying in wait, nurturing her grudge. When we had built the wall without proper permissions, she had promptly reported us, resulting in a fine and a stern reprimand. She had been furious ever since and had been waiting for her chance to get us into serious trouble. And this time, she might have succeeded.

Answering questions and making our own statement took an hour. The room was stark and cold, the walls adorned with faded posters about civic duty and legal procedures. The officer behind the desk listened intently, occasionally jotting down notes as we explained our side of the story.

"So, you're saying this woman has a personal vendetta against you?" the officer asked, looking up from his notes.

"Yes, that's correct," Alex replied, her voice steady but edged with frustration. "She has been waiting for an opportunity to make our lives difficult."

"But you say the mayor gave you permission to build this earth bank?"

"Yes. It was at the village meeting, everyone heard it. We can show you the video. We have it here."

The officer nodded, but his expression remained neutral. "We will take your statement into consideration. For now, any video you may have is not evidence unless it has been verified and a statement obtained from the mayor. Please return to the holding area."

He then called Ilias to give his statement. He soon returned and took his seat.

"Can we go now?" Alex called out.

"No," replied the police chief. "I have to email my report

to police headquarters in Chalkida. I will receive updates on whether you can be set free or imprisoned. It is up to them."

"How long will that take?" Alex asked. We had had no breakfast and were getting hungry.

"Maybe today, or perhaps tomorrow," he replied, and closed his door.

So, not only had we been locked up, but we now faced the depressing prospect of spending the night in the cells.

This was getting out of control. The storms had wiped out most of the village infrastructure and turned our pristine house and garden into a muddy disaster zone. As if that wasn't enough, this vindictive old lady had the audacity to accuse us of intentionally causing the mess. The absurdity of her accusation was mind-boggling. How could anyone in their right mind think that we would willingly subject ourselves to such chaos and destruction? The stupidity of the situation was beyond comprehension. It was infuriating, and Alex's anger was reaching its boiling point.

"If they try to fine us, don't pay it," she told me. "I'd rather rot in jail than give her satisfaction. I want to take a stand against this injustice and show everyone that we won't be beaten. If you pay a fine, then we are admitting we were in the wrong."

I was keen to escape imprisonment, and would have happily paid a fine for freedom, but Alex was correct. It could be construed as an admission of guilt. We were determined to set the record straight. So we agreed to stick to our guns and fight it all the way.

There was a tap on the outside door. An officer opened the hatch. After a muffled conversation, he opened the door. There stood our friend Marily. She had brought breakfast, and came in with a selection of coffees, bottled water, and pastries. It was picnic time in the custody suite.

"I have called the mayor," she said, "but he didn't answer, so I left a message. This is all wrong. You have not broken the law. I heard the mayor tell you it was okay to protect yourself. The entire village heard."

Suddenly, the police chief's door swung open. He stormed out and confronted our friend.

"You may not take photos. Delete them immediately, then leave," he told her.

"I'm not taking photos," she protested.

"But I have just seen you on the CCTV taking photos through the bars. Now go! Or I will arrest you too."

Marily stood up to leave. "Don't worry, I will wait downstairs. They can't hold you for long." The police officer locked the door as she left, and we tucked into our breakfast.

I kept checking my phone, looking for the awaited call from the mayor.

For hours we sat listening for the chief's phone to ring with the decision. Would we ever be set free, or would we be stuck in a Greek jail until our trial date? Greek justice moves slowly. If they committed us, it could take months to get to court. The police chief didn't seem to care either way. It was a routine day at the office for him. But to us, the wait was excruciating.

We had been at the police station for nine hours, when the

call from police headquarters finally came through. We were free to leave, though first we had to sign a document agreeing to remove the earth piled along the riverbank and put it back over our garden.

Rather than feeling relieved at our release, Alex was furious. Thoughts of murder consumed her as she plotted revenge on the old lady. She would find this person and make her suffer.

As promised, Marily was waiting downstairs, her expression a mix of concern and frustration as she told us that she had eventually spoken to the mayor. He had made it clear that he did not wish to get involved in the situation. In fact, he even stated that our arrest was something that had been anticipated. These words shocked and frustrated me. It seemed that even the mayor had broken his promise and was unwilling to support us or intervene on our behalf, despite giving us permission to protect ourselves.

"Our hands are tied," Marily said. "The mayor practically shrugged it off. He said it was expected, and he won't intervene."

I felt a surge of frustration. "How could he say that? We were only trying to protect our property with his explicit permission."

Marily nodded sympathetically. "I know. It's infuriating."

Our arrest and detention had been a horrible experience, compounded by the knowledge that we had done nothing wrong. We had been arrested just after seven in the morning, and it was now past five in the afternoon. We had wasted an entire day being interviewed or sitting in a sterile holding cell, feeling the hours slip away.

The ride back home was silent, each of us lost in our thoughts. As we pulled into the driveway, the sight of our garden, which we had planned to work on today, brought a fresh wave of frustration. But we were relieved to see Mary and the ladies busy in our yard, continuing their work. So the day hadn't been a complete loss.

"Can we come in and see?" Alex asked.

"No, you just stay there. We haven't finished yet. We want you to see it when everything is done," Mary said. "We should be done by tomorrow. Come back and see then."

They refused our offer of a meal, and again refused our offer of help, It was too late to continue with our work in the garden now, so we decided to head to Adonia's taverna for a late lunch.

The drive was short but felt longer with the weight of the day's events hanging over us. As we arrived at Adonia's, the taverna was bustling with activity, the chatter of diners and the clinking of dishes providing a soothing background.

Adonia herself came over as we sat down, her warm smile a stark contrast to the tension we had been feeling all day. "Rough day?" she asked.

"You could say that," Alex replied with a weary smile.

"Well, you're here now." Adonia patted Alex's shoulder. "Let's get you something to eat. How about the usual?"

"That would be perfect," I said, grateful for the familiarity and kindness.

As we waited for our food, we tried to shake off the frustration of the day. The aroma of freshly baked spanakopita and sizzling souvlaki filled the air, enticing everyone's taste buds. The table was soon adorned with an array of colourful dishes, from creamy tzatziki and tangy feta cheese to juicy olives and warm pita bread. As we sat down, Niko brought out a large jug of iced wine and several glasses. The jug glistened in the warm evening sunlight, reflecting the golden hues of the wine within. Niko's hands were steady as he carefully poured the wine, the cold liquid causing the glasses to fog up with condensation. Soon, the influence of the wine helped turn shock and anger into laughter and chatter as we told our story. Adonia was furious at the mean old lady who reported us and wanted to know more. We couldn't help much as we didn't know her name, but we knew where she lived. We explained using a map drawn on a paper napkin.

"Oh her," Adonia exclaimed. "She's really strange. But take my advice and stay away from her. She's trouble."

We already knew that. We hadn't knowingly done anything to offend her. But she had taken a dislike to us and made the crazy accusations for her own reasons.

Others soon joined us, friends and neighbours, and more tables and chairs were brought out. We shuffled around to make space, creating an atmosphere of warmth and togetherness. Friends from all over the village shared stories of the recent flooding.

There was just one topic that no one would discuss with us. Whenever we tried to talk about the horrible old woman who had orchestrated our arrest, everyone fell silent. Their eyes filled with fear and apprehension, as if her name alone sent shivers down their spines. Their avoidance only made us more determined to uncover the truth behind her actions. But it seemed we were alone in our resolve. Perhaps others, burdened by their own experiences with her, were unwilling to confront the haunting memories she had left behind.

Undeterred by the silence and fear that surrounded the mention of the old woman, we pressed on in our quest for answers. It became clear that her presence loomed over the community. As we went deeper into the conversation and the wine kept flowing, we started hearing unsettling stories about people who had encountered her. For instance, there were police raids on those who had enlarged their chicken coops. Even a wall that was just a few centimetres too high had to be taken down because of a complaint from her. In a small village where everyone had some sort of construction that didn't quite follow the plans, people were constantly afraid of being reported and fined.

Now she had turned her attention towards us, it appeared that while the villagers sympathised with our situation, deep down they were relieved that they weren't the ones subjected to the full force of her maliciousness.

Whispers of her manipulative tactics and vindictive nature circulated among those brave enough to speak. It seemed that she held a power over people, instilling a paralysing fear that prevented anyone from openly challenging her.

Still, it was a true testament to the power of Greek food to bring people together and offer comfort in the darkest times. Our worries seemed to melt away with each bite. Surrounded by friends, indulging in the rich flavours of the Mediterranean, we found solace and a reminder of the enduring spirit of community, assuring us that everything would be alright.

CHAPTER 12

Catch Us If You Can

Human behaviour flows from three main sources: desire, emotion, and knowledge.

– Plato

The next day, once again we left our comfortable room in Marily's hotel and drove to our house. Ilias was back, busy complying with the police chief's demands and removing the makeshift earth bank from the river. This would leave us exposed again if another storm came, but we had no option now. We were under the microscope with an uncertain legal future.

As we walked from the garden towards our house, Mary arrived with a radiant smile on her face, clearly eager to share some good news. After the stressful experience with the police the previous day, we desperately needed it. There was a twinkle in her eye as she told us, "We've finished cleaning your house!"

We opened the door and stepped inside. Sunlight poured through the windows, casting a warm glow across the room. The air was filled with a pleasant scent of lemon and lavender, a lingering reminder of the cleaning products used.

The curtains had been washed, ironed, and hung perfectly. Decorative items recovered from the sludge stood neatly arranged on the shelves, their surfaces mud-free and gleaming. Although two of our windows were broken and some of the plasterboard was missing from the walls, the overall atmosphere was uplifting.

Many of our kitchen appliances and units had been thrown away, too damaged to be rescued. Despite this, the kitchen worktops and floor tiles were spotless, reflecting our amazed expressions as we marvelled at the transformation. The living room seemed bigger now, though our old sofa was beyond repair. The bedrooms sparkled but looked bare without the mattresses. Fortunately, the sturdy iron bed frames remained and were clean and polished.

We still needed to redecorate completely and replace the damaged furniture and other possessions lost in the flooding. But the overall effect was one of renewal and hope, a testament to the hard work and dedication of our friends and neighbours.

The stress of the past few days had been tough. But seeing our home clean was lovely. It gave us renewed confidence. We knew that with work, our garden would soon follow.

Alex hugged Mary and thanked her for her hard work. "We couldn't have done this without you," she said, her voice full of gratitude.

I reached into my pocket and took out some money, holding it towards Mary. "Please, take this," I said.

Mary lifted both hands in defence. "Put that money away," she told me, shaking her head firmly. "We did this for you. We don't want payment."

Her words warmed my heart, and I felt a lump in my throat. It wasn't just about the clean house; it was about the kindness and support of our community. These were people who cared about us and showed it through their actions.

"Thank you, Mary," I said. "You have no idea how much this means to us."

Mary put her hand on my shoulder. "We're all in this together. That's what neighbours are for."

We spent the next few minutes chatting with Mary, catching up on village news. It felt good to have a moment of normalcy after the chaos of the past few days.

After Mary left, Alex and I took a slow walk through the house, taking in all the hard work that had been done. The transformation was remarkable. Despite the broken windows and missing plasterboard, the house felt like home again.

"We'll get a new sofa," Alex said, her voice determined. "And new mattresses for the beds. We can replace everything."

I nodded, feeling a surge of determination. "Yes, we will. One step at a time."

As we continued through the house, we made a mental list of what needed to be replaced and repaired. It was a long list, but we felt ready to tackle it together.

I held Alex's hand as we strolled outside again, the garden

still covered in silt. The bulldozer driver had completed his work and moved the earth away from the river. Due to police orders, we were instructed to halt the cleaning. Consequently, Ilias went home, leaving his bulldozer parked in the garden. We walked over the undulating dried mud, looking around our garden. The earth bank had been removed, but the river was still hidden from view. Our garden had raised up significantly, and the river had carved a deeper trench. To see into the river, we needed to stand directly beside it. Surprisingly, the flow had reduced to a trickle, exposing bright white stones at the bottom. The river had also shifted, moving ten metres closer to our home, and was now much wider than the original ditch we discovered when clearing the land.

Before the flooding, we had a lovely lighting arrangement. Lights twinkled in the trees, and spotlights at the end of the garden gave a warm glow, perfect on warm summer nights spent sitting on our patio sipping ouzo and listening to the crickets' song. Now, there was just a tangled mess of cables hanging from trees. Because the river had enlarged and changed course, one of our spotlights was in the middle of the stream and still on its pole.

But that wasn't all we found in our new riverbed. There was also a lady wearing wellington boots, busy taking photographs. It was the horrible old woman who had reported us to the police.

As we approached, she looked up at us with a sour expression. This was too much for Alex. Not only did this objectionable person get us arrested for doing nothing but try to repair the damage caused by the storm, she had also ensured we could not carry on and fix our garden. Now, there she was, standing in our river, taking photographs.

"What the hell are you doing in my garden?" Alex yelled.

"I'm taking photographs of the damage you have caused," she replied.

How could we be responsible? Our island had been hit by the worst storm in a century. The next village experienced mudslides and people were still pumping water out of their homes. Crops were washed away, and trees were felled. The entire village was covered in silt. We stood there, speechless, unsure of how to respond to such an idiotic statement. But clearly, she believed in her own madness.

Alex's demeanour shifted, becoming unusually calm. It dawned on her that she was faced with insanity, leading her to feel a pang of sympathy for the unfortunate woman. Speaking in a gentle tone, she addressed her as a mother would speak to a wounded child.

"Look, come into the house and I will make you a coffee. We can talk about it there."

"No, I won't come near your house. You caused this. You blocked the river!" the woman screeched.

Alex was now losing patience. "We have never touched the river. Look at my garden – we have thousands of euros worth of damage. Do you think we would do this to ourselves?"

The old woman's piercing scream echoed. "God is punishing you for blocking the river! You deserve whatever you receive!"

Alex reached her breaking point. Fuelled by a surge of adrenaline, she mustered every bit of strength within her and propelled herself through the air, landing on the riverbed beside the elderly lady.

I yelled, desperately trying to get Alex's attention, but she couldn't hear me. She was consumed by rage, blind and deaf to everything except her burning fury. Her focus was solely on the person who had abused us on our own land. Vengeance consumed her thoughts as she imagined the damage she could inflict on her. It was terrifying to witness. The old lady deserved her fate, but Alex would get into more trouble if she killed her, as it looked like she might. By the time I reacted and jumped down onto the riverbed myself, she had the woman's arm in a firm grip and was forcefully dragging her bony frame along the river away from our garden.

"Look, you stupid woman. How could we have possibly caused this?" Alex screamed. "You can see the river is still running. There is nothing blocking it except that house over there – and that's yours!"

I seized Alex's shoulder, pulling her towards me. This caused her to release the woman, who swiftly escaped while I restrained my enraged wife.

"That's assault, that is," the old woman yelled as she ran away. "You hurt my arm. I'm reporting you to the police!"

Great, I thought. We had only escaped police custody yesterday. Now, with another, more serious complaint against us, they would throw the book at us, lock us up and throw away the key.

Alex was still trembling as we made our way from the river to our house. I needed to calm her down. I suggested we get away from the house for a while and go for lunch to clear our minds. A good meal at one of our friends' tavernas usually does the trick.

Alex agreed but was reluctant. She thought everyone knew what was going on and that there was a conspiracy of silence, with people reluctant to become involved. She smiled weakly at friends as we took our seats in the taverna.

Theodora and Mary had recently turned part of the village cheese factory into a restaurant for locals. After helping us clean our home, they had reopened their restaurant and were busy cooking. They typify the people in our village: kind, caring and always happy to help. But after her encounter with the horrible old lady in our garden, Alex was in no mood for socialising.

An irate Alex is like a hand grenade. When she explodes, she will scatter shrapnel in all directions without discrimination. When the village priest welcomed us into the taverna, he made the mistake of asking, "How is your house now after the floods?" I watched as she pulled her mental pin and waited the five seconds for the explosion. Suddenly Alex stood up from the table and her chair flew across the floor as she stormed around the room, swearing to herself. The windows shook, and clients dived for cover.

"You all know who did this, don't you?" She pointed an accusing finger at everyone. "You know the river burst its banks because someone built a house in it. You all pretend to know nothing, but you are all in on it. And who suffers? Me."

Theodora put her arm around Alex's shoulder to calm her. But Alex was just warming up. Now her personal floodgates were open, there was no stopping her.

When anger takes over and you can't find a way to release these feelings, it can affect your mental and physical health. Alex would not let this happen to her. She was going to let it all out.

"Not only was our house and garden consumed by the storm," she raged, "the police also arrested us for trying to clean up. Whenever I ask you lot about it, you all close up. What are you doing? I'm Greek, you are Greek; we need to stick together. We need to deal with the river."

The customers sat at their tables and stared into their drinks while Alex continued. They all knew the story but felt powerless to assist, and they all knew Alex's rage wouldn't last long. I know she is a firework; she goes bang quickly and will calm down equally fast, but she needs to express herself first.

I could see Alex was already calming. She retrieved her chair and sat down, and in a quieter voice said to herself, "So, what are we going to do now?"

"You could buy another boat," came a voice from the back.

There was a second of silence before the entire taverna erupted in laughter. Even Alex joined in. We were back in village life. We spent the afternoon eating, drinking the local wine and enjoying ourselves. By the time we left, we were ready for our challenge.

Things were spiralling out of control. Legal advice was necessary. So, we hopped in the car and headed to Istiea in search of a lawyer. We had to intercept this new accusation and prepare ourselves for what could be a more serious charge. I didn't believe Alex had caused any serious harm to the old lady, but I suspected she would bruise easily and would use her injured arm as proof to destroy us once and for all.

The first lawyer we found, we immediately liked. Her name, Sofia, means "wisdom" in Greek, and we certainly needed someone with that quality. Her warm demeanour and attentive nature quickly won us over. Sofia had made the decision to return to our Greek island and work with the local people, a choice that greatly endeared her to the community. She was not only a highly skilled lawyer but also a compassionate individual who genuinely cared about the well-being of others.

As we sat in her office, Sofia listened intently, her eyes widening with each detail. She sat open-mouthed as we shared our story, clearly moved by our ordeal. We told her about the flooding and subsequent arrest, and about the mad old woman who was on her way to the police station to report us yet again.

After hearing our story, Sofia sighed deeply. "This is quite a mess, but don't worry. We'll figure this out together," she said, her voice full of determination. Her words and the sincerity in her eyes reassured us, and we felt a glimmer of hope for the first time since our unexpected legal ordeal began.

"Look. You have to leave for a while. Go back to Glyfada for a few days and let me sort things out here. If you are around when the police come, they may hold you for days. It's best if you are out of the way while I do my work."

Alex folded her arms and pouted. "Why should we leave? We've done nothing wrong. It's the maniac that's up our arses every day. She won't leave us alone."

"Yes, I realise that," Sofia replied. "But if the police receive a complaint, they will arrest you again. They don't care if you did it or not. That's for the court to decide. But assault is a serious charge. You may be locked up. It's best you're not here when they come looking for you."

We went home to pack a bag, knowing we needed to take a temporary leave, though Alex was unhappy with the situation. We didn't want to become fugitives, especially over the irrational ramblings of a mad person. But Greek justice operates differently. In most countries, you are innocent until proven guilty. Here, you are presumed guilty unless you can prove your innocence. Although it was completely obvious to any rational thinker that we could not have possibly caused our village to flood, now that there had been an accusation that we were responsible, it was not enough to simply deny the charges. We had to prove our innocence. Moreover, Alex might be facing an additional charge of assault.

This concept is known as the presumption of guilt. Under this system, the burden of proof lies entirely on the defendant, who is required to provide evidence and arguments to establish their innocence beyond a reasonable doubt. In contrast, the prosecution or police are not obligated to prove guilt, but rather present statements that support their case. If the defendant fails to sufficiently prove their innocence, both the courts and society may assume their guilt. So, this incredible system means that any halfwit can make an outrageous claim against you and report the alleged offence to the police, who will clap you in irons.

Perhaps I could make a complaint about the horrible old lady. She certainly looked like a witch. Perhaps I could report her for that. She would have a real problem trying to prove she hadn't cast a spell on the village. I'd also had a few shooting pains recently. Perhaps she had a voodoo doll with my face on it to stick pins in.

Our brief period of living as fugitives wasn't too terrible. We enjoyed a relaxing day at Glyfada beach and spent another day exploring the charming bookshops of Athens. Surprisingly, life on the run wasn't as challenging as we had anticipated. It afforded us an opportunity to take a step back from our troubles and focus our minds. Often, when you're too immersed in a problem, you become overwhelmed, and everything becomes confused.

A couple of days later, Sofia called.

She assured us that everything was fine now, and we could return. "I have given your statement to the police, so they will stop bothering you while the courts decide if there's a case against you. However, you still need to prove that you are not responsible for flooding the island."

"Did she report us for assault?" Alex asked.

"She tried, but she didn't have a bruise to show them. So, it's just her word against yours. Without evidence, it will never stand up in court. The police are beginning to suspect she's nuts, so fortunately, they ignored that complaint. But here's the good news – you can continue cleaning the garden. Just make sure you stay away from the river."

The news was good indeed. But I wished the river would stay away from us. The course seemed to move every few days. I was happy because I'd successfully kept Alex away from the spiteful woman and prevented her from finishing her off and burying her evil body in the riverbank. We could go back without getting arrested. Even better, we could carry on with our garden. And so, after spending a few soothing days on the run, we returned to Pefki, raring to go again.

We contacted Stamos, the builder, knowing that simply cleaning the garden wouldn't be enough. The damage had been extensive, and we'd need to make significant changes to protect our home from future floods.

But before we could act, we faced the all-too-familiar hurdle of Greek bureaucracy. Permissions were required for any construction near the river, and though recent flooding had prompted some relaxation of the rules, there was no guarantee we'd get approval. The wait was agonising.

"Don't worry," Marily reassured us one evening over coffee. "I know a planning engineer who can help. He's familiar with all the local regulations."

Her practical advice was a lifeline, and within days we were navigating the labyrinthine process of applications and permits. George and Helen also offered their support, reminding us of the importance of doing everything by the book.

"It's a wise decision," George said. "The last thing you need is more trouble with the police."

He was right. We couldn't afford to take any chances. Though the prospect of building a wall and redesigning the garden was daunting, both financially and emotionally, we knew it was the only way to move forward. Still, the uncertainty was a heavy burden.

Would we get permission? And if we did, would Nemesis find a way to interfere again?

CHAPTER 13
Oh No! Another Last Straw

The only true wisdom is in knowing you know nothing.

– Socrates

We still needed approval from the local authorities. The application process had been tedious and time-consuming, requiring us to submit tremendous amounts of seemingly unrelated documents, including archaeologist reports, original plans for our house, and the original permission to build. We had already completed all the necessary paperwork and now had to wait for the building licence.

Our engineer assured us the bureaucratic hurdles would eventually be overcome and we would be able to proceed with our project. In the meantime, we focused on the cleaning, ensuring the site was well-prepared for the construction phase. Despite the setback, we were determined to make the most of this waiting period and ensure that everything was in order once we received the much-awaited permission to build our wall.

But beady eyes were watching us. We didn't want to give the horrible old lady any more excuses to have us arrested again. I still didn't trust Alex to restrain herself if the horrible woman began to creep around our garden again. So it was best if we were out of the way while we waited for our permission to be granted.

After the past few stressful weeks on the island, I longed to leave the village and relax in the familiar comforts and tranquillity of our English home. It had been an incredibly trying time, and the thought of being surrounded by the countryside of my homeland was exactly what we needed to recharge and rejuvenate.

Our life is split between three homes, which might sound like a luxury, but it comes with its own challenges. We have our small home in England, our island home in Pefki, and the family apartment in Glyfada, which is used by the family whenever they visit.

During the floods, many of our neighbours faced the heartbreaking reality of having only one home, which made their losses even more difficult. We felt a mix of emotions. We were grateful to have other places to retreat to, and sympathetic towards those who had no choice but to stay.

As we packed our bags and bid farewell to Greece, a sense

of guilt mingled with relief. We were leaving behind friends who were still grappling with the aftermath of the disaster, but we also knew we needed to restore our energy before we could return and face whatever lay ahead.

"Heading back to England will give us the break we need," Alex said as we loaded the last of our luggage into the car. "We'll come back stronger and ready to tackle everything."

I nodded, looking around at the village one last time before we left. Signs of recovery were visible everywhere. It was hard to leave, but we knew it was the right decision for the moment.

But, as we landed at Heathrow Airport, ready to enjoy our holiday away from it all, Alex's phone rang.

It was Stamos, our builder.

"Come back!" he yelled. "The police have arrived again and arrested Ilias. They've impounded his bulldozer, which means he can't work. He's currently in police custody and they won't release him. They're also searching for you and require your immediate attendance. They have arrested the electrician, who is now sharing a cell with Ilias. I'm not sure why they arrested the electrician, though."

We were both worried. We had only been away for a few hours. In that short time, Pefki had turned into chaos again. Fortunately, we had already passed through Heathrow immigration. This meant that even if Interpol had issued an arrest warrant, we had overcome that obstacle. The Greek police were unaware of our address in England, so we should be relatively safe as long as we remained inconspicuous.

"We have to go back," Alex said.

"What can we do?" I asked her. "If we go back now, we can't do anything. We'll just end up in a police cell with the bulldozer driver and electrician. Also, why did they arrest the electrician?"

Alex called our lawyer and gave her an update, relaying the limited information from Stamos. She asked Sofia to go to the police station and bail Ilias out. We also asked her to find out why he and the electrician had been arrested in the first place. The whole situation was confusing, and we needed answers to understand the events that had unfolded in such a short time. Their sudden detainment had added another layer of confusion to the already perplexing state of affairs.

We had specifically told Ilias to keep away from the river. He knew the situation with the horrible old lady. If he had gone against our instructions, then he deserved all he had coming. But we, being the landowners, would be equally responsible, even though we were sitting on a British Airways aeroplane flying over the Alps at the time. That would be no excuse.

We asked Sofia to keep us informed about our next course of action. Should we return or not? It was a crucial decision, and we relied on her to provide us with the necessary information to make an informed choice of what to do next.

A couple of hours later, she called back and told us she had freed our workers. But the bulldozer had to remain in custody. She still didn't know why they were arrested, but she should receive a police report soon and she would let us know when the paperwork came in. Meanwhile, the arrest warrant for us had been postponed, so we could stay in England for a while.

A few days later, the police report came in.

Unbeknownst to us, the electrician had arrived and asked the bulldozer driver to dig up the cables that connected the garden lights. These cables were buried under the silt and mud. Unfortunately, this required approaching the river.

Within an hour, the police had been back and were swarming around our garden, accompanied by the screeching old lady.

"Look!" she'd screamed. "I told you. They even put lights in the river. See, I told you they blocked the river. There is the evidence."

The electrician attempted to clarify that the lights were not intentionally positioned in the river, but rather, the river had altered its course and engulfed them. Unfortunately, the police dismissed his explanation. From their perspective, the matter seemed straightforward – since the lights were found in the river, they assumed we had deliberately placed them there.

In addition to being persistent offenders, we had now shamelessly ignored the repeated warnings from the police to avoid the river. The authorities had clearly stated that the river was out of bounds, but we disregarded their instructions and, in their eyes, encouraged the breaking of the law once more.

The situation had escalated to a new level. There was no excuse for our actions. It had been pure stupidity on the part of both the electrician and Ilias, who were fully aware of what was going on and the potential consequences. However, the opportunity was seized by the horrible old lady.

At the police station, she not only added to her previous

statement but also accused us of being responsible for flooding our garden and damaging the entire village. Furthermore, she claimed that because we "blocked the river", we should also be held accountable for the damage in the villages upstream.

Our offence had escalated from a misdemeanour to a full-blown crime akin to armed robbery. The gravity of the situation was becoming increasingly serious as the evidence against us mounted and the legal consequences loomed over us. The charges had shifted from a minor infraction to a potentially life-altering offence, leaving us feeling overwhelmed and uncertain about what the future held. We were now facing the harsh reality of the Greek criminal justice system.

We arranged a Zoom meeting with our lawyer, who had a noticeable frown on her face as she spoke, her brows furrowed with concern. The weight of the complaint was palpable in her voice as she emphasised its seriousness. She spoke with empathy and understanding, acknowledging that we were not to blame for the situation at hand. Her reassurance was comforting, but she stressed that simply believing was not enough. Concrete evidence was necessary to support our denial. We needed to provide proof from experts to back up our case and defend ourselves; we needed to prove our innocence beyond any doubt.

We were granted a stay in execution so we could gather evidence for our defence. Proving our innocence required gathering evidence to show that we hadn't caused the damage. This meant hiring experts to analyse weather patterns and geological data to demonstrate that the flooding was a natural disaster, not our doing. It was like trying to prove we hadn't caused a storm – an impossible task made even more difficult by the lack of concrete evidence that could definitively exonerate us. The absurdity of having to explain natural phenomena as part of our defence only added to the frustration. However, the very act of needing to convince others of our innocence made us feel like we were characters in a farce. It seemed ridiculous that we had to go to such lengths to prove something that should have been self-evident. The legal procedures required us to disprove every aspect of the accusations, which were based on nothing more than one person's word. It was an exercise in frustration, as we found ourselves entangled in a bureaucratic web that seemed designed to presume our guilt rather than seek the truth.

But with all this hanging over our heads like a dark cloud, strangely Alex's first thought was for the bulldozer, which was still being held by the police. If we couldn't free it, Ilias would lose his livelihood and be unable to work. Despite knowing he was wrong to go near the river, he was only trying to be helpful. We felt sorry for him and asked Sofia to handle his case and include the expenses on our bill. However, we knew it wouldn't be easy. It seemed that his machine was going to be held as evidence until the prosecutors had decided if there was a case to answer.

Alex loved bulldozers. She would spend hours watching them in action, marvelling at their power and capability. Alex would eagerly ask the operator questions about how it worked, its various functions, and the projects it had been involved in. Her excitement was contagious, and even the operators couldn't help but be impressed by her enthusiasm. Whenever we hired a bulldozer for our garden, Alex would be there, shadowing the operator, observing every movement with wide eyes and a smile that stretched from ear to ear. Her love for bulldozers was more than just a passing interest; it was a genuine passion that brought her joy and excitement every time she saw one.

I first noticed Alex's love for heavy machinery when we started building our apartment block in Glyfada. While I would stop to admire fancy sports cars, Alex was more interested in building sites and the different types of earth moving equipment and cement mixers.

It was truly fascinating to witness her passion for these mechanical beasts. She would enthusiastically explain the intricacies of each machine, from their horsepower to their lifting capacities. I quickly learned that this was not just a passing interest, it was a deep-rooted fascination that brought her immense joy.

Even after our home in Pefki was finished, Alex's passion for heavy machinery remained strong. She would frequently come up with reasons to rent a bulldozer and driver for different tasks on our property. From clearing land to constructing a shed, or simply moving big rocks, she would take advantage of any opportunity to witness their power in action.

Some might find it odd, but I admire Alex's love for heavy machinery. It's one of those quirks that showcases her practical personality in the most amusing way. Forget about fancy cars;

to Alex, a car is just a means of transportation. Who cares about speed or appearance when you could be driving a bulldozer? Yes, a bulldozer.

Alex's eyes light up at the sight of these massive machines. It's like watching a kid in a candy store, but replace the candy with earth moving equipment. Her love for these behemoths represents her determination, attention to detail and unwavering passion. You can see her imagining the power and precision needed to operate one, as if she's conquering mountains with every push of dirt.

This fascination reminds us to embrace our true passions, no matter how unexpected or unconventional they might be. So while others might dream of sleek sports cars, Alex dreams of the roar of a bulldozer's engine and the thrill of moving mountains, one scoop at a time.

"Let's buy it," she suggested.

"What? The bulldozer?" I asked, incredulous. "Why do you want a bulldozer? Neither of us can drive one."

"Look. It's old and rusty. But it's all he has. Now it's been impounded, he can't make a living. If we buy it from him, he can use the money to buy another one. Then when it's released, he can teach me how to drive it. That would be so much fun. You've always wanted a ride-on lawnmower. This will be a step up from that."

I wondered how Alex was expecting me to mow the lawn with a bulldozer, but her enthusiasm was infectious, and I could see the benefits. After all, it would be her birthday soon, and what do you buy a woman who has everything?

I couldn't help wondering if Alex had an alternative motive for wanting her very own bulldozer. The nasty old lady's house was close to the end of our garden. Judging by the gleam in Alex's eye, she was likely considering a small demolition project. Maybe the house that was built in the river would be first on her list.

Alex called Ilias. "Hi, Ilias. How are you?"

"I'm fine," he replied. "I'm really sorry I've got you into so much trouble. I was only trying to find the underground cables. But the crazy woman came back again with the police. Once I get my bulldozer back, I'll come and finish the job for free to make up for it."

The poor chap didn't mention his temporary loss of livelihood. He felt sad for us, but he knew his actions had caused us to face a legal mountain. He chose not to burden us with the knowledge of the financial hardships he and his family would now face. However, we knew it would be devastating.

"Don't worry about that," Alex told him. "Our lawyer is fighting for you, so hopefully everything will work out well. By the way, are there any bulldozers for sale in the village?"

Ilias fell silent as he pondered. "Actually, a friend of mine is selling his. It's the same model and age as mine. Maybe he'll let me borrow it while mine is impounded. I'll ask him."

"That's not why we're asking," Alex said. "How about this: we buy the impounded bulldozer, then you can buy your friend's one. Once yours is released, you can teach me how to drive it. We'll keep it for our garden."

Both bulldozers were old, and the price asked was about

the same as a cheap used car. It was reasonable and well within our budget. So we reached an agreement and sent a bank transfer. We were now the proud owners of a bulldozer, and Ilias could go back to work.

"Don't go near our house yet, though," Alex warned him. "I don't think the police compound is big enough for two bulldozers."

As we prepared to return to Greece, we felt a mix of fear and foreboding. The peaceful English environment had allowed us to recharge and gather our thoughts, but we knew that the challenges awaiting us in Greece would be vastly different. The tranquil countryside had given us time and space to carefully consider our options and fine-tune our plans.

We had analysed every aspect of our situation and were ready to face the stress and pressure that had become part of our new lives in our Greek village. We knew that returning meant diving back into the turbulent sea of bureaucracy and navigating the complex legal system once again. As we made our way to the airport, worries of false accusations filled our minds. But we were determined to prove our innocence.

Travelling to Greece was usually thrilling. We usually felt free as our plane flew towards Athens airport. This time, as we came in to land, we were nervous but ready to face whatever challenges awaited us.

When we arrived in our village, our first stop was to visit

our lawyer in the nearby village of Istiea. We wanted to know the latest updates on the criminal charges against us. Sofia warmly greeted us as we entered her office and immediately started discussing the situation. She showed us a set of well-organised documents, including the complaint filed by the old lady.

We finally learned her name for the first time. Our friends in the village had never told us,. We sensed a feeling of fear from everyone whenever we brought her into a conversation. Almost everyone in the village had built something illegal, such as makeshift chicken houses and barbecues, and sheds that probably needed official permission. If they openly supported us, she might have retaliated against them.

Despite our curiosity, we had respected their decision to keep her name a secret. It only fuelled our focus to unravel the mystery surrounding her.

To protect ourselves and prevent any further legal troubles, it is prudent to keep her real name concealed. Let's call her Nemesis, a fitting name for the dreadful old lady. Nemesis was a Greek goddess known for her cruel and vindictive nature, who took pleasure in causing misery and chaos wherever she went.

All heroes have their nemesis. Where would Sherlock Holmes be without James Moriarty? James Bond needed Ernst Stavro Blofeld, and the ancient text of Homer showed the battle between Poseidon and Odysseus.

Her statement was nasty, vindictive, and read like the incoherent ramblings of a lunatic spitting poison. It was filled with wild accusations, blatant lies and personal attacks that had no basis in reality. Each sentence dripped with malice, twisting the truth and distorting facts to paint us in the worst possible light. It was clear she was out for blood, determined to drag our reputation through the mud and see us suffer, for reasons only she could comprehend.

But Sofia had not left us defenceless. Anticipating the vitriol we would face, Sofia had prepared a counter document on our behalf. Our statement was a masterclass in clarity and reason, meticulously detailing our side of the story. It wasn't just a rebuttal; it was a vehement defence against the baseless accusations thrown our way.

Our statement began by addressing each of her wild claims, systematically dismantling them with cold, hard facts. Where the old woman's words were filled with emotion and rage, ours were calm, composed, and backed by evidence. We included photographs of the river before and after the flood that contradicted her version of events. Every point she made was met with a precise and logical counterpoint, exposing the flaws and inconsistencies in her ramblings.

In contrast to the chaotic and venomous tone of her document, our statement was logical and truthful. Sofia's legal expertise shone through every paragraph.

Our statement closed with a firm yet respectful demand for the matter to be resolved fairly and justly. It called for an end to the baseless attacks, and highlighted our willingness to cooperate in finding a reasonable solution. It was a powerful declaration of our position and a testament to Sofia's skill in navigating the murky waters of legal disputes.

As we reviewed the final draft, we felt a surge of confidence. While her statement had initially left us feeling battered and bruised, our counter document gave us a renewed sense of hope, ready to face whatever came next, with the truth on our side.

Sofia also gave us a document from the prosecutor's office, which requested more information in order for them to decide if our case would go to trial. We would need a land surveyor to back us up with a full survey and report.

We needed to uncover the truth behind the old lady's vendetta and avoid a long, drawn-out legal case. After discussing the matter with Sofia, she recommended a land surveyor named Ajax.

His name was inspired by the legendary Greek warrior. If his work was as impressive as his name, we would be in good hands. We arranged to meet him the next day at his office.

Alex and I could see the look of sympathy in Ajax's eyes as we described how the river had swelled beyond its banks, causing widespread flooding to our home and garden. We told him how the old lady had blamed us for the disaster, accusing us of blocking the river. Ajax listened attentively, occasionally interjecting with questions to gain a better understanding of the situation. His thoughtful nods reassured us he was taking us seriously.

After we finished telling our story, Ajax reclined in his chair and expressed his discontent. "This accusation is foolish," he declared. "I know this river well. It ends right behind your garden. Whatever you did or didn't do, it couldn't have made any difference. It sounds crazy."

Alex flashed me a relieved smile and turned to Ajax. "Could you please provide us with a letter confirming this? It would really help us move forward and get on with our lives."

"It doesn't work that way," he said. "The prosecutor wants a complete topographical study of the area. They need soil samples from upstream and downstream. We will need weather pattern reports. We have to create a map of the previous river location and compare it to the current flow. We need a drone pilot to film the area and prepare a report. After that, I'll compile everything into a formal document, which will then need to be approved by the land registry and formally stamped."

"Wow," I said. "How long will that take?"

"Oh, about three months," he replied. "But unfortunately, it will be rather expensive."

We knew rebuilding our little piece of heaven would come at a hefty price, but the costs were mounting. No one could be held responsible for the devastation caused by the floods, as they were an unforeseen act of God. We had no choice but to accept our unfortunate circumstances and prepare for the work and expenses. However, our local nemesis had caused more trouble and now, in addition, we had legal expenses and land survey costs. There was also a criminal case. On top of all that, we agreed to buy a bulldozer.

Despite everything, we just wanted our home back. We needed to move forward. We discussed the costs with Ajax and agreed with his proposal. Now we needed to find witnesses from our village to support our case. That was going to be another challenge.

CHAPTER 14

The Wicked Witch of the Village

Pay attention to your enemies, as they are the first to discover your mistakes.

– Antisthenes

In Greece, there is an ancient belief that a visitor could actually be one of the gods in disguise. There are stories about the god Zeus dressing up as a commoner and going to villagers' doors to see who would welcome him and who would reject him. Those who turned him away unknowingly brought trouble upon themselves. The ancient Greeks believed that by being kind and hospitable, they would gain favour with Zeus and the other gods, while Zeus would punish those who were found to be inhospitable.

The Greek people are known for their kindness. In ancient times, villagers would often bring fresh fruit to the homes of foreigners or visitors as a gesture of hospitality. Regardless of their social status, Greeks treated guests well by providing them with food, drinks and a place to rest. This tradition continues today, with Greeks helping strangers in need and buying food for the homeless.

Nemesis was certainly an exception to this rule. She had it in for us. We just needed to find out why.

There wasn't much information available about her in the village. We did learn that she had a habit of hiring locals for various tasks like clearing leaves, gardening and doing minor construction work, then found excuses to avoid paying them. People considered her untrustworthy. However, she never went shopping in the village, so she wasn't involved in supermarket gossip. She also never visited any of the tavernas in the village, so most villagers claimed they didn't know much about her.

We managed to gather some scant information. She was of Greek origin, but not born in Pefki. Our friend Marily was born in Gouves, less than a mile away, and she was also considered foreign. Alex, being born in Athens, was positively exotic.

For the locals to not know anything about a resident of the village was difficult to believe. We needed to dig deeper. We quizzed people every day about the horrible lady, but most evaded our probing.

Then one day, we were introduced to the captain, and things changed.

Christos, known in the village as "the captain", was born in

Pefki. He spent a happy childhood here enjoying the simple life and growing up in a safe and loving community. But like most Greeks, when he came of age, he went to sea. Unlike Marily's uncle, Christos went to sea on real ships, not the woolly kind currently chewing grass up in the nearby hills.

Greece is a country of seamen, and Greek ships have sailed to the furthest ends of the earth since the dawn of recorded history. From ancient times, Greece has been known as a nation of skilled seafarers. The Greeks' maritime expertise is a large part of their cultural identity and has shaped the course of their civilisation. Whether it be the legendary voyages of Odysseus or the great naval battles of the Persian Wars, Greece's seafaring tradition is a testament to their skill and determination.

Christos was driven by a deep passion for the sea and a desire to explore new horizons. Despite the allure of joining his friends in the lucrative field of container shipping, he decided to pursue a different path. He chose to enrol in the prestigious Hellenic Naval College in Athens. This decision allowed him to combine his love for the ocean with his thirst for knowledge and adventure. After years of rigorous training and dedication, he achieved his dream and became the captain of his own frigate, patrolling the waters of the Aegean Sea.

Christos served in the navy for over two decades, building a distinguished career filled with numerous voyages and exciting missions. He explored distant shores, navigated treacherous waters, and led his crew through both calm seas and fierce storms. He participated in international naval exercises, representing Greece with pride and forging alliances with other naval forces. His frigate often escorted humanitarian aid ships to war-torn regions, ensuring their safe passage and providing relief to those in need. Christos also played a crucial role in anti-piracy operations, capturing notorious pirate leaders and protecting commercial shipping lanes.

His leadership and bravery earned him respect and recognition, making him a well-known figure in maritime circles. Christos was decorated with numerous medals and awards for his service, including the Hellenic Navy Medal of Merit and the Distinguished Service Cross. He was admired not only for his naval skills but also for his ability to inspire and mentor young sailors, many of whom went on to have successful careers of their own under his guidance.

Eventually, after many years of service, the time came for Christos to retire. He decided to return to his village, seeking a quieter life away from the constant demands of naval life. We met him at Adonia's taverna while we were having lunch. He greeted us warmly and mentioned he had heard about our troubles.

"I heard you dumped a load of earth and concrete in the river," he said. "Is that true?"

Obviously, Nemesis had been spreading her poison around the village in an attempt to alienate us further.

Alex froze with fury. I felt her leg trembling under the table and put my hand on her knee to steady her. "Captain," she said, "just use your common sense. Are we likely to create a dam to block the river and divert it through our own house?" She got up to leave. "Are they all mad in this village?" she muttered to herself as she stormed towards the door.

I rose to follow, but the captain called out, "Alex, please sit down. I didn't say I believed the gossip. However, you deserve to know what some people are saying. I think it's complete nonsense, but it's better to hear the facts directly from you and Peter."

The captain was the mayor we should have had. But he had no interest in the dirty business of politics.

I sat beside him and explained a little about our troubles. "We didn't do anything to cause the flooding of the river. It has always ended at the rear of our garden," I told him. "This crazy woman is obviously insane if she thinks we are responsible for any of this."

"Yes, I know your land," he said. "We all knew the river flooded every time there's a storm. So only an idiot would build a house there."

He laughed and slapped his thigh, and took another swig of tsipouro.

I found myself laughing alongside him, only to realise that I was one of those idiots.

"I don't know her personally, but I have heard stories," he confided.

He told us some of the gossip about her, which was apparently common knowledge in the village. According to the rumours, Nemesis was not so innocent. She had bought her land at a knock-down price, then made a complaint to the person she brought it from because it flooded in the winter. She hired a powerful lawyer in Athens who threatened criminal action against those involved in the sale. She claimed they were aware of the potential for flooding and had fraudulently sold her useless land.

According to the captain, her lawyer successfully got back all the money she paid for the land, plus compensation.

"We have no idea how she got permission to build in the river. Nobody will ever know. But here in Greece, it's always been the same." He tapped the side of his nose knowingly. "A friend of a friend can do wonders if you know the right people."

Somehow she was granted permission to build her house, even though it was directly on the course of the river. Then she built a massive wall. A few other people saw what she had done and cashed in on their land. Soon afterwards, three houses were built side by side, with the garden walls constructed into a cul-de-sac. This allowed the land from there to the seaside to dry out completely. The newly dry land was sold, and more houses built. She had no concern for where the river would redirect its flow. All that mattered to her was keeping her land dry, regardless of the impact on neighbouring homes. Her own well-being was her sole priority.

Then we came along and innocently built a house upstream. If the river had been allowed to maintain its natural course, all would have been fine. But because of Nemesis, we took the consequences.

By the end of lunch, the captain was satisfied that we had nothing to do with the damage to the village. He assured us he would tell others that the poison being spread around by Nemesis was completely unfounded and we were innocent.

After our conversation with the captain, we noticed a remarkable change in the way people treated us, particularly those outside our immediate circle of friends and neighbours. While our close friends had always stood by us, others in the village had previously avoided the topic of our troubles, perhaps out of discomfort or fear of being drawn into the drama. Now, however, it seemed that with the captain's involvement, the stigma had been lifted. Everyone knew about our predicament, and instead of sidestepping the subject, people began to embrace us even more warmly.

It felt like the broader village was collectively trying to make amends, as though they wanted to demonstrate that the actions of one individual did not define their community. In their words, gestures and kind acts it was clear they wanted to show us that we truly belonged.

People started to confide in us, sharing their own problems and letting us into their everyday lives. We felt a deeper connection to the community, a sense of solidarity that had been missing before. Each day, we would open our front door to find baskets filled with fruit, fresh eggs, or home-made pastries wrapped in soft cloth. These gestures were more than just acts of kindness; they were symbols of acceptance and support.

Our neighbours would stop by for a chat, offering words of encouragement and advice. They told us stories of their own struggles with Nemesis, and how they had overcome them, making us feel less isolated in our predicament. Even at Adonia's taverna, where we had first met the captain, the atmosphere had shifted. People greeted us more warmly, inviting us to join their conversations and share their meals. We felt a sense of belonging that had been absent before. Support for us was no longer limited to our close friends and neighbours, who had always stood by us. Now, it felt as though the entire village, people we didn't know well, or who had previously been hesitant to get involved, had decided to rally around us in our time of need.

As we waited for our land surveyor's report, we realised that we were not facing this challenge alone. The support of the village gave us strength and hope. We knew that whatever the outcome of our case, we had found a community that cared for us and stood by us. This new-found sense of belonging was a precious gift, and it made all the challenges we faced feel a little lighter.

One striking example of this community spirit came from the way local businesses and tavernas supported one another, especially during the quieter months. When trade was limited, rather than competing for customers, they saw themselves as part of a larger collective. Instead of fighting over what little business there was, the owners would come together and agree on a plan: most establishments would close for the day, consolidating their resources so that one place could remain open to serve lunch. This thoughtful arrangement not only attracted more customers but ensured that the entire village benefitted. The success of one business became the success of all, showcasing a unity that was truly remarkable.

One day, we went to have lunch at Manya's taverna near the beach. However, we found it closed. So, we decided to drive further into the village to Balarourus's fish restaurant. When we entered, we heard Manya's voice coming from the kitchen. Intrigued, we went to investigate and found her happily cooking. It turned out she had purposely closed her place for the day to support this family business, and rather than take a day off, making it necessary for hungry diners to find another restaurant, she came and did the cooking. Here, most people stuck together and helped each other as much as possible. By now, we had realised that this strong sense of community extended beyond the local residents. We, too, were experiencing the benefits of living in such a welcoming and supportive environment. The villagers didn't treat us as outsiders; instead, they embraced us as part of their extended family.

Stamos called us with some great news. We had finally received permission to move forward with our extensive building project.

"The engineer just called me," he said. "If you want to drive to his office, you can pick up the papers."

The garden's walls would be made of strong concrete to defend against future flooding. The concrete and stone terraces would be carefully arranged to create a visually stunning and durable foundation. Flower beds and trees would be strategically placed to add colour and a touch of nature. Steps leading to higher levels would be designed with both functionality and elegance in mind. Wicker chairs and hammocks would provide lounging areas under the shade of fig trees, and new dining areas would be covered by ornate canopies. The electrician would install pavement lights, spotlights, and other mood lighting options to illuminate the area and create a captivating ambiance for nighttime enjoyment, centrally controlled from a point near the seating area for convenience in adjusting the mood and atmosphere.

We were not allowed to access the back part of our land or go near the river. Our wariness of Nemesis ensured we abided by the rules laid down by the police. We didn't even walk on that part of our garden because we were wary of screeching old ladies and police visits. We decided to stay away from that area until we got more information from our land surveyor and lawyer.

A robust gate would be installed, leading to the back portion of the land and the river beyond. This would also be used as a flood barrier. Once our legal issues were resolved, Alex could freely use her new bulldozer and play with her toy to her heart's content.

The project was set to cost a fortune and would wipe out all our savings. However, one valuable lesson I had learned from being married to Alex was that when we were united, miracles became possible.

Many years had now passed since we started our building project in Glyfada. We'd hired an architect to demolish our old house and build a five-storey apartment block on the land. In exchange for his services, he would keep two apartments and a retail shop, while we would receive the same. But, we would get the most valuable part, the penthouse flat, along with another floor that we could divide into two flats, and our own shop.

The deal seemed great in theory as it wouldn't cost us anything. We had to say goodbye to our beautiful old family home, but we had to think about the future. However, the apartments would be basic, and we would have to decorate and furnish them ourselves. We didn't have much money at the time. I was still working in England and commuting to Athens. The airfare expenses ate into my earnings, and the rest was used for everyday needs. Alex had her small beauty therapy business, but it didn't bring in much money. So, it would take time to turn our new apartment into a home.

One day, we visited one of Alex's wealthy friends, Lydia. She was incredibly rich, owning a yacht with her own captain. Whenever she felt like it, she would set sail and spend weeks cruising the islands. Lydia also had several high-end cars, including a Porsche for the city and a luxurious Range Rover for longer drives. Her large house was close to the sea. It was beautifully decorated with the latest styles and fashions. She had flown in a designer from Paris who dealt with everything without Lydia needing to lift a finger.

Alex and I were sitting in the living room. The room was so perfect and pristine that I felt a little uncomfortable. I was hesitant to sit too hard on the cushions because I didn't want to crease them. I held my coffee in my hand, reluctant to place it on the polished veneered table in case I marked it.

As I gazed out of the window, admiring the glistening Aegean Sea, Alex and Lydia engaged in a conversation about decoration. Alex understood that she would never be able to match that level of sophistication in our new apartment, while I couldn't help but feel a pang of guilt, knowing that I would never possess the wealth necessary to provide such opulence. Nevertheless, Alex seemed to be gathering some inspiration and ideas for our own space. Alex took a sip of her coffee and looked at the curtains.

"Oh, I love those." Alex pointed at the ruffled drapes hanging majestically across the window.

Lydia sneered and looked down her nose at Alex. "They are not for you," she told her. "I got those in Rome. They are way beyond your price range."

I stopped looking at the sea. Instead, I stared directly into Lydia's eyes. I was furious. How could she? This woman had never worked a day in her life. Her money came from inheritance. She had no clue about the troubles and stresses of regular people who had to save up for things beyond the necessities. And yet, there she was, telling my amazing wife that the curtains were too expensive for her.

If Alex desired the curtains, I would damn well walk to Rome and fetch them. This was the motivation I needed. On that day, I made a decision: Alex deserved the best. Whatever she wanted, I would find a way to provide it.

We threw away the old kitchen appliances from our old house. We ordered and paid for new fridges and freezers. Our new kitchen would have a state-of-the-art cooker. We replaced the ceramic tiles with the best pink marble floors. The bathroom ceiling would be adorned with hand-painted clouds on a blue sky, with cherubs made from ornate plaster. Alex wanted decorative Corinthian columns, so we got them. I even built a replica Parthenon on our roof. Nothing was too good for our new home, and we had learned that with the correct motivation, we could do anything.

Achieving this transformation wasn't easy, but we managed to balance our budget with creativity and resourcefulness. We sourced high-quality materials at discounted prices, hunted for sales, and sometimes even repurposed items. Alex's eye for design and my knack for DIY allowed us to create a luxurious feel without always resorting to expensive options. We learned to find beauty in unexpected places. I found an dried-up branch of an olive tree lying beside the road. I strapped it to the top of my car, took it home and set about placing light bulbs around the twigs, before hoisting it to the ceiling to use as a chandelier. It looked incredible. A natural piece of rural Greece in a new home gave us an authentic feel, and we loved it. So with other ideas, including saving driftwood from the beach to turn into lamps or pieces of furniture, or using cheap fabric to make curtains ourselves, we made our dream home a reality without breaking the bank.

When our home was complete, Alex and I stood there, hands intertwined, admiring our beautiful penthouse. I popped open a bottle of champagne and poured it into two glasses. We raised our glasses in unison, toasting to Lydia. Without her, we would have never achieved this incredible feat. She would never know the part she played in our lives.

Perhaps Nemesis would be the unlikely inspiration we needed here in our little Greek village.

CHAPTER 15

Truth Beneath the Surface

Justice will overtake fabricators of lies and false witnesses.

– Heraclitus

The next morning, our lawyer, Sofia, called.

"I need you both to come to my office for a meeting right away," she said. "I have news."

Alex pressed her for more information. "Is it good or bad news?" she asked.

Sofia refused to elaborate. "Just come, I will explain everything when you arrive."

As we approached the next village and the lawyer's office, a feeling of dread washed over us. What if there was more evidence against us? Could Nemesis have come up with additional charges? We had purposely avoided going near our land by the river, not even setting foot on it. Surely, she couldn't accuse us of anything else. We were already under investigation for a crime. What else could she throw at us? We had given Stamos a large deposit, and after meticulously coordinating plans with his team, he was set to begin work tomorrow. The long wait for everything to fall into place, permits, approvals and preparations, was finally over. Knowing that the rebuilding would soon begin brought a mixture of relief and anticipation. While we had faced countless delays and frustrations, the thought of seeing progress in our garden made it all seem worthwhile. Could more charges put a stop to our recovery plans and force us to live in a mud pit for years? All these thoughts raced through our minds as we parked outside the office and cautiously climbed the dark staircase.

Sofia had company. Ajax, our land surveyor, sat on a chair next to her, his face set in a serious expression. His shoulders were slightly hunched, his eyes scanning through a stack of papers on the desk in front of him. Sofia, our steadfast lawyer, mirrored his seriousness, her lips pressed into a thin line. The room was quiet, save for the occasional rustle of paper and the distant hum of traffic outside.

Alex and I sat facing Sofia and Ajax. The room felt small and tense, and as we waited I tried to distract myself. I studied the walls which were adorned with framed certificates and legal awards, a testament to Sofia's expertise and dedication. A large oak desk separated us from them, its surface cluttered with legal documents, a few pens and a half-empty coffee cup.

The sunlight streaming through the window did little to lift the mood. It cast long shadows across the room, accentuating the lines of worry on everyone's faces. I glanced at Alex, who was fidgeting slightly, her fingers tapping a nervous rhythm on the arm of her chair. She caught my eye and gave a small, reassuring smile, but I could see the tension in her eyes.

Ajax cleared his throat, breaking the silence. He shuffled his papers once more, then looked up, meeting our gazes with a steady, determined look. Sofia leaned forward, her hands clasped together on the desk, ready to dive into the matter at hand.

The meeting had begun.

Ajax opened a thick file on the desk in front of him and took out a series of photographs. They included old drawings, grainy black and white images, and more up-to-date photos. He picked one from the pile. It was an aerial photograph showing our house under construction. He pointed to the dry riverbed originating from the next village. It snaked its way towards our land, then abruptly disappeared into the undergrowth. It was clear the land hadn't been touched in years. The river simply disappeared.

"This was before you cleared your land. At that time, the river ended there." He pointed at the photograph indicating the boundary of our property.

He took out an older photograph. This was taken in the nineteen sixties, showing the land from Artemision all the way to the sea before any houses were built. This clearly showed the river running in an unbroken line all the way past our plot and discharging into the sea.

Then, another photograph was produced. This showed the river passing our land, then abruptly stopping at a huge white wall which had completely stopped the flow. This was the house of Nemesis.

"So please explain," Alex said. "What are you showing us?"

"What I am showing you is the end of your legal troubles." He smiled. "You could not possibly have blocked the river. This photograph proves what you have been saying all along. Now it's no longer just your word; this confirms it. It was already blocked." He went on to explain, "The construction of this house downstream obstructed the natural flow of the river, causing silt to accumulate in its bed. This accumulation led to a situation where, during periods of heavy rain, the river was unable to stay on its original course and instead diverted towards the point of least resistance. At times, it would follow roads, while other times it would cut through the olive grove that stands opposite your garden. Unfortunately, during this particular flood, the river changed its course and struck your home with great force." Reaching for his glass, he took a slow sip of water, his gaze flicking between us, measuring our reaction.

"You had nothing to do with it. You were the innocents here. This woman who had you arrested and made your life a living hell is the one responsible for everything. This file proves it."

He sat back and allowed us to digest this information.

Alex could no longer hold herself and burst into tears. The stress of the past few months had taken its toll, but as the tears streamed down her face, they carried with them a flood of relief. It felt as though a crushing weight had been lifted, allowing her to breathe freely for the first time in months. She turned to me and said, her voice trembling, "Is it really over? Can we finally move on?"

I didn't answer immediately. Could it be possible? Would we at long last be able to prove our innocence? Relief, disbelief and cautious hope swirled within me. For months, we had lived under constant pressure, like a storm cloud was hanging over us, threatening to break at any moment. The sleepless nights, the endless anxiety, the fear of what might come next, all of it had consumed us. And now, could this truly be the end?

Alex's tears mirrored what I felt but struggled to express. While relief washed over us, a simmering anger still lingered. Yes, we had endured, but the injustice we had faced wasn't so easily forgotten. As I watched Alex wipe her face and attempt a shaky smile, I felt a new determination rising within me. We had weathered the storm, but the echoes of what we had endured would take time to fade.

Sofia looked up from her desk, smiled, and passed Alex a tissue. Reaching across the desk, she took Alex's hand in hers and gave it a reassuring squeeze.

"It's nearly over now," Sofia assured her. "She no longer has power over you. You are in control of what happens next."

Sofia's words hung in the air, heavy with implications.

"It is clear that if the case goes to court, we will win. But there are other things we need to do. Ajax needs to complete his official report. Then it has to be presented to the planning office for the stamp of approval. Meanwhile, I will rewrite your defence and hold on to it until we have Ajax's full report typed up and notarised. Then we can decide what we are going to do. When we meet again after the official report, let's discuss the next step. However, for the time being, this conversation is a secret," she warned us. "Don't tell anyone. We don't want Nemesis to find out what we've discovered. Let her rant and complain all she wants. She will only be digging herself into a deeper grave."

As she spoke, a wave of relief washed over me, but it was quickly followed by a surge of anxiety. The idea of keeping this under wraps, of living with this secret, made my heart race. I glanced sideways at Alex and took a deep breath, trying to steady my nerves. The path ahead was clear, but it was fraught with uncertainty and risk. The thought of Nemesis continuing her tirades while we held this trump card gave me a strange mix of satisfaction and dread. We had the upper hand, but the stakes were high.

"I understand," I said, my voice steadier than I felt. "We'll keep this between us. We trust your judgement, Sofia."

Alex squeezed my hand, a silent signal of her support. We were in this together, ready to face whatever came next with a united front.

We left the meeting and headed home. We had a plan, but it required patience and secrecy. The sun outside seemed brighter, the world continuing as normal, oblivious to the storm brewing in our lives. But with Sofia and Ajax on our side, I felt a glimmer of hope. We could do this. We just had to stay strong and stick to the plan.

Finally, after months of stress and worry, it seemed we were going to be free from all our troubles. Now that the situation had changed, we started to think about what we should do about the horrible old lady. The possibilities of revenge seemed delightful as we relished the thought of turning the tables back onto Nemesis.

But this would come later. Tomorrow, Stamos would be arriving to start work.

The next day, we woke up to the familiar sound of bulldozers in our garden. We had missed that wonderful sound. We made coffee and went out to our patio. The air smelled of fresh concrete as the workers poured it into frames for our new walls. Stamos was everywhere, making sure everything was done precisely. The sound of drilling and hammering filled the air as workers placed metal rods for reinforcement. Throughout the day, Alex and I were amazed at the transformation happening in front of us. Stamos and his team were turning our vision into reality.

Suddenly, a police siren sounded as two police cars skidded to a halt on the road outside our house. Three police officers jumped out of the cars, followed by their passenger. It was Nemesis, here to torment us further, or so she thought.

"Look!" she screamed. "I told you, they are building walls. Look, they are blocking the river again! They are not allowed to do it. Arrest them, arrest them all!"

This time, Alex and I just watched and grinned. This infuriated the horrible old lady even more.

"Look!" she shrieked, pointing her bony finger at us. "They're laughing at me. Arrest them now. They are blocking the river!"

The police chief looked at Nemesis and told her to be quiet. "I will deal with this," he said. He walked over to us with a resigned look on his face.

"I don't want to arrest you again. But you're leaving me little choice. I've already told you that you can't do anything to your land without official permission." He lowered his voice. "And this woman is driving us all crazy at the station."

"Is this what you're looking for?" Stamos yelled, his voice echoing across the construction site. He had stormed off to his van and returned triumphantly, waving a file in the air. It contained our official building permission, the very document that could put an end to this madness.

Marching up to the officer, Stamos thrust the file into his hands. "Here," he said defiantly. "Take a good look."

The officer flipped through the pages, his expression unreadable. A tense silence settled over the scene as everyone watched, waiting for his verdict. Stamos crossed his arms and stood back, daring the officer to find a flaw.

After what felt like an eternity, the officer handed the documents back to Stamos. "Yes, everything seems fine. You can continue now," he confirmed, his tone almost reluctant. "But you should have posted it on the wall for everyone to see."

Stamos let out a hearty laugh. "That's next on my list," he replied. "We don't have a wall yet to nail it to. But don't worry, when we build it, we'll proudly display the permission for all to see." He turned and winked at Nemesis.

The officer turned to Nemesis. "You can go home now. Everything is in order," he told her, a hint of finality in his voice. She was furious. She grabbed his sleeve to pull him towards the back of the garden.

"But the river!" she screamed. "They are blocking the river again!"

The officer pulled his arm away from her and walked to his car. The other officers followed, and the cars disappeared along the road, leaving Nemesis in the middle of our building site, with spittle on the corner of her mouth, muttering, "The river, but the river …"

Alex walked towards her.

"Excuse me, but do you know you are on private land? Now fuck off."

Alex turned and gave me a satisfied smile as Nemesis slunk off, muttering and swearing to herself.

Stamos watched her retreat, then turned to the gathered workers and neighbours. "All right, everyone!" he called out. "Let's get back to work. We've got a wall to build and a permission to display!"

The tension lifted, and the sounds of construction resumed. Stamos clapped me on the back, grinning. "Never underestimate the power of having your paperwork in order," he said with a chuckle.

The next day, the police released the impounded bulldozer. Even though Ilias no longer owned it, he was happy to collect it and drive it home. Alex was thrilled with her new toy and insisted that Ilias start her driving lessons immediately.

We still had piles of mud and silt near the river, and Alex couldn't wait to use her new machine to level the land. However, we were under strict instructions to leave that part of our land untouched for now, as neither the police nor Nemesis knew we had proved our innocence. We had to be cautious and not give them any reason to charge us again. So, Ilias drove Alex's bulldozer to the beach, and we followed in our car, to begin her lesson.

Pefki beach is one of the longest in Greece, stretching over two kilometres along the seafront from Asmini to Artemision. Even in peak summer, you can stroll along the nearby road and discover your own private beach. It's a perfect spot to unwind without any other people around.

Alex had a great first lesson in operating a bulldozer. During winter, JCBs come to the beach and dig furrows in the sand to enable the wet ground to drain into the sea. In summer, some of the furrows are filled to create a large area of sand and shingle for beachgoers and swimmers to enjoy the hot Greek sun. Some of these furrows still needed to be filled and others opened, ready for the forthcoming winter. Ilias sat Alex in the cab and explained the controls. The seat could swivel to the front or rear, depending on whether you were using the front blade as a plough or the rear bucket for digging.

She drove her machine slowly over the sand. Ilias hung

from the side and gave instructions through the open door. The blade dipped and the motor strained as it pushed a pile of sand across the beach. The bulldozer turned for another run. I could see Alex's face. She had a wide grin and a look of pure concentration. She ploughed the sand into smooth, flat lines. She was having a great time.

Cars passing by stopped as people got out to watch. While they were accustomed to seeing construction vehicles on the beach, now they were watching a beautiful woman with flowing golden hair that shimmered in the sunlight, her piercing brown eyes sparkling with determination. Her slender figure was clad in a dusty, oversized construction suit, but even the bulky attire couldn't hide Alex's natural grace. As she expertly manoeuvered the bulldozer through the sandy terrain, it was clear that she was getting the hang of it.

Alex soon became skilled at using the blade to push sand up and down the beach. Now it was time to learn how to use the hydraulic arm with the bucket on the back. Ilias took charge and turned the seat to face the arm. He then lowered the bucket towards a pile of shingle. The arm reached over, collected a full load, and effortlessly lifted it into the air. Finally, it tipped the contents into the waiting trench. Alex and Ilias swapped places. She was now in control. Within moments, Alex had mastered it. Ilias left her and came to join me. By now, the few passing motorists had turned into a small crowd. A round of applause and whoops of delight emanated every time Alex successfully filled the bucket and deposited its contents into the trench.

However, when I glanced over my shoulder at the beach, my eyes widened in surprise. Standing amidst the spectators was a hefty man in a police uniform. It was none other than the chief of police himself. My stomach tightened with apprehension, but then I noticed something unexpected: a smile on his face as he watched Alex and her bulldozer.

I approached cautiously, half expecting a reprimand. "Good afternoon, Chief," I greeted him, trying to sound more confident than I felt.

"Good afternoon," he replied, his eyes still on Alex. "She's quite something, isn't she?"

I chuckled nervously. "Yes, she certainly is. I hope we're not breaking any laws."

The chief shook his head. "Not at all. In fact, it's nice to see someone taking initiative. It's not often we get such energy around here."

I relaxed a little, relieved by his words. "We're just trying to make things better for the village. This part of the beach needed a good clean anyway."

The chief nodded thoughtfully. "I can see that. Alex has a way of drawing people in. Maybe this will inspire others."

Alex must have noticed us talking because she hopped down from the bulldozer and joined us, her face flushed with excitement. "Hello, Chief!" she greeted cheerfully.

"Hello, Alex," the chief said, still smiling. "You've got quite an audience."

Alex glanced around at the crowd. "The more, the merrier. Do you fancy a go on the bulldozer? It's great fun!"

The chief chuckled. "No, but you're doing a fine job of it. Just make sure to keep everything within the rules, and I'll stay out of your way."

"Absolutely," Alex agreed. "We'll keep everything above board."

With a nod, the chief turned back to the crowd and gave a small wave, signalling that everything was fine. The tension that had hung over the gathering dissipated, and the atmosphere became even more festive as people returned their attention to Alex's work.

"Yes," I agreed proudly. "Once we get permission to clean our remaining land, she will be ready."

He shrugged his shoulders.

"That could be a long time coming," he said. "That old lady really has it in for you. If it was up to me, you could do anything you wanted. But I have bosses. They are far away in Chalkida, so they don't know what's going on here. All they see is the official complaints, which make you look as guilty as hell. They tell me what to do and I have to follow their orders. But there is a way you might be able to make progress."

He looked around to make sure no one was in earshot. He lowered his voice and whispered over the sound of the distant bulldozer engine, and gave me some very valuable advice.

In many regions of Greece, including the one where we lived, the local government, or municipality, is responsible for managing natural deposits such as mud and debris that wash down from the mountains into residential areas. According to Greek law, the municipality is required to ensure that such materials are cleared from private properties to prevent any damage or disruption. This law is intended to protect property owners from the natural but potentially destructive consequences of living near rivers or mountains.

As our property had been affected by mud washed down from the river, the accumulation was technically municipal property, since it originated from a public waterway. It was therefore the local government's responsibility to remove it.

"I am not telling you this," the chief whispered conspiratorially, glancing around to ensure no one else could overhear. "We all know the river problem has nothing to do with you."

He leaned in closer and continued to offer his advice. "The river has deposited mud onto your garden, which technically belongs to the municipality and is on your land illegally. Your lawyer can demand its removal, and they would have to come and take it away. However, they will probably ignore the request, as they always do."

He explained that the bureaucracy always leads to delays or inaction. "You can set a time limit of ten days. If they fail to comply, you will have the right to remove it yourself," he suggested. "But, before you do anything, you must get a paper from the mayor's office granting you the authority. When you have the paper, no one can stop you. This paper is a formal permit providing legal protection and proof that you were acting within your rights. Once you have formal permission, even if the old woman screams, Alex can still play with her bulldozer," he added with a wry smile.

I couldn't wait to tell Alex the news. But she was still busy making the beach look nice.

The following day, we arranged a meeting with Sofia to discuss the issue of the mud in our garden. We explained that the mud technically belonged to the municipality and was illegally encroaching on our land.

Initially, Sofia appeared doubtful as we outlined our request. "You want to demand that the local council remove the mud from your property?" she asked, raising an eyebrow. Her scepticism was understandable, as getting local authorities to act promptly was impossible.

"We know that," Alex told her. "But this way, we can clear it ourselves legally without getting arrested again."

Sofia smiled knowingly. "I see now. Ingenious."

Sofia agreed to draft a formal demand letter to the local council. The letter would cite the relevant laws and emphasise their duty to maintain public waterways and remove natural debris from private properties. She planned to set a clear deadline for the council to respond and take action.

By taking this legal route, we aimed to ensure the council couldn't ignore our request. "Once the demand is in place, and if they fail to act within the given time frame, you'll have the right to remove the mud yourselves, with full legal backing," Sofia assured us.

We were slowly getting ahead of our legal troubles. Little victories were being achieved and were satisfying as we looked forward to more. Even though we had secretly proven our innocence, it was still likely that our case could go to court, so Sofia was still working on our defence.

We required witness statements for the changes in the river's course over the years. Sofia instructed us to talk to our friends and neighbours who were familiar with the river. She made it clear that these statements were not meant to condemn Nemesis. Instead, they would serve as background showing the historical record of the river's transformations from eye witnesses who lived here and knew the seasonal changes in direction, and had seen the flooding over the years. The statements would be used alongside the land surveyor's report. This would be the final piece of evidence which could be presented at any future court hearing. But this would have an additional benefit as it would be presented to the local authority to spur them on to do something about the river and hopefully come up with a solution, which everyone in the village wanted.

Nemesis had already provided a list of witnesses against us. There were only two names on the list. One was the old man we met at the police station when we were arrested. However, he had withdrawn his complaint, so we were unsure why his name was included. The other name was even more intriguing. It belonged to one of our neighbours who had Alzheimer's. But here's the catch – he was dead. He had passed away in an Athens hospital over a year ago. Unless Nemesis had supernatural abilities to communicate with the spirit world, this witness wouldn't be able to testify against us.

We reached out to our friends and neighbours for help. Our troubles had naturally become well known in the village. Everyone was talking about Nemesis and realised that they had been misled by malicious gossip.

Now that they knew the truth, the villagers were eager to help. They offered to contribute to our defence, sharing any information they had about the river and its natural flow. People began coming forward with stories, documents, and even old photographs that could help prove our innocence. They wanted to make up for their earlier suspicions and show us that we truly belonged in their community.

The captain's intervention had turned the tide in our favour, transforming suspicion into solidarity. The village rallied around us, ready to stand by our side and support us in any way they could.

Alex and I decided to invite everyone in our immediate area to a meeting at our home. They had all been affected by the river at some point. We wanted to gather as much support and as many statements in our defence as possible. On the day of the meeting, we set up our patio for the gathering. We brought in extra chairs from the dining room and arranged them in a circle around the table to ensure everyone felt included.

The patio was fresh and airy. It offered a view of our muddy garden and had banks of earth piled high. The damage was visible for everyone to see. We hoped that with the evidence right in front of them, people would realise the suffering we had endured. On a side table, we had refreshments set up, including coffee, tea, beer and ouzo. Plates of pastries from the local bakery were arranged. Despite the seriousness of the situation, the atmosphere was warm and welcoming. Alex and I had personally knocked on each neighbour's door. We invited them to join us and briefly explained the situation, asking for their support. Everyone we spoke to was more than willing to help and showed genuine concern.

As our neighbours arrived, they filled the chairs, chatting quietly among themselves. Our lawyer and land surveyor sat at opposite ends of the table, their faces serious but approachable.

Twelve of our neighbours came to support us. Seeing so many smiling faces eager to help was touching. They knew we had been falsely accused, and their presence showed a united front. It was unthinkable for one of their own to go against their beliefs in hospitality and kindness to strangers, especially a foreigner. They felt ashamed that we had been treated so unfairly and were determined to assist us as much as possible.

As everyone settled in, Alex stood up to open the meeting.

"Thank you all for coming," she began, her voice steady but filled with emotion. "Your support means everything to us."

After she finished, she nodded towards Ajax, inviting him to speak. Ajax stood up, adjusting his glasses. His presence commanded attention, and everyone fell silent.

"I appreciate everyone being here today," Ajax said, his voice clear and authoritative. "We're here to discuss the situation and gather your statements about the river, and in doing so to support Alex and her husband. This is not just about defending them, but also about standing up for our community values."

He paused, looking around, making eye contact with each person. "If anyone has any questions or observations, now is the time to speak up."

Ajax asked the first question, breaking the ice. "Can anyone share if they've noticed any changes in the river's flow over the past few months?"

Maria raised her hand and began to speak. "I've lived here for twenty years, and I can tell you the river has always been unpredictable. But I've never seen anything like this before. It wasn't their fault."

Her statement was met with nods of agreement. Each neighbour took turns sharing their observations and support, their voices filled with sincerity and conviction. They spoke about the river, the sudden changes, and how they had seen nothing that could implicate us in causing the flooding.

As the meeting went on, the sense of community and solidarity grew stronger. Ajax and our lawyer took notes, asking follow-up questions and guiding the conversation.

"Does anyone here believe that Alex or Peter could have done anything to cause the river to burst its banks? If so, put your hand up," Ajax said.

Not one hand rose. Our neighbour George was the first to speak.

"Listen to me," he said. "The flood had a severe impact on me. I lost all my garden furniture, and my outbuildings were wrecked. The damage amounted to thousands of euros. If I believed they were responsible, I would have been the first to file a complaint. So, no, I won't be raising my hand."

I smiled at George and nodded my thanks as the next neighbour spoke. Her name was Athina, and she owned a house a few doors down from us. Athina was a kind and friendly neighbour. I had seen her around but we had never officially met until now. As she started speaking, I couldn't help but notice her warm smile and gentle disposition.

She began by expressing her gratitude for the sense of community that we all shared. Athina mentioned how she appreciated the support and camaraderie among our friends, which made our neighbourhood feel like a close-knit family.

Listening to Athina, I couldn't help but feel a sense of pride. It was evident that she genuinely cared about the well-being of everyone living here. She mentioned how she loved the peacefulness and tranquillity of our village, and how it had become a true sanctuary for her.

Athina also touched upon her love for gardening. She shared stories of how the flooding had affected her garden.

"I too had lots of damage. This river has always been a problem. It's nothing to do with them. It's the other houses down there that are blocking it. It can't go anywhere. So it just flows through our houses and gardens."

It had transformed her garden into a terrible mess, losing her plants and garden furniture and ruining her once beautiful garden. "I'm happy we are meeting," she said. "It is long past the time when the river should have been fixed."

As she continued speaking, Athina emphasised the importance of helping one another. She highlighted the numerous times she had witnessed acts of kindness within our community, from lending a helping hand to offering a listening ear. Her words resonated with me, reminding me of the lovely people of the village who had already given us so much.

As the meeting continued, more neighbours shared their

experiences and concerns. Each story painted a clearer picture; the river had been a persistent issue for many years, long before we arrived. The recent storm of the century had only made things worse, highlighting the existing problems and the need for a solution.

Sofia moved around the table, speaking with each person individually. She asked pointed questions, her pen moving swiftly across her notebook as she recorded every detail. Her meticulous nature was evident as she carefully noted down their statements, ensuring that nothing was missed. Each statement was then securely filed away.

The atmosphere was one of solidarity and shared purpose. Our neighbours' willingness to help and their collective testimony provided a powerful counter to the false accusations we faced. As the meeting drew to a close, Alex stood up once more, her voice filled with emotion.

"Thank you all for your support," she said. "Your kindness and willingness to stand with us mean more than words can express. Together, we will overcome this challenge, and maybe this will finally encourage the council to do its duty and protect us in the future."

The meeting ended with a sense of accomplishment and hope. As our neighbours began to leave, many of them stopped to offer a few final words of encouragement. Alex and I stood by the door, thanking each one personally.

Once everyone had left, Alex turned to me, her eyes shining with determination. "We've got this," she said firmly.

We were already aware that we had done nothing wrong,

but it felt wonderful to have the support of our friends and neighbours. We also knew that this meeting of twelve people would not keep it secret. They would go their separate ways, visiting others in the village to spread the word. This would go far, dispelling any lingering doubts other villagers may have had about our guilt. Then they would all focus their anger on where it truly belonged.

Nemesis would soon be in big trouble.

Our lawyer had presented our request to have the mud removed from our land ten days previously. As expected, it was ignored. We collected the document from Sofia and brought it to the mayor's office. The official read the request and confirmed that the council did not contest it or take any action to comply. As a result, he stamped it, granting us permission to remove the mud ourselves.

This victory was significant. It allowed Alex to use her new bulldozer and finish reclaiming our garden. I warned her not to disturb the river. It was still illegal to disrupt the river's flow, wherever it may be. The river had already changed its course multiple times since the flood. It now cut diagonally across our land, no longer marking our boundary. We still needed to keep away from it. However, both banks were now part of our garden.

I sat on the patio while Alex climbed into the cab. The roar of the diesel engine radiated across the garden as the beast came to life. Alex's smiling face radiated pleasure as she engaged the gears and trundled away from me to begin her project.

The sun glimmered brightly overhead as Alex skilfully manoeuvred the bulldozer through the garden, effortlessly turning the soil with each pass. The sound of the engine hummed in the air, mingling with the crisp breeze that rustled the leaves of nearby trees. As the bulldozer moved, clouds of dust billowed up, creating a mesmerising dance in the sunlight. It was evident that Alex had a deep connection with the land, as if the earth responded to her touch, eagerly awaiting transformation.

Then, over the sound of the engines, came the expected scream. Nemesis had heard the bulldozer from her house and had come to investigate. Her voice reverberated through the air, filled with triumph. Her eyes gleamed with satisfaction as she pointed an accusing finger at Alex. "I have you now," she screeched, her voice laced with anger and vindication. "You know the police banned you from touching this land, don't you? And now, by doing this, you're in even bigger trouble."

Alex switched off the engine and calmly exited the cab. Clutched tightly in her hand was a photocopy of the official document granting us the authorisation to clear our land. She extended it towards Nemesis, who swiftly snatched it from Alex's grasp and scanned the contents.

She was furious. "It can't be. This is wrong! You're blocking the river again, you're breaking the law. This document means nothing. I'm going to the police. You will be sorry." She tore the document into pieces and threw it in front of a grinning Alex.

"You are trespassing again," Alex told the furious old woman. "If you don't get off my land now, this bulldozer may accidentally bury your evil bones in the river. Now, I have told you before. Fuck off."

Alex calmly climbed back into the cab, started the engine, and continued to make our garden beautiful again.

The old lady's complaints went unheeded; the police never came. Nemesis was at last beginning to see her plans for us unravelling. But unknown to her, we were only getting started. We were quickly gaining the upper hand, and the consequences for her could be devastating.

After that confrontation, everything went quiet on the Nemesis front.

Stamos and his team pressed on with the rebuilding. Over the next few weeks, they constructed sturdy stone walls – not just for decoration, but as much-needed flood protection. He laid intricate stone paving, replacing what was once plain lawn with beautifully crafted spaces.

Around each tree, he created small, raised garden beds, blending them seamlessly into the new landscape. The thick layers of silt and mud were too extensive to remove entirely, so Stamos worked with it, incorporating the higher ground into his design. The result was not just practical but striking, with elevated seating areas that gave us a fresh perspective on our surroundings.

To tie it all together, he added a series of tiered patios, connected by ornate stone staircases. What had once been a battered, mud-covered garden was now transformed into a space full of character, depth and unexpected beauty.

The result of Stamos's labour was a harmonious blend of nature and human craftsmanship. The meticulously constructed walls, the intricate stone paving, and the thoughtfully designed seating areas and patios transformed the landscape into a masterpiece. Now, we could revel in the beauty of the surroundings while enjoying the comfort and elegance of the newly created spaces.

The electrician had been busy collaborating with Stamos to install fresh cables within the walls and beneath the solid concrete floors. Above us, the trees were adorned with radiant lights, casting a gentle glow. At ground level, pavement lights illuminated the area from below, creating a captivating sight. Along the perimeter, wall lights emitted a soft, warm glow, embracing our garden with a myriad of enchanting hues.

Our new garden was a dream. It far surpassed our previous space. Instead of a natural oasis, it now resembled an enormous extension of our living room. We kept the wilder part of the garden, which was now farther back on the other side of our new walls, roughly as it was. This area was always at risk of flooding, so we decided not to build anything permanent. Instead, we simply laid grass and added a few more trees.

The gods had presented us with a challenge, and we rose to the occasion. The devastation inflicted upon our beautiful Greek island home had been truly heart-wrenching. We had endured months filled with stress, anger and worry. However, the outcome was here, right before our eyes. This dramatic chapter in our lives ultimately became a blessing. We were satisfied with our home before, but due to necessity, we were compelled to rebuild – and this time, it turned out even better.

Nemesis was important in building our determination. If it weren't for the constant fear of legal battles and the delays and suffering caused by her, we might have just levelled the land and planted more grass seeds. Our new masterpiece, which had unfolded before our eyes, would not exist.

But we were not yet ready to raise our glasses in a toast to Nemesis. We still had unfinished business.

CHAPTER 16
The Turning Tide

Prefer a loss to a dishonest gain; the one brings pain at the moment, the other for all time.

– Chilon of Sparta

Our garden was finally finished, but we needed to buy new furniture as everything had been lost in the floods. Our village had everything we needed, except for shops that sold garden furniture. Alex suggested that we go back to Glyfada for a few days to do some shopping.

Because Glyfada had become a booming city over the past few years, its impersonal nature was somehow strangely refreshing. We only realised how exhausted we were when we sat on our terrace roof in our Glyfada home. From there, we could see the blue Aegean Sea beyond the buildings. We watched the ferries leaving white lines in the sea as they departed from the port of Piraeus to reach Greek islands nearby and far away. We knew that no visitors would come to disturb our peace. The phone wouldn't ring with demands for our company at a nearby taverna. We were unlikely to be bothered by screeching old ladies, and it was highly improbable that we would be arrested today. It was just perfect.

With the influx of tourists and new residents, Glyfada offered a refreshing sense of freedom. The anonymity of the crowds and the vibrant pace of city life allowed us to escape the constant scrutiny of Pefki. In Glyfada, we could walk unnoticed through the bustling streets, blending in with the flow of urban energy. Here, we felt an exhilarating release from the village's watchful eyes and endless curiosity.

Back in Pefki, our battles with Nemesis had turned us into a local spectacle, fuelling gossip and speculation. But in Glyfada, there was no expectation, no pressure – just the simple joy of being anonymous. For a while, we left the stir of village drama behind and relished the peace of urban obscurity.

On Sofia's advice, we hadn't shared the reports from our lawyer and land surveyor proving our innocence with anyone. The village still believed that we were in legal trouble. We kept our cards hidden to prevent Nemesis from realising her impending failure. We wanted her to believe she had the upper hand and remain determined for what she considered justice. Our aim was to trap her.

After a few days, we felt rejuvenated and ready to visit Leroy Merlin, the biggest supplier of garden furniture in Athens.

Our priority was a new dining set for the patio, where we

loved to enjoy evening meals under the stars. We picked out a sturdy yet elegant wicker and glass-topped table, accompanied by matching chairs with weather-resistant cushions. The wicker promised durability and a touch of natural charm, perfectly suited for our island home.

Next, we turned our attention to creating a cosy lounging area. We chose a large, comfortable sofa with plush, washable cushions. The sofa was modular, allowing us to rearrange the pieces to fit our needs, whether we were hosting friends or just relaxing with a book.

To add a splash of colour and a bit of flair, we selected a set of bright outdoor rugs and scatter cushions in shades of blue and green, reflecting the sea and sky. We also picked out a couple of stylish sun loungers with adjustable backs, perfect for sunbathing or taking an afternoon nap in the shade.

No Greek garden would be complete without a spot for enjoying a morning coffee or an evening drink. For this, we found a charming bistro set – a small round table with two matching chairs, ideal for tucking into a quiet corner of the garden.

We also considered practicality and convenience. A large, weatherproof storage box would keep our cushions and garden tools safe from the elements. Finally, to add ambiance and ensure we could enjoy our garden day and night, we selected a variety of outdoor lighting. String lights to drape across the stone arch, solar-powered path lights to illuminate the walkways, and a few elegant lanterns to place around the seating areas.

After making our selections, we arranged for everything to be delivered to the island. Leroy Merlin's delivery service was efficient, and they assured us that our new garden furniture would arrive promptly. As we left the store, we felt a renewed sense of excitement and anticipation. Our garden was on its way to becoming a beautiful, welcoming sanctuary once again.

Then Sofia called to tell us that Ajax had finished the report and the topographical study. It had been submitted to the land registry. Now it had an official stamp of approval, it became a legally binding document.

Sofia wanted us to understand our options and determine if we were ready to launch a legal attack on our nemesis. The sun was setting and a warm, golden glow radiated over the island as we arrived on the ferry from the mainland. The journey had been long, and we were both anxious and eager to get to Sofia's office.

We drove straight from the port, navigating the winding roads that led to the heart of the village. The streets were quiet, with only a few locals strolling about, enjoying the cool evening breeze. As we pulled up to Sofia's office, the last light of day was fading, and the streetlights began to flicker on, casting long shadows on the cobblestones.

Inside Sofia's office, the atmosphere was markedly different. The fluorescent lights hummed softly, illuminating the room with a stark, almost clinical brightness. Sofia sat behind her desk, her expression serious yet welcoming. She gestured for us to take a seat.

Ajax was already there, waiting for us with a thick pile

of documents. The papers were neatly organised, each one representing a piece of the complex puzzle we were about to tackle. He looked up as we entered, giving us a nod of acknowledgement.

"Good evening," Sofia began, her voice calm and reassuring. "I wanted to go over our options and see if you're ready to move forward with a legal attack."

We settled into our chairs, the tension in the room palpable. Ajax spread the documents out on the table before us, his meticulous nature evident in the careful arrangement of papers.

"These are the reports, statements and evidence we've gathered," Ajax said, tapping the top of the stack. "It's all here for you to read through."

Sofia leaned forward, her eyes scanning our faces. "We need to decide our next steps carefully. This isn't just about defending yourselves any more; it's about holding her accountable for the damage she's caused."

The gravity of the situation was clear. We spent the next few hours poring over the documents, guided by Ajax's detailed explanations and Sofia's strategic insights. The clock on the wall ticked steadily, marking the passage of time as we delved deeper into the case.

We read and digested the information diligently assembled in our complete legal report: a comprehensive analysis of our case, including all relevant statutes, regulations and precedents. The report also contained in-depth research on similar cases and potential strategies. By the end, we were more than impressed by the work Ajax and Sofia had done. They had proved beyond any legal doubt that all the complaints and charges brought against us were completely unfounded, and the case against us would likely be dismissed immediately.

Not only would the documents completely clear our names, but they would be damning to Nemesis.

Ajax pointed out that building her house had changed the course of the river, but it didn't block it, just redirected it. This act was illegal, but she was granted permission. However, it seemed that the permission was obtained through back channels. The local planning office would never have issued formal permission, although we couldn't prove it yet. To investigate further, Sofia would need to examine the official records and identify those involved in approving the plans. It would be a lengthy process, but she was determined to uncover the truth in the end if we wanted to go that far.

But something had been proven without any doubt: long before our house was built and our land developed, Nemesis had constructed a concrete wall across the natural path of the river. This wall didn't just divert the river, it completely blocked it, creating a dead end. Ajax and Sofia had searched the official planning records and found no evidence that she ever received permission for that construction. She had gone ahead anyway. Building the house had diverted the river, but building the garden wall had blocked it.

She had caused the water to back up and overflow into our community. The excess water had nowhere to go, leading to flooding that engulfed our homes and neighbouring farmland.

The floods had destroyed years of hard work and investment, leaving many of us with significant damage. It became clear that the construction of Nemesis's wall was the direct cause of our catastrophic floods.

Not only had she subjected us to months of pain and suffering, but she had also tried to strip the local tradesmen of their means of living just because they were helping us. She caused our arrest and the detainment of our bulldozer driver; she spread deceitful allegations and toxic rumours designed to alienate the entire village from us. But she failed in her ultimate ambition. We would not be convicted as common criminals. We now had the tools to turn everything against her.

We had realised the potential risks from the beginning when we first exposed a dry ditch in our garden. I walked upstream and saw the size of the wide and deep river's course. When I returned, I found level land and the end of the river. It was clear to anyone that there could be future problems. Even during our worst troubles, we could point and say, "Look, it's obvious we didn't cause this." However, legally, common sense is not a defence. We had to provide proof. Finally, common sense needed the aid of an expensive lawyer and land surveyor. It was no longer just an opinion or observation. It was now a proven fact, officially documented, and it would be upheld in any court.

But how would we use our new power? Sofia began to explain our options.

Alex shook her head in frustration. "I can't believe she did this, then blamed us. All our hard work … gone."

"I know," I said, my voice tinged with anger. "It's infuriating. We knew this all along, but now we can prove it. We have to stay focused."

"We have the evidence we need," said Sofia. "Ajax's report clearly shows how the wall caused the water to back up. We can prove it in court."

This meant that we could not only demand the removal of her unlawfully constructed wall, but also seek compensation for the damage to our home. Also, if we chose to further investigate her initial planning consent, we might be able to establish that her house was unlawfully built and demand its demolition.

But for the river to be restored to its natural course, other houses would have to go too. These people had innocently purchased dry building land, which was reclaimed from the river by the meddling of Nemesis. They had no idea they were inadvertently part of the drama which had occurred further upstream. They didn't even realise they had built their homes on an old river course. If we were determined to have our revenge against Nemesis, they would also suffer.

Indeed, I had endured my fair share of anger and frustration towards Nemesis. The power to get even was now within my grasp, a tempting prospect after all we had suffered. But as Sofia and Ajax continued to explain the full extent of her wrongdoing, I found my thoughts drifting. I pictured her not as the scheming, vindictive woman who had caused us so much harm, but as the bitter, lonely old woman she truly was. Her constant meddling, her baseless accusations – what had driven her to this? Had her life been so empty and joyless that tormenting us had become her only purpose?

A sense of pity began to stir, softening my anger. For all her malice, what did she really have? No community rallying behind her, no friends coming to her aid. Just an isolated existence, defined by resentment and spite. Was she truly an enemy, or was she a sad figure, clinging to whatever power she thought she still had?

Later that evening, Alex and I sat on the patio, the night air cool and still, the sky speckled with stars. As we sipped our wine, the pressure of the day hung between us. "I can't stop thinking about her," I admitted, breaking the silence. "All this time, I've been so angry, but … can't you see it? She's just a bitter, sad old woman. I thought winning would feel better than this."

Alex set her glass down, her expression thoughtful. "I've been thinking the same," she said. "At first, I wanted to bury her face-down in the river mud for what she's done to us. But now, all I see is someone whose life is already miserable enough. What would destroying her really accomplish?"

We talked late into the night, sharing our feelings and debating the choices before us. By the time we headed inside, we had reached a decision. Not from a place of weakness or reluctance, but from a deeper understanding of what true strength and justice really meant. Forgiveness wasn't just for her; it was for us, too. A way to finally move on and reclaim the peace that Nemesis had tried to steal from us.

If we were to exercise our rights and pursue this matter

to its ultimate conclusion, we could strip her of everything she possessed, potentially rendering her homeless and utterly destitute. This realisation weighed heavily on our conscience.

As we stood at this crossroads, we realised that true strength lies not in the ability to cause harm, but in the capacity to show compassion and mercy. Despite the suffering we had endured, we had no right to destroy another human being out of vengeance.

In that moment, we made a choice to let go of our desire for retribution and instead look for a way to defuse the situation. She had started a war, but we were prepared to end it.

Our home had not only been restored to its former glory thanks to the wonderful ladies of the village, but thanks to the recent improvements of the outdoor areas, it had surpassed our wildest expectations.

It had been expensive. Legal costs, surveyor's fees and building work had left us without savings. But we had been poor before, so that didn't worry us.

That evening, after our long discussion on the patio, Alex and I both felt lighter, as though some of the emotional burden we'd been carrying for months had started to lift. Forgiveness wouldn't erase what Nemesis had done, but it would allow us to take back control of our lives.

The next morning over coffee, Alex suggested we call Sofia. "Let's make it official," she said. "There's no point letting this drag on any longer."

I nodded in agreement, and a few moments later, I dialled Sofia's number. She picked up almost immediately, her voice calm and professional. "Good morning. What's the update?"

"We've made a decision," I said. "We don't want to escalate things further. Please go ahead and submit our final defence to the prosecutors. Once they see Ajax's report, the case should collapse. That's all we want, for it to be over."

There was a pause on the line, as if Sofia were processing our words. "I see," she said finally. "You're sure about this? You're not planning to pursue anything else?"

"We're sure," Alex chimed in. "We've been through enough. All we want now is to move forward and leave this behind us."

Sofia's tone softened. "I think you're making the right choice. I'll file everything this afternoon. Once the prosecutors review the evidence, I expect the charges will be dropped quickly. I'll let you know as soon as I hear back."

"Thank you, Sofia," I said. "For everything."

After we hung up, Alex and I exchanged a look. The phone call felt like a turning point. Not just legally, but emotionally. By choosing to end the fight, we were finally taking back our peace.

Sofia assured us that once the prosecutors received it, the case would likely be closed. A court case would go nowhere. Ultimately, Nemesis would receive a copy of our documents. That should scare her when she understood the implications of our investigations.

If we claimed against this old lady, knowing ourselves we would carry the burden of regret and self-blame for the rest of our lives. All we wanted was to be left alone to enjoy our village paradise and continue our lives in this beautiful part of

Greece. But would she let us be?

We had to make sure she was aware of the danger she was facing, but without resorting to legal action. Once a complaint had been made against her, it would be out of our hands, as the Greek legal system would take over. So how would we let her know?

CHAPTER 17

The Olive Branch Strategy

There is no forgiveness, only forgivingness. There is a benevolent willingness to understand how it is that people cannot help doing bad things, because they are ignorant or irrational, or are overwhelmed by untamed or negative forces within them.

The cool morning breeze rustled the leaves as we sat on our patio, nestled in our comfortable wicker chairs, savouring steaming cups of coffee. The serene beauty of the surrounding nature provided a calming backdrop for our intense brainstorming session. The sun's rays filtered through the lush green canopy, casting dappled shadows on the table, adding an almost ethereal quality to our contemplative space.

As we exchanged thoughtful glances, the burden of our next move hung heavily in the air. We both knew its significance – it could either bring us closer to the village or alienate us completely. The silence was palpable, punctuated only by the occasional chirping of birds. Time seemed to stand still as we delved deep into our thoughts, contemplating various possibilities and weighing up their potential risks and rewards.

Nemesis had proven herself to be both nasty and vindictive. Her constant interference in our lives had caused us untold worry and sadness. We could no longer continue living under the scrutiny of someone whose sole intention seemed to be to destroy us and drive us away. Her actions had cost us a fortune in legal fees and surveyor costs, compounding the disaster of the flooding many times over and striking us at our weakest moment.

"She really knows how to hit where it hurts," Alex murmured, breaking the silence, her eyes reflecting the turmoil we both felt. "Every time we thought we had made progress, she found a way to set us back."

I nodded, taking a deep breath. "If she ever has the opportunity to make our lives more miserable in the future, we can be sure she'll seize it with relish."

We fell silent again, the gravity of our situation settling over us like a heavy blanket. The papers on the table before us were not just evidence, they were our lifeline, our means of fighting back against the relentless storm Nemesis had unleashed upon us.

"We need to be strategic," I said. "This isn't just about winning a battle; it's about reclaiming our peace and our lives."

Alex leaned forward, her eyes narrowing with determination. "We can't let her drive us out. We need to scare her off.

But how?"

Our resolve strengthened, we continued our planning, the cool breeze and peaceful surroundings contrasting sharply with the intensity of our discussion. We knew the road ahead would be fraught with challenges, but we were determined to face them head-on. The future of our home and our place in the village depended on it.

As the morning wore on, our strategy took shape, each point meticulously planned and noted. The sun climbed higher in the sky, its warmth a reminder that despite the shadows Nemesis had cast over our lives, there was still light to be found.

"We need to make sure she understands the danger she's facing. But we can't risk getting the legal system involved," Alex told me.

"I know," I replied. "Once a complaint is filed, it's out of our hands. The Greek legal system will take over, and who knows where that will lead?"

"So, how do we let her know without making it official?"

"Easy. We tell Maria." I laughed. "Then we make sure the news will spread by telling her to keep it to herself."

"That will do the trick." Alex giggled.

Alex called Maria and invited her for a coffee and to tell her our latest news. Maria arrived within three minutes, eager for some fresh gossip.

I made a coffee and brought three cups to the table. Alex glanced around to make sure no one else was nearby. "Maria, we need to talk to you about something important. But it has to stay between us. Do you promise?"

Maria raised an eyebrow. "Sounds serious. You have my word. I won't tell a soul. What's going on?"

Alex lowered her voice and leaned towards Maria. "Our lawyer has told us that we have the right to demand Nemesis's house be removed to free the river."

"Wow." Maria looked at us wide-eyed. "Really? That would be a huge deal. Are you actually going to do it?"

Alex shared a quick look with me. "Let's just say we're angry enough to. And it would certainly be an end to the problems with the river. All our neighbours would be safe from it in the future. We're not doing this out of spite or revenge. We just want to protect our home, and we can't really see another way."

I could see Maria's mind working. This was the best gossip she had ever heard. As gossip goes, it was the Olympic gold medal winner. But she had foolishly agreed not to tell anybody. Yet this was far too good to keep to herself. She had been at ground zero and heard the plans directly from the horse's mouth. Something as monumental as this just had to be shared with the village.

She smiled and stood up from the table, leaving her coffee half finished. Her usual visits lasted over two hours; this time she had only been here for a few moments. She looked like she was about to explode.

"I've just remembered I need something from the village shop. Do you need anything?" she asked.

"No," Alex replied. "But remember to keep this conversation secret."

"Then tha vgálo áchna (I won't breathe a word)," she told

Alex as she hurried towards the village.

The plan worked. Maria, being the gossip of our village, could spread information faster than a wildfire. We just needed to bide our time and wait.

Rumours of Nemesis's wrongdoings had been circulating for weeks, fuelling the anger and resentment of the villagers. Whispers of her mistreatment of others, especially her abuse of the cardinal rule of Greek hospitality, were on everyone's lips. She had upset the foreigners, and for that crime, there was no forgiveness.

The Greek god Zeus is sometimes referred to as Zeus Xenios because he played the role of protector of strangers. In ancient times, treating a stranger poorly was considered a sin, as hospitality was always extended regardless of social class or wealth. In modern-day Greek language, many words have roots derived from the term "xeno". Kindness to the xeno is a way of life that Greeks have cherished and practised for centuries.

The term "filoxenia" means "friend to stranger" in literal translation. However, its true meaning extends beyond mere hospitality. It embodies the act of helping lost strangers by inviting them to accompany you on your own journey and guiding them to their desired destination. In a village, if while walking you encounter someone working in their garden, they may invite you into their home for a cup of coffee, which often leads to dinner, wine and conversation. Often, these encounters lead to lifelong friendships.

Nemesis had violated this sacred tradition. Her actions

were more than just personal attacks against us – they were an affront to the very essence of Greek culture. She had broken the first rule of Greek hospitality, and in doing so had dishonoured the spirit of filoxenia. She had failed to extend kindness and respect to the xeno, choosing instead to spread malice and discord.

In Greek culture, the gods highlight the importance of respect by demonstrating the consequences of breaking xenia. If someone violates xenia, the gods will punish them by either striking them down or cursing them. The villagers understood this well, and their growing disdain for Nemesis was rooted in the knowledge that her actions had invited divine retribution.

As the sun dipped below the horizon, it became clear that Nemesis's days of unchecked tyranny were numbered. The community, bound by a shared sense of justice and the ancient traditions of their ancestors, stood united against her. The message was unmistakable: those who dishonour the sacred laws of hospitality and kindness will face the consequences, both from their fellow villagers and from the gods themselves.

As our carefully crafted gossip reached the old men at the kafenio, it of course became distorted and exaggerated, taking on a life of its own. The story now claimed that a fleet of menacing bulldozers was en route to Nemesis's house, with the sole purpose of razing it to the ground. The anticipation among the townspeople grew, with eager faces lining the streets, yearning to witness the downfall of the troublesome old woman who had tormented them for far too long.

We had no such intention. But our plan to spread the

rumour around the village to scare her off seemed to be gaining traction.

We let the gossip simmer and mature for two days, until it was ready to be savoured, like a fine wine. Villagers were keen to pump us for information, offering mezes and glasses of tsipouro in an attempt to get us to talk. It was surprising that no one defended Nemesis. Everyone wanted to see the bulldozers come and demolish her house. They had all been affected by her malice or knew of others who had suffered because of her.

The old men of the kafenio were clearly trusted more than us, though. They seemed to have all the answers, but we didn't mind. The gossip must have filtered through to Nemesis by now. We were curious about how she was feeling. It was time to execute the next part of our plan.

We had to be sure of our next step. We had no intention of taking the matter any further, but it was important for our own sanity that we could calm things down and at last enjoy our life in the village. This meant ensuring Nemesis would be disarmed and lose all her power over us and everyone else. Our reluctance to take the matter further might not save her in the end, anyway. Once our land surveyor's report was available, it would be a public document available for all to read. People of the village who she had abused over the years might take a different view and use it to take their own revenge. But this was out of our control. She had forced this upon us with her unfounded charges against us. We had been instructed by the police to provide an independent report because of the charges she brought against us. It was an unfathomable act of stupidity.

She must have realised that her actions would necessitate a full-scale enquiry of not only our home, but others near the river. But she seemed blinded by her rage, and logic had become a stranger to her.

In my home country of England, family matters are normally discussed over a cup of tea. Here, when Alex and I need to discuss something important, we do it Greek-style. This involves large plates of food and wine, concluding with sticky sweets. It was crowded when we arrived at Balarourus's taverna. This meant we needed to pass several tables before we found an available one.

As we walked past other diners, they looked up from their meals and smiled. Some were familiar faces, while others were strangers. A man I had never met before stood up, shook my hand, smiled and sat back down. By the time we reached our table, several people had greeted us. Alex even received a kiss on the cheek. We started to feel like celebrities. It seemed that we had unintentionally become heroes in the village. We had confronted the wicked witch, and it appeared to the villagers that we had emerged victorious, without being turned into toads.

As we took our seats, Mr Balarourus arrived at our table with a jug of wine and two glasses.

"It's from the mayor," he told us and waved his hand towards a nearby table.

We looked in the direction of the wave and recognised Athanasios, our mayor, who was sitting with three other men. As I raised my hand in thanks, he rose from his chair and made his way to our table.

"Yahsoo Peter, yahsoo Alex. I'm glad I bumped into you. What a coincidence! I was just about to visit you at your house," he said. "I have some great news for you."

Alex glanced at him, refraining from offering a smile or greeting, sensing that he had ulterior motives. The broken promises he had made were unforgivable. It was based on his assurance that we had proceeded to construct a barrier as a safeguard against the river. When Marily had attempted to reach him from the police cell, he deliberately ignored her call. After our arrest, he had vanished from our lives. He had never answered our calls or returned our messages. Now, here he was, standing at our table as if nothing had happened.

The phrase "Timeō Danaōs et dōna ferentēs" is from a Latin epic poem written by Virgil. It is spoken by Trojan priest Laocoön. He expresses his fear of the Greeks, even when they come bearing gifts. This is in reference to the Trojan Horse that was used by the Greeks during the Trojan War. We needed to be on our guard here, but we were still curious to hear his "great news".

Alex pouted as I offered him a seat at our table. He sat and began to speak.

He told us that after the flooding, he knew our house was the worst affected in the village. "I couldn't just sit back and do nothing. I knew something had to be done. When the Greek government's minister of the interior announced a visit to assess the damage in North Evia, I saw an opportunity. I arranged for the minister's tour to include a stop at your house."

He sat back in his chair to allow us to absorb this

information.

"I wanted to make sure the minister saw the full extent of the devastation," he explained. "Your home was a perfect example of the damage that was done."

As he recounted the day, his eyes lit up with pride. "I intentionally took the minister to your house. I guided him through the flooded rooms, pointing out the soaked furniture, the ruined walls and the muddy floors. I showed him how the water had reached almost to the ceiling in some places."

This was news to us. We had no idea we had received a ministerial visit. Why was he telling us all this now? He must have been aware of our legal troubles. He certainly knew we had been arrested. It was only a phone call to let us know what was going on.

The mayor smiled and continued with his account.

"I could see the horror in his eyes as he walked through your home," he continued. "He kept shaking his head, unable to comprehend the level of destruction. I made sure to tell him about the years of hard work you had put into making that house a home."

He paused, looking at us intently. "Because of what he saw, because of your story, the minister was moved to take action. He understood that this wasn't just about property damage – it was about people's lives being turned upside down."

He proudly explained that because of his efforts, the minister left our village with a clear picture of the dire situation. "Last week, the government held an emergency meeting. The minister shared what he had seen, and they quickly approved funding to reroute the river. They knew they couldn't let this happen again."

His voice softened. "I know it doesn't make up for what you went through, but I hope it brings you some comfort to know that your suffering led to real change. The new river route will prevent future floods from devastating all the homes near the river. It's all because of you. We begin work next month." He leaned back in his chair, giving us time to process what he'd said.

We suspected the mayor's motives. On the surface, it seemed like good news. The rerouting of the river would mean it would never torment us again. We would be safe, even if we were subjected to another storm of the same force. However, we couldn't shake the feeling that the mayor might have had his own agenda. His eagerness to showcase our home to the minister seemed a bit too convenient. Was he using our misfortune to gain favour or political leverage? The mayor's sudden interest in our plight, after months of indifference, raised more questions than it answered.

Even as he spoke with pride about the government's decision, we wondered if there was more to the story. Had he truly been moved by our suffering, or was this just a strategic move to secure funding and improve his standing with the government? We couldn't tell for sure, but the doubts lingered.

As he finished his tale, we exchanged glances, silently agreeing to stay cautious. While the rerouting of the river was undoubtedly a positive development, we knew better than to take everything at face value. We would remain vigilant, keeping a close eye on how things unfolded, aware that not all good news comes without strings attached.

We thanked Athanasios. Alex gave him a weak smile, and I shook his hand, expecting him to leave our table now he had delivered the news. But he remained seated.

There were a few seconds of awkward silence before he spoke again.

"How are your legal troubles?" he asked. "I hear they may be resolved."

"Fine, thank you," Alex replied. "No thanks to you."

The mayor looked down into the wine jug, refusing to meet Alex's accusing stare.

"But Alex, as mayor, I cannot get involved with individual squabbles. I must rise above this. I was powerless to assist in this matter."

"I was not asking you to take sides," Alex told him. "All I wanted was for you to confirm you gave us permission to build the protection. That was all. But you let us down." Indeed, I had filmed the exchange at the village meeting in front of hundreds of people. "When asked to confirm it to the police, you stood back and let us take the consequences."

"I'm truly sorry, Alex. It was a difficult time for everyone. I made mistakes; you made mistakes. Nobody is perfect."

Alex thawed. She had received a long overdue apology. She smiled, took his hand and squeezed it gently in a sign of forgiveness.

"But now I hear you are thinking about taking drastic action," he said. "Please think before you do something you regret. Nemesis is an old lady who has lost her marbles. She can't hurt you any more. I have even spoken to the police, who have agreed to ignore her ravings in the future. Let's just let it be and move on."

He had no idea what we were planning to do. Nobody did. But it was clear that Nemesis had friends in high places. Threats and legal charges against us had backfired against her. Now she was panicking and had clearly sent the mayor to reason with us.

"Do you realise what she has cost us?" Alex said. "It's not only about the money. She made our lives a misery. Now you want to reason with us, but where were you during our darkest moments? Who is going to foot the bill? You? The government? Of course not."

The mayor leaned in, his tone shifting from casual to earnest. "Alex, I know you have suffered," he began, his voice heavy with concern. "But I've heard you're considering some really serious legal action. You may be within your rights to proceed legally, but think of the damage to the village. So many people could lose their homes. It would be devastating."

He scanned our faces for understanding, and we could sense the weight of the responsibility he was placing on our shoulders. "I understand that what you've been through is unimaginable. The flooding, the loss, the heartache – it's all real, and it's unfair. But taking legal action against Nemesis could have far-reaching consequences beyond your immediate situation. If the court rules in your favour and decides that the house must be torn down, it won't just affect Nemesis. Innocent families who have lived here for years could find themselves homeless overnight."

He gestured to the people sitting in the taverna. "This village is more than just buildings and streets. It's the people, the relationships, the history. Legal battles can tear all of that apart. We could see neighbours turning against each other, long-standing friendships broken, and a sense of mistrust and resentment seeping into every corner."

Alex and I exchanged glances. We knew he was right about the potential for widespread impact. But he had no idea of our plans, so we just nodded along and looked thoughtful.

"But, Athanasios," Alex said, "our home was at the epicentre of this disaster, and Nemesis's actions pushed us to the brink. If we let this go, she will be crawling up our arses for the rest of our lives."

The mayor leaned back, his expression softening. "I'm not saying you shouldn't seek justice. You deserve that much. But maybe there's a way to resolve this without causing more harm. A way to find a solution that protects everyone, not just your interests."

He sighed deeply, the strain clear in his eyes. Although we had no intention of doing anything to harm the village, our plan seemed to be working even better that we had hoped. So we remained noncommittal and gave nothing away.

"Think about it, please. Before making any decisions, consider the bigger picture. This village has weathered many storms, but another legal battle could be the one thing that finally breaks it."

"Look," I said. "Even if we back down now, the surveyor's report has already been lodged with the planning office. It's public knowledge; anyone can read it. She has clearly made lots of enemies in the village. Anyone could use it to launch an attack on her. It's not only us who have suffered at her hands."

The mayor gave us a knowing look. "I wouldn't worry about that. Files get lost all the time. The planning office is an administration nightmare. I wouldn't be surprised if it disappeared completely."

Wow! They must be getting worried, I thought. What did Nemesis have on him? Why was he so keen to protect her? But perhaps he was just genuinely concerned. If we did take action, it would certainly be devastating for the village. Although we would likely win the battle, it was clear that our actions would have far-reaching consequences, and perhaps even end the mayor's political future.

"Thank you for your words, Athanasios. I know you're trying to do the best for the village," Alex said, her tone firm. "But it's about time somebody made a stand."

The mayor sighed, realising he wasn't going to change Alex's mind. He returned to his table and began a whispered conversation with his friends. They kept glancing at us with worried expressions.

During our conversation with the mayor, the usual noise of the taverna had ceased. People strained to eavesdrop, their ears tuned to every word being discussed. Over the past week or two, we had noticed that public opinion had certainly swayed in our favour. The people sitting in the taverna seemed to be revelling in the conflict, most wearing satisfied smiles.

One older man leaned over to his companion. "Did you hear that? They're finally standing up to Nemesis."

A woman at a nearby table looked over approvingly, her eyes fixed on us. "It's about time someone did. We've all suffered because of her."

The taverna buzzed with quiet murmurs of agreement. It was clear that the villagers were tired of Nemesis's antics and were rallying behind us. The solidarity we felt was reassuring, a small beacon of hope in our ongoing struggle.

As we prepared to leave, a young couple approached us. "We just wanted to say thank you," the woman said, her voice filled with sincerity, "for standing up for what's right. We're behind you."

Her partner nodded in agreement. "If you need any help, don't hesitate to ask. The whole village is with you."

We thanked them, deeply touched by their support. It was clear that the tide had turned. The village was no longer willing to tolerate Nemesis's behaviour, and they were ready to support us in our fight for justice. As we walked out of the taverna, we felt a renewed sense of purpose and determination, bolstered by the solidarity of our community.

We gave it one more day for the news of our encounter with the mayor to filter through the village. Everyone was certain we were gunning for Nemesis and keenly awaited the outcome.

Nemesis had now been tenderised, trussed up, and was ready for the oven. And we were primed for the last part of our plan.

CHAPTER 18
Peace Among the Ruins

*The highest form of knowledge is empathy,
for it requires us to suspend our egos
and live in another's world.*

– Plato

We drove to the next village to meet our lawyer and explain our intentions.

Sofia greeted us in her office, a look of curiosity mixed with concern on her face. "Are you sure about this?" she asked, raising an eyebrow as she shuffled the papers on her desk. "I can see the logic. If we did proceed with a legal case against her, the fallout for the village could be disastrous. But you have your legal rights, and most would use these rights to get closure."

Alex and I exchanged a glance before I spoke up. "We've thought long and hard about this, Sofia. It's not just about legal rights. It's about moving forward and healing."

Alex continued. "We believe that showing compassion,

even in the face of everything she's done, might be the only way to truly resolve this."

Sofia leaned back in her chair, studying us for a moment. "It's a bold move. But if anyone can pull it off, it's you two. I'll be standing by for news. Just be careful."

On the way back, we stopped by the bakery and picked up a cake. The warm scent of freshly baked goods filled the car, wrapping us in a sense of comfort and quiet optimism. Next, we visited the florist, selecting a bouquet bursting with colour – not just a peace offering, but a symbol of new beginnings.

We pulled up outside Nemesis's house and turned off the engine. For a moment, neither of us moved. The village had been buzzing with speculation, and we knew this moment was crucial. Alex exhaled sharply, gripping the cake box a little tighter. I drummed my fingers on my knee, wondering – for the hundredth time – if this was a terrible idea. But we needed peace in our lives.

With a shared nod, we stepped out of the car. The air felt heavy, thick with unspoken words. As we approached the door, I took a deep breath and knocked. The sound echoed through the quiet street.

The door creaked open, and there she stood, a shadow of her former self. Her once fiery demeanour had been replaced by a timid and broken look. The sight of her in such a state took us aback, stirring unexpected sympathy within us.

Alex stepped forward, a kind smile on her face, and handed her the bouquet. "We thought you might like these," she said gently.

I held out the cake. "And we brought you this. Just a little something to brighten your day."

Nemesis hesitated, her eyes darting between us and the gifts. Her hands trembled slightly as she took the flowers from Alex.

"I'm not going to say any more," Alex continued. "But rest assured, we are not holding any anger towards you. As far as we are concerned, the situation between us goes no further and ends now. We don't want to have any more bad feelings between us. When you are ready, please come to our house for a coffee. You will be welcome."

Nemesis didn't reply. She simply took the flowers, her eyes softening a little. I placed the cake on the table in her porch, giving her a reassuring nod.

"We hope you enjoy the flowers and the cake," I said, trying to convey our sincerity.

She looked at us, her expression unreadable, but the tension seemed to ease slightly. We smiled at her, then turned and walked away, leaving her to process our gesture.

As we walked back to our car, the stress of the past weeks began to lift. We had made our peace, and now it was up to Nemesis to decide how to respond. The resolution of this conflict was not just about ending hostilities but about moving forward with a sense of understanding and compassion.

The villagers were perplexed. They had expected us to follow through with the final blow, but instead we had chosen to show compassion. The confusion grew as word spread throughout the village about our illogical actions. However, little did they know our decision was not out of weakness or hesitation. It was a deliberate choice to demonstrate that victory doesn't always have to come at the expense of others. We had achieved a significant victory by defeating the enemy and rendering her helpless, but we wanted to prove that our strength lay not only in physical power but also in our ability to show mercy. So, instead of exercising our rights to claim compensation and insisting on removal of the structure that caused the flooding, we surprised her with flowers and cake. It was a gesture of forgiveness and a symbol of our commitment to peace.

The village, although initially confused, soon began to admire our unexpected act of kindness, and over the following months it seemed to spark a ripple of change in their own attitudes towards conflict resolution.

At first, our neighbours couldn't quite believe what we had done. They had been eagerly awaiting a dramatic showdown, with harsh words and legal battles resulting in fleets of bulldozers knocking down houses built on the river. Instead, they saw us extend an olive branch. Whispers of our visit to Nemesis spread quickly through the narrow streets and bustling tavernas. The sight of us, the wronged foreigners, bringing flowers and cake to our adversary left many stunned and introspective.

One afternoon, as we sat in the village square, sipping coffee under the shade of an ancient olive tree, we noticed something remarkable. Eleni, who had held a grudge against Stavros for as long as anyone could remember, was sitting across from him at a small table. The two were sharing a glass of tsipouro, their conversation punctuated by laughter and the occasional nostalgic sigh. It was a sight that would have been unthinkable just weeks earlier.

"Eleni and Stavros, drinking together?" Alex murmured, nudging me gently. "I never thought I'd see the day."

I was equally amazed. "If we can forgive Nemesis, then maybe they realised they could let go of their grudges too."

Over the next few months, this shift in the village's atmosphere was palpable. Old rivalries seemed to soften, and long-standing disputes were approached with new-found patience and understanding. The baker, Dimitri, who had been at odds with the blacksmith, Nikos, over a trivial boundary dispute, was now seen delivering fresh bread to Nikos's forge. Children who had been told to avoid certain families now played together in the sun-dappled streets, their laughter echoing off the stone walls of the houses.

Our act of kindness had set off a chain reaction. People began to reflect on their own relationships and conflicts, questioning the necessity of their long-held animosities. The village elders, who had witnessed generations of feuds, started to speak about the importance of unity and community during their evening gatherings.

One evening, our neighbour Maria approached us with a warm smile. "Your gesture to Nemesis has reminded us all of what truly matters," she said, her eyes shining with gratitude. "We had forgotten that forgiveness is a strength, not a weakness."

Her words resonated deeply with us. It was heartening to see that our decision had not only defused our own conflict but also inspired others to seek peace in their lives. As the days passed, the village became a more harmonious place. Shared meals and communal gatherings became more frequent, filled with joy and camaraderie.

In the end, our act of kindness towards Nemesis did more than just resolve our personal dispute. It healed wounds we never knew existed and brought a sense of togetherness that the village hadn't seen in years. The villagers learned that forgiveness could build bridges where there were once walls, and that even the most bitter enemies could find common ground over a simple gesture of goodwill.

The transformation was profound. We had not only found peace for ourselves but had also helped to weave a stronger, more compassionate fabric within the community. It was a powerful reminder that sometimes the smallest acts of kindness can have the most far-reaching effects.

A few days later, our land surveyor, Ajax, came to visit with news. The mayor had been honest with us at last. The Greek government had indeed sent a minister to assess the damage caused by the devastating flooding. The minister, understanding the urgency of the matter, had visited nearby villages and took the time to speak directly with residents and businesses affected by the disaster. This proactive approach surprised many, as politicians are often seen as only showing concern for publicity. However, the minister's actions instilled a glimmer of hope in the hearts of the people, as it seemed that this time genuine action would be taken.

The mayor had indeed chosen our home as an example of the river's destructive power. The once beautiful and serene landscape was now a chaotic mess of mud and debris. Our beloved garden, which we had nurtured with care, lay in ruins. The scene was enough to break anyone's heart, but it seemed to be the last straw needed to spur the government into action. An application for funding was passed unanimously through the parliament and the work to redirect the river was approved.

The commitment to action offered a glimmer of hope amidst the destruction. There was comfort in knowing that the disaster that had struck our home would lead to a safer future for the village.

"Do you realise the impact of your actions here?" Ajax asked us. "If it weren't for the damage to your house, the minister would have just gone back to Athens and forgotten about our village. But when he witnessed the chaos caused to your home and heard the story of an innocent foreigner being persecuted by the Greek justice system due to the lack of proper infrastructure, it was too shameful for him to ignore. So, both you and Alex have altered the course of our village's history."

I sat and reflected on this. We were happy before the flooding. We had a lovely home and garden. Then the storm came and took it all away. Yes, we had suffered months of agony. Not only had we lost our home, we had also been blamed for causing the devastation.

The remarkable statement from Nemesis would still haunt

us forever: "God has punished you for blocking the river," she had told Alex.

But, despite the mountain of challenges, we rebuilt. And this time it was bigger and better than we could ever had expected. Now that the river will never be a problem again, land value has rocketed. Our community, once plagued by adversity, has become a beacon of possibility. The obstacles we faced were merely stepping stones on the path to a brighter future. Through our tragedy and suffering, we have not only overcome the past but have also helped build a foundation for a thriving and vibrant community.

Without the accusations of Nemesis and the stressful legal examination, this might never have happened. We would have put our home back together and gone back to enjoy it, but always looking over our shoulder for the next disaster. Now we would at last be safe in the knowledge that the river would never come back to ruin our lives again.

It's been a roller coaster ride since moving to Greece, marrying my Greek goddess and settling down here. Despite everything we have been through, I've never once regretted it.

Our story began when I was a smitten teenager, daydreaming about the beautiful girl who would walk past every morning on her way to school. I didn't realise it then, but Greece was already a part of me. As a kid, I was hooked on tales of Greek heroes – Hercules's adventures, Achilles's bravery, and

Odysseus's epic sea journeys after he insulted Poseidon.

My transition into Greek life was made easy by the love of my new Greek family, especially my mother-in-law, Debbie, who became a mother to us all. She showed me a better way to live, for which I will be eternally grateful. When I first arrived on the scene, she naturally had some suspicion of me. However, she never showed it. Her eyes were always full of love and understanding for my cultural difficulties, and she could see that I meant well. Her suspicion was not based on any offence I had committed but rather stemmed from her tremendous love for her only daughter, whom she cherished above all else.

Over the years, I slowly earned her trust. Debbie watched as Alex and I worked together to create a better future for ourselves, seeing the love in her daughter's eyes reflected in mine. She observed as we built homes and strived to create rather than destroy, understanding that our relationship was built on mutual respect and partnership.

Through countless shared meals, family gatherings, and conversations that stretched late into the night, Debbie saw our dedication to building a life together. She witnessed our efforts to contribute positively to the family and watched as we faced challenges with determination and resilience. She realised that Alex and I as a team were an unstoppable force, and came to understand that her daughter was safe in my hands.

This was my ultimate gift to Debbie. As she left this world, she knew with certainty that her family was going to be fine. She departed with the peace of knowing that the love and values she had instilled in her daughter would continue to flourish in our home. It was a bond of trust that had taken years to build, but one that was unshakeable by the end. She could rest easy, knowing her legacy would live on in the family she cherished so deeply.

Over the last twenty or so years, I have come to deeply respect our shared culture. Greece to me has been an eye-opening experience, at times exasperating with the incredible burdens of bureaucracy forced upon people. But in hindsight, perhaps this is needed in some perverse way. Greeks are free spirits. Without control, where would they be?

In such a relaxed and laid-back society, it is easy to assume that anything goes. When Alex and I fell foul of the law, it was a difficult episode in our lives, but the result was surprising. Our experience taught us many things, not least compassion and love. If we had been permitted to do anything we wanted, would anything ever really be learned?

Greek culture has long been characterised by a blend of individualism. Ancient Greece was a cradle of democracy and philosophy, celebrating free thought while maintaining social order through laws and civic duties. The balance between personal freedom and societal responsibilities was essential to its success. A certain level of control can promote accountability, ensuring that people obey laws designed to protect the common good. In Greece, the historical legacy of philosophers, artists and thinkers is a testament to the power of free thought and expression. However, absolute freedom without any constraints can lead to excess and self-destruction. The notion of "free spirits" might imply a tendency towards impulsivity, which, if unchecked, could lead to societal breakdown.

Societies function best when there is a balance between freedom and control. Too much of either can lead to dysfunction. A society with no rules may descend into chaos, while one with too many restrictions can become oppressive. It's crucial for bureaucratic systems to adapt and evolve to meet the changing needs of society. Although it can be mind-numbingly frustrating, Greece seems to have got the balance right.

But above all, there is love. Not just the kind that comes from sharing a life or navigating daily routines, but something deeper. An unshakeable connection that feels guided by destiny. It's as if our souls are intertwined, each one incomplete without the other, bound together by forces beyond time and space.

From the moment Alex and I met, there was an undeniable pull, a sense that we weren't meeting for the first time but reconnecting after lifetimes apart. That feeling of wholeness, of finding the missing piece I didn't know I lacked, has never faded. It's as though an invisible thread has drawn us together in every lifetime, ensuring our paths always cross and our spirits always unite.

This love is a sanctuary, a source of strength that transcends all obstacles. It's the kind of connection that fuels great adventures and quiet assurances alike, reminding us that no matter what the world throws our way, we face it together. In Alex, I haven't just found a partner. I've found the other half of myself, someone who truly understands me and makes life's journey endlessly meaningful.

On a warm evening that summer, as we gathered with friends and neighbours to celebrate the harmony we had rediscovered, we raised our glasses, not just to our victories or our resilience, but to love – the constant thread that had guided us through it all.

"Thank you, Nemesis," I said with a smile, acknowledging the unexpected catalyst she had been in our journey. *"Stin ygeiá sas – to your health."*

The End

Author's Note

All books tell a story. Some are written from imagination, others from personal experience, and many from a mixture of both. Yet authors are guided by a couple of simple rules: "Write what you know" and "Know your genre". When I sat down to write this book, I had already ticked the first box. The second was less clear.

As I look at the finished work, I find myself struggling to categorise it. It begins like a romance and continues like narrative fiction: a thriller at times, or perhaps even a horror story? It could be seen as a journey of self-discovery and the resolution of conflict. Maybe it's a fairy tale with a wicked witch intent on causing as much pain as possible to the village. The book contains elements of storytelling that seem to blur the lines between reality and imagination.

But at its core, the book is a personal journey of self-discovery, highlighting the moral and ethical dilemmas faced by the characters, and exploring themes of identity, belonging and transformation.

Whatever category we ultimately place this book in, it is important to note that, for legal reasons, I have changed some names, altered locations and adapted some conversations to protect the identities of those involved. Despite these changes, the events described are all true – they actually happened. Therefore, perhaps the most fitting label is a memoir.

Credits and Gratitude

Writing a book is never a solo journey, and this one is no exception. There are a few incredible people without whom this story would never have made it onto the page – people to whom I owe my deepest gratitude.

First and foremost, my heartfelt thanks go to my editor, Nicky Taylor. If there were an award for patience and wizardry with words, she would have a shelf full of trophies. Her skill, insight and unwavering attention to detail transformed my tangled ramblings into a book I can be truly proud of. Without her, this would be a very different read – probably one with a lot more typos and a lot less coherence.

To my daughter, Charly Alex Fuller, who designed the stunning cover artwork. You didn't just create a book cover, you gave it a face, a soul, and a presence on the shelf. Thank you for bringing my words to life in a way only you could.

To Barbara "Eagle-Eyed" Charlton, my brilliant proofreader. Your sharp attention to detail gave me the confidence to publish this book, knowing it was free of those sneaky little errors. I'm truly grateful for your keen eye and unwavering patience!

To the amazing members of the We Love Memoirs Facebook group, the friendliest corner of the internet. Your encouragement, support and willingness to share my books with memoir lovers everywhere mean more than I can say. You've cheered me on, made me laugh, and helped bring my stories to new readers. I am incredibly grateful for each and every one of you.

And of course, my wife, Alexandra Schinas. Without her, I wouldn't have written a single word. She is my muse, my inspiration, my greatest adventure. Every story I tell, every page I write, carries a piece of her – the fire, the laughter, the unwavering spirit. She is the reason these books exist, and for that I will be forever grateful.

www.ingramcontent.com/pod-product-compliance
Ingram Content Group UK Ltd.
Pitfield, Milton Keynes, MK11 3LW, UK
UKHW021847060325
455777UK00011B/145